THE ANARCHIST
COLLECTIVES

THE ANARCHIST COLLECTIVES

Edited by Sam Dolgoff

Workers'
Self-management
in the Spanish
Revolution
1936-1939

Introductory
Essay by
Murray
Bookchin

FREE LIFE
EDITIONS

THE ANARCHIST COLLECTIVES:
Workers' Self-management in
the Spanish Revolution (1936-1939)

Copyright © 1974 by Sam Dolgoff
Introductory Essay © 1974 by Murray Bookchin

First Edition

Published 1974 by Free Life Editions, Inc.
41 Union Square West
New York, N.Y. 10003

Canadian edition published by Black Rose Books by arrangement
with Free Life Editions, Inc.
Black Rose Books
3934 St. Urbain
Montreal 131, Quebec

Library of Congress Catalog Card Number: 73-88239
ISBN: 0-914156-02-0 paperback
ISBN: 0-914156-03-9 hardcover

Manufactured in the United States of America
Faculty Press, Inc. Brooklyn, N.Y. 159

To the heroic workers and peasants of Spain!
To my comrades, the Spanish Anarchists,
        who perished fighting for freedom!
To the militants who continue the struggle!

Contents

Appendices appear on pages 11, 29, 30, 71, and 81.
Photographs and posters appear on pages 4, 15, 25, 34, 45, 64, 72,
97, 103, 104, 110, 117, 141, 142, 157, 158, 173, and 197.

Preface

The Spanish Social Revolution has been long neglected in English language works. Its importance as a revolutionary event and model, and as a concrete example of workers' self-management by the people is just not recognized. My purpose in this collection is to provide an introduction to this unique experience. In my first chapter and friend Bookchin's introductory essay, a general overview and context is presented. Most important, of course, is that this was a real experience for the people who took part. Through their words and deeds and the observations of the authors used in this collection, it is hoped that the reader will gain a meaningful understanding of the aims and organization of the anarchist collectives.

The material has been divided into two main sections. The first provides essential background information: the nature of the Spanish Revolution, the collectivist tradition, the development of the libertarian labor movement in Spain, and the historical events leading up to and then culminating in the destruction of the collectives.

The second, and main, section deals with the actual social revolution—the overall characteristics of agrarian collectivization and industrial socialization. It begins with a discussion about economic coordination, the place and nature of money in the collectives, and includes statistics on the number of collectives. It then deals with actual descriptions of life in the collectives, first under industrial socialization, and then in the rural collectives: how the new institutions were established, how they functioned, how production and distribution were handled; about coordination, exchange, relations between collectives, and between collectivized and non-collectivized areas. The book ends with a short evaluation of the anarchist collectives with some comments on their relevance and lessons.

The glossary, bibliography and appendices add to the overall usefulness of this volume. The photographs reproduced within begin to correct the visual bias that has left a plethora of war scenes but very little reflecting the constructive aspects of the Spanish Social Revolution. Most of the pictures are from contemporary sources held by the editor. I would like to thank Victor Berch, Special Collections Librarian at Brandeis University for permission to use the pictures on pages 104, 141, and 142.

The observers speaking in these selections visited the same regions and often the same collectives at different times within the short span of approximately two years. Since each observer stressed what seemed most important to him, their accounts supplement each other, thus providing a more balanced view of/the new way of life than any single observer could have done. Under these circumstances, though, some repetition is inevitable. The translations I have made are strict to the meaning, but are not literal, for I have also been concerned with giving the spirit of the words, and with reducing repetitions.

Finally I would like to express my thanks to all the farsighted and brave people whose work I have used in putting together this collection. (A short biography on each is included in the bibliography.) Their efforts have immortalized a social experience of momentous importance. My object has been to present them to the English reader within a context that will be useful.

ACKNOWLEDGEMENTS

It is with the deepest appreciation that I acknowledge the contributions to the present work of the following persons:

My friend, Chuck Hamilton, for his tireless technical and editorial labors in turning a poorly typed manuscript into the finished book.

To my friend, Dr. Paul Avrich, for reading the manuscript and making valuable suggestions.

To my comrade, Murray Bookchin, who first encouraged me to undertake this project.

Last, but by no means least, my wife Esther who scrupulously examined the manuscript as it was being written and detected many errors.

New York City
January, 1974

Introductory Essay
by Murray Bookchin

In the morning hours of July 18, 1936, General Francisco Franco issued the *pronunciamiento* from Las Palmas in Spanish North Africa that openly launched the struggle of Spain's reactionary military officers against the legally elected Popular Front government in Madrid.

The Franco *pronunciamiento* left little doubt that, in the event of victory by the Spanish generals, a parliamentary republic would be replaced by a clearly authoritarian state, modelled institutionally on similar regimes in Germany and Italy. The Francista forces or "Nationalists," as they were to call themselves, exhibited all the trappings and ideologies of the fascist movements of the day: the raised open-palm salute, the appeals to a "folk-soil" philosophy of "order, duty, and obedience," the avowed commitments to smash the labor movement and end all political dissidence. To the world, the conflict initiated by the Spanish generals seemed like another of the classic struggles waged between the "forces of fascism" and the "forces of democracy" that had reached such acute proportions in the thirties. What distinguished the Spanish conflict from similar struggles in Italy, Germany, and Austria was the massive resistance the "forces of democracy" seemed to oppose to the Spanish military. Franco and his military co-conspirators, despite the wide support they enjoyed among the officer cadres in the army, had grossly miscalculated the popular opposition they would encounter. The so-called "Spanish Civil War" lasted nearly three years—from July 1936 to March 1939—and claimed an estimated million lives.

For the first time, so it seemed to many of us in the thirties, an entire people with dazzling courage had arrested the terrifying success of fascist movements in central and southern Europe. Scarcely three years earlier, Hitler had pocketed Germany without a shred of resistance from the massive Marxist-dominated German labor movement. Austria, two years before, had succumbed to an essentially authoritarian state after a week of futile street-fighting by Socialist workers in Vienna. Everywhere fascism seemed "on the march" and "democracy" in retreat. But Spain had seriously resisted—and was to resist for years despite the armaments, aircraft, and troops which Franco acquired from Italy and Germany. To radicals and liberals alike, the "Spanish Civil War" was being waged not only on the Iberian peninsula but in every country where "democracy" seemed threatened by the rising tide of domestic and international fascist movements. The "Spanish Civil War," we were led to believe, was a struggle between a liberal republic that was valiantly and with popular support trying to defend a democratic parliamentary state against authoritarian generals—an imagery that is conveyed to this very day by most books on the subject and by that shabby cinematic documentary, *To Die in Madrid*.

What so few of us knew outside of Spain, however, was that the "Spanish Civil War" was in fact a sweeping social revolution by millions of workers and peasants who were concerned not to rescue a treacherous republican regime but to reconstruct Spanish society along revolutionary lines. We would scarcely have learned from the press that these workers and peasants viewed the republic almost with as much animosity as they did the Francistas. Indeed, acting largely on their own initiative against "republican" ministers who were trying to betray them to the generals, they had raided arsenals and sporting-goods stores for weapons and with incredible valor had aborted the military conspiracies in most of the cities and towns of Spain. We were almost totally oblivious to the fact that these workers and peasants had seized and collectivized most of the factories and land in republican-held areas, establishing a new social order based on direct control of the country's productive resources by workers' committees and peasant assemblies. While the republic's institutions lay in debris, abandoned by most of its military and police forces, the workers and peasants had created their own institutions to administer the cities in republican Spain, formed their own armed workers' squads to patrol the streets, and established a remarkable revolutionary militia force to fight the Francista forces—a voluntaristic militia in which men and women elected their own commanders and in which military rank conferred no social, material, or symbolic distinctions. Largely unknown to us at that time, the Spanish workers and peasants had made a sweeping social revolution. They had created their own revolutionary social forms to administer the country as well as to wage war against a well-trained and well-supplied army. The "Spanish Civil War" was not a political conflict between a liberal democracy and a fascistic military corps, but a deeply socio-economic conflict between the workers and peasants of Spain and their historic class enemies, ranging from the landowning grandees and clerical overlords inherited from the past to the rising industrial bourgeoisie and bankers of more recent times.

The revolutionary scope of this conflict was concealed from us—by "us" I refer to the many thousands of largely Communist-influenced radicals of the "red" thirties who responded to the struggle in Spain with the same fervor and agony that young people of the sixties responded to the struggle in Indochina. We need not turn to Orwell or Borkenau, radicals of obviously strong anti-Stalinist convictions, for an explanation. Burnett Bolloten, a rather politically innocent United Press reporter who happened to be stationed in Madrid at the time, conveys his own sense of moral outrage at the misrepresentation of the Spanish conflict in the opening lines of his superbly documented study, *The Grand Camouflage*:

> Although the outbreak of the Spanish Civil War in July, 1936, was followed by a far-reaching social revolution in the anti-Franco camp—more profound in some respects than the Bolshevik Revolution in its early stages—millions of discerning people outside of Spain were kept in ignorance, not only of its depth and range, but even of its existence, by virtue of a policy of duplicity and dissimulation of which there is no parallel in history.
>
> Foremost in practicing this deception upon the world, and in misrepresenting in Spain itself the character of the revolution, were the Communists, who, although but an exiguous minority when the Civil War began, used so effectually the manifold opportunities which that very upheaval presented that before the close of the conflict in 1939 they became, behind a democratic frontispiece, the ruling force in the left camp.

The details of this deception would fill several large volumes. The silence that gathers around Spain, like a bad conscience, attests to the fact that the events are very much alive—together with the efforts to misrepresent them. After nearly forty years the wounds have not healed. In fact, as the recent revival of Stalinism suggests, the disease that produced the purulence of counter-revolution in Spain still lingers on the American left. But to deal with the Stalinist counter-revolution in Spain is beyond the scope of these introductory remarks. Fortunately, the bibliography furnished by Sam Dolgoff provides the English-speaking reader with a number of the more important works on this subject. It might be useful, however, to examine the revolutionary tendencies that unfolded prior to July 1936 and explore the influence they exercised on the Spanish working class and peasantry. The collectives described in this book were not the results of virginal popular spontaneity, important as popular spontaneity was, nor were they nourished exclusively by the collectivist legacy of traditional Spanish village society. Revolutionary ideas and movements played a crucial role of their own and their influence deserves the closest examination.

The Spanish generals started a military rebellion in July 1936; the Spanish workers and peasants answered them with a social revolution—and this revolution was largely anarchist in character. I say this provocatively even though the Socialist UGT was numerically as large as the anarcho-syndicalist CNT.[1] During the first few months of the military rebellion, Socialist workers in Madrid often acted as radically as anarcho-syndicalist workers in Barcelona. They established their own militias, formed street patrols, and expropriated a number of strategic factories, placing them under the control of workers' committees. Similarly, Socialist peasants in Castile and Estramadura formed collectives many of which were as libertarian as those created by anarchist peasants in Aragon and the Levant. In the opening "anarchic" phase of the revolution, so similar to the opening phases of earlier revolutions, the "masses" tried to assume direct control over society and exhibited a remarkable élan in improvising their own libertarian forms of social administration.

Looking back beyond this opening phase, however, it is fair to say that the durability of the collectives in Spain, their social scope and the resistance they offered to the Stalinist counter-revolution, depended largely on the extent to which they were under anarchist influence. What distinguishes the Spanish Revolution from those which preceded it is not only the fact that it placed much of Spain's economy in the hands of workers' committees and peasant assemblies or that it established a democratically elected militia system. These social forms, in varying degrees, had emerged during the Paris Commune and in the early period of the Russian Revolution. What made the Spanish Revolution unique is that

---

[1] Both the UGT and the CNT probably numbered over a million members each by the summer of 1936. The officious, highly bureaucratic UGT tended to overstate its membership figures. The more amorphous decentralized CNT—the most persecuted of the two labor federations—often exercised much greater influence on the Spanish working class than its membership statistics would seem to indicate.

workers' control and collectives had been advocated for nearly three generations by a massive libertarian movement and became the most serious issues to divide the so-called "republican" camp, (together with the fate of the militia system). Owing to the scope of its libertarian social forms, the Spanish Revolution proved not only to be "more profound" (to borrow Bolloten's phrase) than the Bolshevik Revolution, but the influence of a deeply rooted anarchist ideology and the intrepidity of anarchist militants virtually produced a civil war within the civil war.

Indeed, in many respects, the revolution of 1936 marked the culmination of more than sixty years of anarchist agitation and activity in Spain. To understand the extent to which this was the case, we must go back to the early 1870's, when the Italian anarchist, Giuseppi Fanelli, introduced Bakunin's ideas to groups of workers and intellectuals in Madrid and Barcelona. Fanelli's encounter with young workers of the *Fomento de las Artes* in Madrid, a story told with great relish by Brenan, is almsot legendary: the volatile speech of the tall bearded Italian anarchist who hardly knew a word of Spanish to a small but enthusiastic audience that scarcely understood his free-wheeling mixture of French and Italian. By dint of sheer mimicry, tonal inflections, and a generous use of cognates, Fanelli managed to convey enough of Bakunin's ideals to gain the group's adherence and to establish the founding Spanish section of the International Working Men's Association or so-called "First International." Thereafter, the "Internationalists," as the early Spanish anarchists were known, expanded rapidly from their circles in Madrid and Barcelona to Spain as a whole, taking strong root especially in Catalonia and Andalusia. Following the definitive split between the Marxists and Bakuninists at the Hague Congress of the IWMA in September 1872, the Spanish section remained predominantly Bakuninist in its general outlook. Marxism did not become a significant movement in Spain until the turn of the century and even after it became an appreciable force in the labor movement, it remained largely reformist until well into the thirties. During much of its early history, the strength of the Spanish Socialist Party and the UGT lay in administrative areas such as Madrid rather than in predominantly working-class cities like Barcelona.[2] . Marxism tended to appeal to the highly skilled, pragmatic,

---

[2] Madrid, although with a largely Socialist labor movement, was the home of an intensely active anarchist movement. Not only were the Madrid construction workers strongly anarchosyndicalist, but at the turn of the century, many Madrid intellectuals were committed to anarchism and established a renowned theoretical tradition for the movement that lingered on long after anarchist workers had cut their ties with the Spanish intelligentsia.

rather authoritarian Castilian; anarchism, to the unskilled, idealistic Catalans and the independent, liberty-loving mountain villagers of Andalusia and the Levant. The great rural masses of Andalusian day-workers or *braceros*, who remain to this day among the most oppressed and impoverished strata of European society, tended to follow the anarchists. But their allegiances varied with the fortunes of the day. In periods of upheaval, they swelled the ranks of the Bakuninist IWMA and its successor organizations in Spain, only to leave it in equally large numbers in periods of reaction.

Yet, however much the fortunes of Spanish anarchism varied from region to region and from period to period, whatever revolutionary movement existed in Spain during this sixty-year period was essentially anarchist. Even as anarchism began to ebb before Marxian social-democratic and later Bolshevik organizations after the First World War period, Spanish anarchism retained its enormous influence and its revolutionary élan. Viewed from a radical standpoint, the history of the Spanish labor movement remained libertarian and often served to define the contours of the Marxist movements in Spain. "Generally speaking, a small but well-organized group of Anarchists in a Socialist area drove the Socialists to the Left," observes Brenan, "whereas in predominantly Anarchist areas, Socialists were outstandingly reformist." It was not socialism but rather anarchism that determined the metabolism of the Spanish labor movement—the great general strikes that swept repeatedly over Spain, the recurring insurrections in Barcelona and in the towns and villages of Andalusia, and the gun battles between labor militants and employer-hired thugs in the Mediterranean coastal cities.

It is essential to emphasize that Spanish anarchism was not merely a program embedded in a dense theoretical matrix. It was a way of life: partly, the life of the Spanish people as it was lived in the closely-knit villages of the countryside and the intense neighborhood life of the working class barrios; partly, too, the theoretical articulation of that life as projected by Bakunin's concepts of decentralization, mutual aid, and popular organs of self-management. That Spain had a long tradition of agrarian collectivism is discussed in this book and examined in some detail in Joaquin Costa's *Colectivismo Agrario en Espagna*. Inasmuch as this tradition was distinctly pre-capitalist, Spanish Marxism regarded it as anachronistic, in fact, as "historically reactionary." Spanish socialism built its agrarian program around the Marxist tenet that the peasantry and its social forms could have no lasting revolutionary value until they were "proletarianized" and "industrialized." Indeed, the sooner the village decayed the better and the more rapidly the peasantry became a hereditary proletariat, "disciplined, united, organized by the very mechanism of the process of capitalist production itself" (Marx)—a distinctly hierarchical and authoritarian "mechanism"—the more rapidly Spain would advance to the tasks of socialism.

Spanish anarchism, by contrast, followed a decisively different approach. It sought out the precapitalist collectivist traditions of the village, nourished what was living and vital in them, evoked their revolutionary potentialities as liberatory modes of mutual aid and self-management, and deployed them to vitiate the obedience, hierarchical mentality, and authoritarian outlook fostered by the factory system. Ever mindful of the "embourgeoisment" of the proletariat (a term continually on Bakunin's lips in the late years of his life), the Spanish anarchists tried to use the pre-capitalist traditions of the peasantry and working class against the assimilation of the workers' outlook to an authoritarian industrial rationality. In this respect, their efforts were favored by the continuous fertilization of the Spanish proletariat by rural workers who renewed these traditions daily as they migrated to the cities. The revolutionary élan of the Barcelona proletariat—like that of the Petrograd and Parisian proletariat—was due in no small measure to the fact that these workers never solidly sedimented into a herditary working class, totally removed from pre-capitalist traditions, whether of the peasant or the craftsman. Along the Mediterranean coastal cities of Spain, many workers retained a living memory of a non-capitalist culture—one in which each moment of life was not strictly regulated by the punch clock, the factory whistle, the foreman, the machine, the highly regulated workday, and the atomizing world of the large city. Spanish anarchism flourished within the tension created by these antagonistic traditions and sensibilities. Indeed, where a "Germanic proletariat" (to use another of Bakunin's cutting phrases) emerged in Spain, it drifted either toward the UGT or the Catholic unions. Its political outlook, reformist when not overtly conservative, often clashed with the more *déclassé* working class of Catalonia and the Mediterranean coast, leading to conflicting tendencies within the Spanish proletariat as a whole.

Ultimately, in my view, the destiny of Spanish anarchism depended upon its ability to create libertarian organizational forms that could synthesize the precapitalist collectivist traditions of the village with an industrial economy and a highly urbanized society. I speak here of no mere programmatic "alliance" between the Spanish peasantry and proletariat, but more organically, of new organizational forms and sensibilities that imparted a revolutionary libertarian character to two social classes who lived in conflicting cultures. That Spain required a well-organized libertarian movement was hardly a matter of doubt among the majority of Spanish anarchists. But would this movement reflect a village society or a factory society? Where a conflict existed, could the two be melded in the same movement without violating the libertarian tenets of decentralization, mutual aid, and self-administration? In the classical era of "proletarian socialism" between 1848 and 1939, an era that stressed the "hegemony" of the industrial proletariat in all social struggles, Spanish anarchism followed a historic trajectory that at once revealed the limitations of the era itself and the creative possibilities for anarchic forms of organization.

By comparison with the cities, the Spanish villages that were committed to anarchism raised very few organizational problems. Brenan's emphasis on the *braceros* notwithstanding, the strength of agrarian anarchism in the south and the Levant lay in the mountain villages, not among the rural proletariat that worked the great plantations of Andalusia. In these relatively isolated villages, a fierce sense of independence and personal dignity whetted the bitter social hatreds engendered by poverty, creating the rural "patriarchs" of anarchism whose entire families were devoted almost apostolically to "the Idea." For these sharply etched and rigorously ascetic individuals, defiance to the State, the Church, and conventional authority in general was almost a way of life. Knitted together by the local press—and, at various times, there were hundreds of anarchist periodicals in Spain—they formed the sinews of agrarian anarchism from the 1870's onwards and, to a large extent, the moral conscience of Spanish anarchism throughout its history.

The accounts of the agrarian collectives which Dolgoff translates from Peirats, Leval, and Souchy in the latter half of this book reflect to a remarkable extent the organizational forms which the anarchists fostered among all the villages under their influence before the 1936 revolution. The revolution in rural communities essentially enlarged old IWMA and later CNT nuclei, membership groups, or quite simply clans of closely knit anarchist families into popular assemblies. These usually met weekly and formulated the policy decisions of the community as a whole. The assembly form comprised the organizational ideal of village anarchism from the days of the first truly Bakuninist congress of the Spanish IWMA in Cordova in 1872, stressing the libertarian traditions of Spanish village life.[3] Where such

---

[3]I would not want to argue, here, that the Spanish village formed a *paradigm* for a libertarian society. Village society differed greatly from one region of Spain to another—in some areas retaining undisturbed its local democratic traditions, in others ruled tyrannically by the Church, the nobility, caciques, and custom. Quite often, both

popular assemblies were possible, their decisions were executed by a committee elected from the assembly. Apparently, the right to recall committee members was taken for granted and they certainly enjoyed no privileges, emoluments, or institutional power. Their influence was a function of their obvious dedication and capabilities. It remained a cardinal principle of Spanish anarchists never to pay their delegates, even when the CNT numbered a million members.[4] Normally, the responsibilies of elected delegates had to be discharged after working hours. Almost all the evenings of anarchist militants were occupied with meetings of one sort or another. Whether at assemblies or committees, they argued, debated, voted, and administered, and when time afforded, they read and passionately discussed "the Idea" to which they dedicated not only their leisure hours but their very lives. For the greater part of the day, they were working men and women, *obrera consciente*, who abjured smoking and drinking, avoided brothels and the bloody bull ring, purged their talk of "foul" language, and by their probity, dignity, respect for knowledge, and militancy, tried to set a moral example for their entire class. They never used the word "god" in their daily conversations (*salud* was preferred over *adios*) and avoided all official contact with clerical and state authorities, indeed, to the point where they refused to legally validate their life-long "free unions" with marital documents and never baptized or confirmed their children. One must know Catholic Spain to realize how far-reaching were these self-imposed mores—and how quixotically consistent some of them were with the puritanical traditions of the country.[5]

---

tendencies co-existed in a very uneasy equilibrium, the democratic still vital but submerged by the authoritarian.

[4] In the case of the CNT there were exceptions to this rule. The National Secretary was paid an average worker's salary, as was the clerical staff of the National Committee and the editors and staffs of daily newspapers. But delegates to the national, regional, and local committees of the CNT were not paid and were obliged to work at their own trades except when they lost time during working hours on union business. This is not to say that there were no individuals who devoted most of their time to the dissemination of anarchist ideas. "Travelling about from place to place, on foot or mule or on the hard seats of third-class railway carriages, or even like tramps or ambulant bullfighters under the tarpaulins of goods wagons," observes Brenan, "whilst they organized new groups or carried on propagandist campaigns, these 'apostles of the idea,' as they were called, lived like mendicant friars on the hospitality of the more prosperous workers"—and, I would add, "villagers." This tradition of organizing, which refers to the 1870's, did not disappear in later decades; to the contrary, it became more systematic and perhaps more securely financed as the CNT began to compete with the UGT for the allegiance of the Spanish workers and peasants.

[5] Yet here I must add that to abstain from smoking, to live by high moral standards, and to especially abjure the consumption of alcohol was very important at the time.

It is appropriate to note at this point that the myth, widely disseminated by the current sociological literature on the subject, that agrarian anarchism in Spain was anti-technological in spirit and atavistically sought to restore a neolithic "Golden Age" can be quite effectively refuted by a close study of the unique educational role played by the anarchists. Indeed, it was the anarchists, with inexpensive, simply written brochures, who brought the French enlightenment and modern scientific theory to the peasantry, not the arrogant liberals or the disdainful Socialists. Together with pamphlets on Bakunin and Kropotkin, the anarchist press published simple accounts of the theories of natural and social evolution and elementary introductions to the secular culture of Europe. They tried to instruct the peasants in advanced techniques of land management and earnestly favored the use of agricultural machinery to lighten the burdens of toil and provide more leisure for self-development. Far from being an atavistic trend in Spanish society, as Hobsbawm (in his *Primitive Rebels*) and even Brenan would have us believe, I can say with certainty from a careful review of the issue that anarchism more closely approximated a radical popular enlightenment.

In their personal qualities, dedicated urban anarchists were not substantially different from their rural comrades. But in the towns and cities of Spain, these urban anarchists faced more difficult organizational problems. Their efforts to create libertarian forms of organization were favored, of course, by the fact that many Spanish workers were either former villagers or were only a generation or so removed from the countryside.[6] Yet the prospect for libertarian organization in the cities and factories could not depend upon the long tradition of village collectivism—the strong sense of community—that existed in rural anarchist

Spain was going through her own belated industrial revolution during the period of anarchist ascendancy with all its demoralizing features. The collapse of morale among the proletariat, with rampant drunkenness, venereal disease, and the collapse of sanitary facilities, was the foremost problem which Spanish revolutionaries had to deal with, just as black radicals today must deal with similar problems in the ghetto. On this score, the Spanish anarchists were eminently successful. Few CNT workers, much less committed anarchists, would have dared to show up drunk at meetings or misbehave overtly among their comrades. If one considers the terrible working and living conditions of the period, alcoholism was not as serious a problem in Spain as it was in England during the industrial revolution.

[6] In "black" (purely anarchistic) Saragossa, where the working class was even more firmly committed to anarchist principles than the Barcelona proletariat, Raymond Carr quite accurately emphasizes that "strikes were characterized by their scorn for economic demands and the toughness of their revolutionary solidarity: strikes for comrades in prison were more popular than strikes for better conditions."

areas. For within the factory itself—the realm of toil, hierarchy, industrial discipline, and brute material necessity—"community" was more a function of the bourgeois division of labor with its exploitative, even competitive connotations, than of humanistic cooperation, playfully creative work, and mutual aid. Working class solidarity depended less upon a shared meaningful life nourished by self-fulfilling work than the common enemy—the boss—who exploded any illusion that under capitalism the worker was more than an industrial resource, an object to be coldly manipulated and ruthlessly exploited. If anarchism can be partly regarded as a revolt of the individual against the industrial system, the profound truth that lies at the heart of that revolt is that the factory routine not only blunts the sensibility of the worker to the rich feast of life; it degrades the worker's image of his or her human potentialities, of his or her capacities to take direct control of the means for administering social life.

One of the unique virtues that distinguished the Spanish anarchists from socialists was their attempt to *transform* the factory domain itself—a transformation that was to be affected in the long run by their demand for workers' self-management of production, and more immediately, by their attempt to form libertarian organizations that culminated in the formation of the syndicalist CNT. However, the extent to which workers' self-management can actually *eliminate* alienated labor and *alter* the impact of the factory system on the worker's sensibilities requires, in my view, a more probing analysis than it has hitherto received. The problem of the impact of the factory system on workers became crucial as the proletarian element in the CNT grew, while the anarchists sought to develop characteristics of initiative and self-management that were directly opposed to the characteristics inculcated by the factory system.

No sizable radical movement in modern times had seriously asked itself if organizational forms had to be developed which promoted changes in the most fundamental behavior patterns of its members. How could the libertarian movement vitiate the spirit of obedience, of hierarchical organization, of leader-and-led relationships, of authority and command instilled by capitalist industry? It is to the lasting credit of Spanish anarchism—and of anarchism generally—that it posed this question.[7] The term "integral personality" appears repeatedly in Spanish anarchist documents and tireless efforts were made to develop individuals who not

---

[7] For Marx and Engels, organizational forms to change the behavioral patterns of the proletariat were not a problem. This could be postponed until "after the revolution." Indeed, Marx viewed the authoritarian impact of the factory ("the very mechanism of the process of capitalist production itself") as a positive factor in producing a "disciplined, united" proletariat. Engels, in an atrocious diatribe against the anarchists

only cerebrally accepted libertarian principles but tried to practice them. Accordingly, the organizational framework of the movement (as expressed in the IWMA, the CNT, and the FAI) was meant to be decentralized, to allow for the greatest degree of initiative and decision-making at the base, and to provide structural guarantees against the formation of a bureaucracy. These requirements, on the other hand, had to be balanced against the need for coordination, mobilized common action, and effective planning. The organizational history of anarchism in the cities and towns of Spain—the forms the anarchists created and those which they discarded—is largely an account of the pull between these two requirements and the extent to which one prevailed over the other. This tension was not merely a matter of experience and structural improvization. In the long run, the outcome of the pull between decentralization and coordination depended on the ability of the most dedicated anarchists to affect the consciousness of the workers who entered anarchist-influenced unions—specifically unions of a syndicalist character whose aims were not only to fight for immediate material gains but also to provide the infrastructure for a libertarian society.

Long before syndicalism became a popular term in the French labor movement of the late 1890's, it already existed in the early Spanish labor movement. The anarchist-influenced Spanish Federation of the old IWMA, in my opinion, was distinctly syndicalist. At the founding congress of the Spanish Federation at Barcelona in June, 1870, the "commission on the theme of the social organization of the workers" proposed a structure that would form a model for all later anarcho-syndicalist labor unions in Spain, including the CNT. The commission suggested a typical syndicalist dual structure:organization by trade and organization by locality. Local trade organizations (*Secciones de oficio*) grouped together all workers from a common enterprise and vocation into large occupational federations (*Uniones de oficio*) whose primary function was to struggle around economic grievances and working conditions. A local organization of miscellaneous trades gathered up all those workers from different vocations whose numbers were too small to constitute effective organizations along vocational lines. Paralleling these vocational organizations, in every community and region where the IWMA was represented, the different local

---

titled "On Authority," explicitly used the factory structure—its hierarchical forms and the obedience it demanded—to justify his commitment to authority and centralization in working class organizations. What is of interest, here, is not whether Marx and Engels were "authoritarians" but the way in which they thought out the problem of proletarian organization—the extent to which the matrix for their organizational concepts was the very economy which the social revolution was meant to revolutionize.

Secciones were grouped together, irrespective of trade, into local geographic bodies (*Federaciones locales*) whose function was avowedly revolutionary—the administration of social and economic life on a decentralized libertarian basis.

This dual structure forms the bedrock of all syndicalist forms of organization. In Spain, as elsewhere, the structure was knitted together by workers' committees, which originated in individual shops, factories, and agricultural communities. Gathering together in assemblies, the workers elected from their midst the committees that presided over the affairs of the vocational *Secciones de oficio* and the geographic *Federaciones locales*. They were federated into regional committees for nearly every large area of Spain. Every year, when possible, the workers elected the delegates to the annual congresses of the Spanish Federation of the IWMA, which in turn elected a national Federal Council.

With the decline of the IWMA, syndicalist union federations surfaced and disappeared in different regions of Spain, especially Catalonia and Andalusia. The first was the rather considerable Workers' Federation of the 1880's. Following its suppression, Spanish anarchism contracted either to non-union ideological groups such as the Anarchist Organization of the Spanish Region or to essentially regional union federations like the Catalan-based Pact of Union and Solidarity of the 1890's and Workers' Solidarity of the early 1900's. Except for the short-lived Federation of Workers' Societies of the Spanish Region, established in 1900 on the initiative of a Madrid bricklayers' union, no major national syndicalist federation appeared in Spain until the organization of the CNT in 1911. With the establishment of the CNT, Spanish syndicalism entered its most mature and decisive period. Considerably larger than its rival, the UGT, the CNT became the essential arena for anarchist agitation in Spain.

The CNT was not merely "founded;" it developed organically out of the Catalan Workers' Solidarity and its most consolidated regional federation, the Catalan federation (*Confederación Regional del Trabajo de Cataluña*.) Later, other regional federations were established from local unions in each province—many of them lingering on from the Federation of Workers' Societies of the Spanish Region—until there were eight by the early 1930's. The national organization, in effect, was a loose collection of regional federations which were broken down into local and district federations, and finally, into *sindicatos*, or individual unions. These *sindicatos* (earlier, they were known by the dramatic name of *sociedades de resistencia al capital*—resistance societies to capital) were established on a vocational basis and, in typical syndicalist fashion, grouped into geographic and trade federations (*federaciones locales* and *sindicatos de oficio*). To coordinate this structure, the annual congresses of the CNT elected a National Committee which was expected to occupy itself primarily with correspondence, the collection of statistics, and aid to prisoners.

The statutes of the Catalan regional federation provide us with the guidelines used for the national movement as a whole. According to these statutes, the organization was committed to "direct action," rejecting all "political and religious interference." Affiliated district and local federations were to be "governed by the greatest autonomy possible, it being understood by this that they have complete freedom in all the professional matters relating to the individual trades which integrate them." Each member was expected to pay monthly dues of ten centimes (a trifling sum) which was to be divided equally among the local organization, Regional Confederation, National Confederation, the union newspaper (*Solidaridad Obrera*—"Workers' Solidarity"), and the all-important special fund for "social prisoners."

By statute the Regional Committee—the regional equivalent of the CNT's National Committee—was expected to be merely an administrative body. Although it clearly played a directive role in coordinating action, its activities were bound by policies established by the annual regional congress. In unusual situations, the Committee could consult local bodies, either by referendums or by written queries. In addition to the annual regional congresses at which the Regional Committee was elected, the Committee was obliged to call extraordinary congresses at the request of the majority of the local federations. The local federations, in turn, were given three months notice before a regular congress so that they could "prepare the themes for discussion." Within a month before the congress, the Regional Committee was required to publish the submitted "themes" in the union newspaper, leaving sufficient time for the workers to define their attitudes toward the topics to be discussed and instruct their delegates accordingly. The delegations to the congress, whose voting power was determined by the number of members they represented, were elected by general assemblies of workers convened by the local and district federations.

These statutes formed the basis for the CNT's practice up to the revolution of 1936. Although they notably lacked any provision for the recall of the committee members, the organization in its heroic period was more democratic than the statutes would seem to indicate. A throbbing vitality existed at the base of this immense organization, marked by active interest in the CNT's problems and considerable individual initiative. The workers' centers (*centros obreros*), which the anarchists had established in the days of the IWMA, were not only the local offices of the union; they were also meeting places and cultural centers where members went to exchange ideas and attend lectures. All the affairs of the local CNT were managed by committees of ordinary unpaid workers. Although the official union meetings were held only once in three months, there were "conferences of an instructive character" every Saturday night and Sunday afternoon. The solidarity of the *sindicatos* was so intense that it was not always possible to maintain an isolated strike. There was always a tendency for a strike to trigger off others in its support and generate active aid by other *sindicatos*.

In any case, this is the way the CNT tried to carry on its affairs and during favorable periods actually functioned. But there were periods when repression and sudden, often crucial, turns in events made it necessary to suspend annual or regional congresses and confine important policy-making decisions to plenums of leading committees or to "congresses" that were little more than patchwork conferences. Charismatic leaders at all levels of the organization came very close to acting in a bureaucratic manner. Nor is the syndicalist structure itself immune to bureaucratic deformations. It was not very difficult for an elaborate network of committees, building up to regional and national bodies, to assume all the features of a centralized organization and circumvent the wishes of the workers' assemblies at the base.

Finally, the CNT, despite its programmatic commitment to libertarian communism and its attempt to function in a libertarian manner, was primarily a large trade union federation rather than a purely anarchist organization. Angel Pestaña, one of its most pragmatic leaders, recognized that roughly a third of the CNT membership could be regarded as anarchists. Many were militants rather than revolutionaries; others simply joined the CNT because it was the dominant union in their area or shop. And by the 1930's, the great majority of CNT members were workers rather than peasants. Andalusians, once the largest percentage of members in the anarchist-influenced unions of the previous century, had dwindled to a minority, a fact which is not noted by such writers as Brenan and Hobsbawm who over-emphasize the importance of the rural element in the anarcho-syndicalist trade unions.

With the slow change in the social composition of the CNT and the growing supremacy of industrial over village values in its leadership and membership, it is my view that the confederation would have eventually turned into a fairly conventional Latin-type of trade union. The Spanish anarchists were not oblivious to these developments. Although syndicalist unions formed the major arena of anarchist activity in Europe, anarchist theorists were mindful that it would not be too difficult for reformist leaders in syndicalist unions to shift organizational control from the bottom to the top. They viewed syndicalism as a change in focus from the commune to the trade union, from all of the oppressed to the industrial proletariat, from the streets to the factories, and, in emphasis at least, from insurrection to the general strike.

Malatesta, fearing the emergence of a bureaucracy in the syndicalist unions, warned that "the official is to the working class a danger only comparable to that provided by the parliamentarian; both lead to corruption and from corruption to death is but a short step." Although he was to change his attitude toward syndicalism, he accepted the movement with many reservations and never ceased to emphasize that "trade unions are, by their very nature, reformist and never revolutionary." To this warning he added that the "revolutionary spirit must be introduced, developed and maintained by the constant actions of revolutionaries who work from within their ranks as well as from outside, but it cannot be the normal, natural definition of the Trade Union's function."

Syndicalism had divided the Spanish anarchist movement without really splitting it. Indeed, until the establishment of the FAI, there was rarely a national anarchist organization to split.[8] Yet a Spanish anarchist movement held together on two levels: by means of well-known periodicals like *La Revista Blanca* and *Tierra y Libertad*, and in the form of small circles of dedicated anarchists, both inside and outside the syndicalist unions. Dating as far back as the 1880's these typically Hispanic groups of intimates, traditionally known as *tertulias*, met at favorite cafes to discuss ideas and plan actions. They gave themselves colorful names expressive of their high-minded ideals (*Ni Rey ni patria*) or their revolutionary spirit (*Los Rebeldes*) or quite simply their sense of fraternity (*Los Afines*). The Anarchist Organization of the Spanish Region to which I have already alluded, founded in Valencia in 1888, consciously made these *tertulias* the strands from which it tried to weave a coherent movement. Decades later, they were to reappear in the FAI as *grupos de afinidad* (affinity groups) with a more formal local and national structure.

Although Spanish anarchism did not produce an effective national

---

[8] The disappearance of Bakunin's Alliance of Social Democracy in Spain scattered the forces of Spanish anarchism into small local nuclei which related on a regional basis through conferences, periodicals, and correspondence. Several regional federations of these nuclei were formed, mainly in Catalonia and Andalusia, only to disappear as rapidly as they emerged.

movement until the founding of the FAI, the divisions between the anarcho-syndicalists and anarcho-communists were highly significant.[9] The two tendencies of Spanish anarchism worked in very different ways and were mutually disdainful of each other. The anarcho-syndicalists functioned directly in the unions. They accepted key union positions and placed their emphasis on organizing, often at the expense of propaganda and ideological commitment. As "practical men," Catalan anarcho-syndicalists such as José Rodriguez Romero and Tomás Herreros were ready to make compromises, more precisely, to form alliances with "pure-and-simple" trade unionists.

The anarcho-communists were the "fanatics over there"—in the editorial offices of *Tierra y Libertad*—"purists" like Juan Barón and Francisco Cardinal, who regarded the anarcho-syndicalists as deserters to reformism and held faithfully to the communist doctrines that formed the basis of the old Anarchist Organization of the Spanish Region. They were not disposed to trade union activism and stressed commitment to libertarian communist principles. It was not their goal to produce a large "mass movement" of workers who wore lightly the trappings of libertarian ideals, but to help create dedicated anarchists in an authentically revolutionary movement, however small its size or influence. Once fairly influential, their terrorist tactics at the turn of the century and the ensuing repression had greatly depleted their numbers.

The founding of the FAI in the summer of 1927 was expected to unite these two tendencies. Anarcho-syndicalist needs were met by requiring that every faista become a member of the CNT and by making the union the principle arena of anarchist activity in Spain. The needs of the anarcho-communists were met by the very fact that an avowedly anarchist organization was established nationally, apart from the CNT, and by making the affinity group the basis for a vanguard movement avowedly dedicated to the achievement of libertarian communism.[10] *Tierra y Libertad* was adopted as the FAI's organ. But by establishing an anarchist organization

---

[9] See pages 29 and 30 for useful definitions.

[10] I employ the word "vanguard" provocatively, despite its unpopularity in many libertarian circles today, because this term was widely used in the traditional anarchist movement. Some anarchist publications even adopted it as a name. There can be no doubt that an anarchist *obrera consciente* regarded himself or herself as an "advanced person" and part of a small *avant-garde* in society. In its most innocuous sense, the use of this term meant that such a person merely enjoyed a more advanced social consciousness than the majority of less developed workers and peasants, a distinction that had to be overcome by education. In a less innocuous sense, the word provided a

for the express purpose of controlling the CNT or, at least, to keep it from falling into the hands of reformists or infiltrators from the newly founded Spanish Communist Party, the anarcho-syndicalists had essentially enveloped the anarcho-communists in syndicalist activity. By 1933, the FAI's control over the CNT was fairly complete. Systematic organizational work had purged the union of Communists, while its reformist leaders either left on their own accord or had defensively camouflaged themselves with revolutionary rhetoric. No illusion should exist that this success was achieved with an overly sensitive regard for democratic niceties, although the militancy of the *faistas* unquestionably attracted the greated majority of CNT workers. But the FAI's most well-known militants—Durruti, the Ascaso brothers, Garcia Oliver—included terrorism in their repertory of direct action. Gun play, especially in "expropriations" and in dealing with recalcitrant employers, police agents, and blacklegs, was not frowned upon. These *atentados* almost certainly intimidated the FAI's less prominent opponents in the CNT, although "reformists" like Pestana and Peiró did not hesitate to publicly criticize the FAI in the harshest terms.

Despite its influence in the CNT, this remarkable anarchist organization remained semi-secret up to 1936 and its membership probably did not exceed 30,000. Structurally, it formed a near-model of libertarian organization. Affinity groups were small nuclei of intimate friends which generally numbered a dozen or so men and women. Wherever several of these affinity groups existed, they were coordinated by a local federation and met, when possible, in monthly assemblies. The national movement, in turn, was coordinated by a Peninsular Committee, which ostensibly exercised very little directive power. Its role was meant to be strictly administrative in typical Bakuninist fashion.

Affinity groups were in fact remarkably autonomous during the early thirties and often exhibited exceptional initiative. The intimacy shared by the *faistas* in each group made the movement very difficult for police agents to infiltrate and the FAI as a whole managed to survive the most severe repression with surprisingly little damage to its organization. As time passed,

---

rationale for elitism and manipulation, to which some anarchist leaders were no more immune than their authoritarian Socialist opponents.

The word "leader," on the other hand, was eschewed for the euphemism "influential militant," although in fact the more well-known anarchist "influential militants" were certainly leaders. This self-deception was not as trifling as it may seem. It prevented the Spanish anarchists from working out the serious problems that emerged from real differences in consciousness among themselves or between themselves and the great majority of undeveloped *ceneteistas*.

however, the Peninsular Committee began to grow in prestige. Its periodic· statements on events and problems often served as directives to the entire movement. Although by no means an authoritarian body, it eventually began to function as a central committee whose policy decisions, while not binding in the organization, served as more than mere suggestions. Indeed, it would have been very difficult for the Peninsular Committee to operate by fiat; the average *faista* was a strong personality who would have readily voiced disagreement with any decision that he or she found particularly unpalatable. But the FAI increasingly became an end in itself and loyalty to the organization, particularly when it was under attack or confronted with severe difficulties, tended to mute criticism.

There can be no question that the FAI raised enormously the social consciousness of the average *ceneteista*. More than any single force apart from employer recalcitrance, it made the CNT into a revolutionary syndicalist organization, if not a truly anarcho-syndicalist one. The FAI stressed a commitment to revolution and to libertarian communism and gained a considerable following within the CNT (a more dedicated following in anarchist Saragossa than in syndicalist Barcelona). But the FAI was not able to completely rid the CNT of reformist elements (the union attracted many workers by its militant fight for improved economic conditions) and the sedimentation of the CNT along hierarchical lines continued.

In its attempt to control the CNT, the FAI in fact became a victim of the less developed elements in the union. Peirats quite rightly emphasizes that the CNT took its own toll on the FAI. Just as reformists inside the union were predisposed to compromise with the bourgeoisie and the State, so the FAI was compelled to compromise with the reformists in order to retain its control over the CNT. Among the younger, less experienced *faistas*, the situation was sometimes worse. Extravagant militancy which fetishized action over theory and daring over insight rebounded, after failure, in the crudest opportunism.

In the balance: the CNT had provided a remarkably democratic arena for the most militant working class in Europe; the FAI added the leavening of a libertarian orientation and revolutionary deeds within the limits that a trade union could provide. By 1936, both organizations had created authentically libertarian structures to the extent that any strictly proletarian class movement could be truly libertarian. If only by dint of sheer rhetoric—and, doubtless, considerable conviction and daring actions—they had keyed the expectations of their memberships to a revolution that would yield workers' control of the economy and syndicalist forms of social administration. This process of education and class organization, more than any single factor in Spain, produced the collectives described in this book. And to the degree that the CNT-FAI (for the two organizations now became fatally coupled after July 1936) exercised the major influence in an area, the collectives proved to be generally more durable, communistic, and resistant to Stalinist counter-revolution than in other republican-held areas of Spain.

Moreover, in the CNT-FAI areas, workers and peasants tended to show the greatest degree of popular initiative in resisting the military uprising. It was not Socialist Madrid that first took matters into its own hands and defeated its rebellious garrison: it was anarcho-syndicalist Barcelona that can lay claim to this distinction among all the large cities of Spain. Madrid rose against the Montana barracks only after sound trucks broadcast the news that the army had been defeated in the streets and squares of Barcelona. And even in Madrid, perhaps the greatest initiative was shown by the local CNT organization, which enjoyed the allegiance of the city's militant construction workers.

The CNT-FAI, in effect, revealed all the possibilities of a highly organized and extremely militant working class—a "classical" proletariat, if you will, whose basic economic interests were repeatedly frustrated by a myopic intransigent bourgeoisie. It was out of such "irreconcilable" struggles that anarcho-syndicalism and revolutionary Marxism had developed their entire tactical and theoretical armamentorium.

But the CNT-FAI also revealed the limitations of that type of classical struggle—and it is fair to say that the Spanish Revolution marked the end of a century-long era of so-called "proletarian revolutions" which began with the June uprising of the Parisian workers in 1848. The era has passed into history and, in my view, will never again be revived. It was marked by bitter often uncompromising struggles between the proletariat and bourgeoisie, an era in which the working class had not been admitted into its "share" of economic life and virtually denied the right to form its own protective institutions. Industrial capitalism in Spain was still a relatively new phenomenon, neither affluent enough to mitigate working class unrest nor sure of its place in political life—yet still asserting an unqualified right to ruthlessly exploit its "hired hands." But this new phenomenon was already beginning to find its way if not toward traditional European liberal political forms, then towards authoritarian ones which would give it the breathing space to develop.

The economic crisis of the thirties (which radicals throughout the world viewed as the final "chronic crisis" of capitalism), coupled with the myopic policies of the Spanish liberals and ruling classes turned the class struggle in

Spain into an explosive class war. The agrarian reform policies of the early thirties republic turned out to be farcical. The liberals were more preoccupied with baiting the Church than dealing seriously with the long-range or even short-range economic problems of the peninsula. The Socialists, who joined the liberals in governing the country, were more concerned with promoting the growth of the UGT at the expense of the CNT than in improving the material conditions of the working class as a whole. The CNT, strongly influenced by volatile *faistas* whose radical education had been acquired in the *pistolero* battles of the early twenties, exploded into repeated insurrections—uprisings which its leaders probably knew were futile, but were meant to stimulate the revolutionary spirit of the working class. These failures by all the elements of Spain in the early republican years to meet the promise of reform left no recourse but revolution and civil war. Except for the most dedicated anarchists, it was a conflict that no one really wanted. But between 1931, when the monarchy was overthrown, and 1936, when the generals rebelled, everyone was sleep-walking into the last of the great proletarian revolutions—perhaps the greatest in terms of its short-lived social programs and the initiative shown by the oppressed. The era seemed to have collected all its energies, its traditions, and its dreams for its last great confrontation—and thereafter was to disappear.

It is not surprising that the most communistic collectives in the Spanish Revolution appeared in the countryside rather than the cities, among villagers who were still influenced by archaic collectivistic traditions and were less ensnared in a market economy than their urban cousins. The ascetic values which so greatly influenced these highly communistic collectives often reflected the extreme poverty of the areas in which they were rooted. Cooperation and mutual aid in such cases formed the preconditions for survival of the community. Elsewhere, in the more arid areas of Spain, the need for sharing water and maintaining irrigation works was an added inducement to collective farming. Here, collectivization was also a technological necessity, but one which even the republic did not interfere with.

What makes these rural collectives important is not only that many of them practiced communism, but that they functioned so effectively under a system of popular self-management. On this score, I can offer no substitute for Dolgoff's translations and remarks. The accounts themselves totally belie the notion held by so many authoritarian Marxists that economic life must be scrupulously "planned" by a highly centralized state power and the odious canard that popular collectivization, as distinguished from statist nationalization, necessarily pits collectivized enterprises against each other in competition for profits and resources.

In the cities, however, collectivization of the factories, communications systems, and transport facilities took a very different form. Initially, nearly the entire economy in CNT-FAI areas had been taken over by committees elected from among the workers and were loosely coordinated by higher union committees. As time went on. this system was increasingly tightened. The higher committee began to pre-empt the initiative of the lower, although their decisions still had to be ratified by the workers of the facilities involved. The effect of this process was to tend to centralize the economy of CNT-FAI areas in the hands of the union. The extent to which this process unfolded varied greatly from industry to industry and area to area, and with the limited knowledge we have at hand, generalizations are very difficult to formulate. With the entry of the CNT-FAI into the Catalan government in 1936, the process of centralization continued and the union-controlled facilities became wedded to the state. By early 1938, a political bureaucracy had largely supplanted the authority of the workers' committees in all "republican"-held cities. Although workers control existed in theory, it had virtually disappeared in fact.

If the commune formed the basis for the rural collectives, the committee formed the basis for the industrial collectives. Indeed, apart from the rural communes, the committee system predominated wherever the State power had collapsed—in villages and towns as well as factories and urban neighborhoods. "All had been set up in the heat of action to direct the popular response to the military coup-d'etat," observe Broué and Témime:

"They had been appointed in an infinite number of ways. In the villages, the factories, and on the work sites, time had sometimes been taken to elect them, at least summarily, at a general meeting. At all events, care had been taken to see that all parties and unions were represented on them, even if they did not exist before the Revolution, because the Committee represented at one and the same time as the workers a whole and the sum total of their organizations: in more than one place those elected 'came to an understanding' as to who was to represent one or another union, who would be the 'Republican' and who the 'Socialist.' Very often, in the towns, the most active elements appointed themselves. It was sometimes the electors as a whole who chose the men to sit on the Committee of each organization, but more often the members of the Committee were elected either by a vote within their own organization or were quite simply appointed by the local governing committees of the parties and union."

The nearly forty years that separate our own time from the Spanish revolution have produced sweeping changes in western Europe and America, changes that are also reflected in Spain's present social development. The classical proletariat that fought so desperately for the minimal means of life is giving way to a more affluent worker whose major concern is not material survival and employment, but a more human way of life and meaningful work. The social composition of the labor force is changing as well—proportionately, more toward commercial, service, and professional vocations than unskilled labor in mass manufacturing industries. Spain, like the rest of western Europe, is no longer predominantly an agricultural country; the majority of its people live in towns and cities, not in the relatively isolated villages that nourished rural collectivism. In a visit to working class Barcelona during the late sixties, I seemed to see as many American-style attaché cases as lunch boxes.

These changes in the goals and traits of the non-bourgeois classes in capitalist society are the products of the sweeping industrial revolution that followed the Second World War and of the relative affluence or expectations of affluence that have brought all the values of material scarcity into question. They have introduced a historic tension between the irrationality of present lifeways and the utopian promise of a liberated society. The young workers of the late sixties and early seventies tend to borrow their values from relatively affluent middle class youth, who no longer hypostasize the work ethic, puritanical mores, hierarchical obedience, and material security, but rather free time for self-development, sexual liberation in the broadest sense of the term, creative or stimulating work as distinguished from mindless labor, and an almost libidinal disdain for all authority. In Spain it is significant that the privileged university students, who tended to play such a reactionary role in the thirties, are among the most radical elements of society in the sixties and seventies. Together with young workers and intellectuals in all fields, they are beginning to accept in varying degrees the personalistic and utopistic goals that make the puritanical and overly institutionalized anarcho-syndicalism of the CNT-FAI seem anachronistic.

The limitations of the trade union movement, even in its anarcho-syndicalist form, have become manifestly clear. To see in trade unions (whether syndicalist or not) an inherent potentiality for revolutionary struggle is to assume that the interests of workers and capitalists, *merely as classes*, are intrinsically incompatible. This is demonstrably untrue if one is willing to acknowledge the obvious capacity of the system to remake or to literally create the worker in the image of a repressive industrial culture and rationality. From the family, through the school and religious institutions, the mass media, to the factory and finally trade union and "revolutionary" party, capitalist society conspires to foster obedience, hierarchy, the work ethic, and authoritarian discipline in the working class as a whole; indeed, in many of its "emancipatory" movements as well.

The factory and the class organizations that spring from it play the most compelling role in promoting a well-regulated, almost unconscious docility in mature workers—a docility that manifests itself not so much in characterless passivity as in a pragmatic commitment to hierarchical organizations and authoritarian leaders. Workers can be very militant and exhibit strong, even powerful character traits in the most demanding social situations; but these traits can be brought as much, if not more readily, to the service of a reformist labor bureaucracy as to a libertarian revolutionary movement. They must break with the hold of bourgeois culture on their sensibilities—specifically, with the hold of the factory, the locus of the workers' very *class* existence—before they can move into that supreme form of direct action called "revolution," and further, construct a society they will *directly* control in their workshops and communities.

This amounts to saying that workers must see themselves as human beings, not as class beings; as creative personalities, not as "proletarians," as self-affirming individuals, not as "masses." And the destiny of a liberated society must be the free commune, not a confederation of factories, however self-administered; for such a confederation takes a part of society—its economic component—and reifies it into the totality of society. Indeed, even that economic component must be humanized precisely by bringing an "affinity of friendship" to the work process, by diminishing the role of onerous work in the lives of the producers, indeed, by a total "transvaluation of values" (to use Neitzsche's phrase) as it applies to production and consumption as well as social and personal life.

Even though certain aspects of the libertarian revolution in Spain have lost their relevance, anarchist concepts themselves that can encompass and fully express a "post-scarcity mentality," can be much more relevant to the present than the authoritarian ideologies of the 1930's, despite the tendency of these ideologies to fill the vacuum left by the absence of meaningful libertarian alternatives and organizations. Such anarchist concepts could no longer rely in practical terms on the collectivist traditions of the countryside; these traditions are virtually gone as living forces, although perhaps the memory of the old collectivist traditions lives among Spanish youth in the same sense that American youth have turned to the tribal traditions of the American Indians for cultural inspiration. With the decline of the nuclear family and in reaction to urban atomization, the commune has everywhere acquired a new relevance for young and even older people—a shared, mutually supportive way of life based on *selective* affinity rather than kinship ties. Burgeoning urbanization has posed more shrply than ever the need for decentralistic alternatives to the megalopolis; the gigantism of the city, the need for the human scale. The grotesque bureaucratization of life, which in Camus' words reduces everyone to a functionary, has placed a new value on non-authoritarian institutions and direct action. Slowly, even amidst the setbacks of our time, a new self is being forged. Potentially, this is a libertarian self that could intervene directly in the changing and administration of society—a self that could engage in the self-discipline, self-activity, and self-management so crucial to the development of a truly free society. Here, the values prized so highly by traditional anarcho-communism establish direct continuity with a contemporary form of anarcho-communism that givess consciousness and coherence to the intuitive impulses of this new sensibility.

But if these goals are to be achieved, contemporary anarcho-communism cannot remain a mere mood or tendency, wafting in the air like a cultural ambience. It must be organized—indeed, *well*-organized—if it is to effectively articulate and spread this new sensibility; it must have a coherent theory and extensive literature; it must be capable of dueling with the authoritarian movements that try to denature the intuitive libertarian impulses of our time and channel social unrest into hierarchical forms of organization. On this score, Spanish anarchism is profoundly relevant for our time and the Spanish Revolution still provides the most valuable lessons in the problem of self-management that we can cull from the past.

To deal with these problems, perhaps I can best begin by saying that there is little, in fact, to criticize in the *structural* forms that the CNT and the FAI tried to establish. The CNT, almost from the outset, organized its locals as factory rather than craft unions, and the nation-wide occupational federations (the *Uniones de oficio* or "internationals" as we would call them) which emerged with the IWMA were abandoned for local federations (the *Federaciones locales*). This structure situated the factory in the community, where it really belonged if the "commune" concept was to be realistic, rather than in an easily manipulatable industrial network that easily lent itself to statist nationalization. The *centros obreros*, the local federations, the careful mandating of delegates to congresses, the elimination of paid officials, the establishment of regional federations, regional committees, and even a National Committee, would all have been in conformity with libertarian principles had all of these institutions lived up their intentions. Where the CNT structure failed most seriously was in the need to convene frequent assemblies of workers at the local level, and similarly, frequent national and regional conferences to continually re-evaluate CNT policies and prevent power from collecting in the higher committees. For, as frequent as meetings may have been—committees, subcommittees, and regional and national committee meetings—the regular and close communication between workers and the "influential militants" did tend to become ruptured.

Confusion developed over the crucial problem of the locus for making policy decisions. The real place for this process should have been shop assemblies, regular congresses, or when events and circumstances required rapid decisions, conferences of clearly mandated and recallable delegates elected for this purpose by the membership. The sole responsibility of the regional and national committees should have been administrative—that is, the coordination and execution of policy decisions formulated by membership meetings and conference or congress delegates.

Nevertheless, the structure of the CNT as a syndicalist union and that of the FAI as an anarchist federation was, in many respects, quite admirable. Indeed, my principal criticisms in the pages above have been not so much of the forms themselves, but of the departures the CNT and the FAI made from them. Perhaps even more significantly, I've tried to explain the social limitations of the period—including the mystique about the classical proletariat—that vitiated the realization of these structural forms.

Another issue that was a crucial problem for the FAI and which is still a source of confusion for anarchists at the present time is the problem of the "influential militant"—the more informed, experienced, "strong," and oratorically gifted individuals who tended to formulate policy at all levels of the organization.

It will never be possible to eliminate the fact that human beings have different levels of knowledge and consciousness. Our prolonged period of dependence as children, the fact that we are largely the products of an acquired culture and that experience tends to confer knowledge on the older person would lead to such differences even in the most liberated society. In hierarchical societies, the dependence of the less-informed on the more-informed is commonly a means of manipulation and power. The older, more experienced person, like the parent, has this privilege at his or her disposal and, with it, an alternative: to use knowledge, experience, and oratorical gifts as means of domination and to induce adulation—or for the goal of lovingly imparting knowledge and experience, for equalizing the relationship between teacher and taught, and always leaving the less experienced and informed individual free to make his or her decisions.

Hegel brilliantly draws the distinction between Socrates and Jesus: the former a teacher who sought to arouse a quest for knowledge in anyone who was prepared to discuss; the latter, an oracle who pronounced "truth" for adoring disciples to interpret exegetically. The difference, as Hegel points out, lay not only in the character of the two men but in that of their "followers." Socrates' friends had been reared in a social tradition that "developed their powers in many directions. They had absorbed that democratic spirit which gives an individual a greater measure of independence and makes it impossible for any tolerably good head to depend wholly and absolutely on one person.... They loved Socrates because of his virtue and his philosophy, not virtue and his philosophy because of him." The followers of Jesus, on the other hand, were submissive acolytes. "Lacking any great store of spiritual energy of their own, they had found the basis of their conviction about the teaching of Jesus principally in their friendship with him and dependence on him. They had not attained truth and freedom by their own exertions; only by laborious learning had they acquired a dim sense of them and certain formulas about them. Their ambition was to grasp and keep this doctrine faithfully and to transmit it equally faithfully to others without any addition, without letting it acquire any variations in detail by working on it themselves."

The FAI—illegal by choice, sometimes terrorist in its tactics, and aggressively "macho" in its almost competitive daring—developed deeply personal ties within its affinity groups. Durruti's grief for the death of Francisco Ascaso revealed real love, not merely the friendship that stems from organizational collaboration. But in the FAI either friendship or love was often based on a demanding association, one that implicitly required conformity to the most "heroic" standards established by the most "daring" militants in the group. Such relationships are not likely to shatter over doctrinal disagreements or what often seem like "mere" points of theory. Eventually, these relationships produce leaders and led; worse, the leaders tend to patronize the led and finally manipulate them.

To escape this process of devolution, an anarchist organization must be aware of the fact that the process *can* occur and it must be vigilant against its occurrence. To be effective, the vigilance must eventually express itself in more positive terms. It cannot co-exist with an adulation of violence, competitive daring, and mindless aggressiveness, not to speak of an equally mindless worship of activism and "strong characters." The organization must recognize that differences in experiences and consciousness *do* exist among its members and handle these differences with a wary consciousness—not conceal them with euphemisms like the term "influential militant." The taught as well as the teacher must *first* be taught to ask himself or herself whether domination and manipulation is being practiced—and not deny that a systematic teaching process is taking place. Moreover, everyone must be fully aware that this teaching process is unavoidable within the movement if relationships are eventually to be equalized by imparted knowledge and the fruits of experience. To a large extent, the conclusions one arrives at about the nature of this process are almost intuitively determinable by the behavior patterns that develop between comrades. Ultimately, under conditions of freedom, social intercourse, friendship, and love would be of the "free-giving" kind that Jacob Bachofen imputes to "matriarchal" society, not the demanding censorius type he associates with patriarchy. Here, the affinity group or commune would achieve the most advanced and libertarian expression of its humanity. Merely to strive for this goal among its own brothers and sisters would qualitatively distinguish it from other movements and provide the most assurable guarantee that it would remain true to its libertarian principles.

Our period, which stresses the development of the individual self as well as social self-management, stands in a highly advantageous position to assess the authentic· nature of libertarian organization and relationships. A European or American civil war of the kind that wasted Spain in the thirties is no longer conceivable in an epoch that can deploy nuclear weapons, supersonic aircraft, nerve gas, and a terrifying firepower against revolutionaries. Capitalist institutions must be hollowed out by a molecular historical process of disengagement and disloyalty to a point where any popular majoritarian movement can cause them to collapse for want of support and moral authority. But the kind of development such a change will produce—whether it will occur consciously or not, whether it will have an authoritarian outcome or one based on self-management—will depend very much upon whether a conscious, well-organized libertarian movement can emerge.

Sam Dolgoff's book presents a feast of historical experience that is invaluable to anyone who seeks non-authoritarian alternatives to the present society. His discussion and his selected accounts of the Spanish anarchist collectives must be studied not merely as history, but as raw material from which we can construct a realistic vision of a libertarian society. Whatever may have been its limitations in other spheres, Spanish anarchism's achievements in the economic sphere boggle all the conventional perspectives of liberal and socialist thought. In Spain, millions of people took large segments of the economy into their own hands, collectivized them, administered them, even abolished money and lived by communistic principles of work and distribution—all of this in the midst of a terrible civil war, yet without producing the chaos or even the serious dislocations that were and still are predicted by authoritarian "radicals." Indeed, in many collectivized areas, the efficiency with which an enterprise worked by far exceeded that of a comparable one in nationalized or private sectors. This "green shoot" of revolutionary reality has more meaning for us than the most persuasive theoretical arguments to the contrary. On this score it is not the anarchists who are the "unrealistic day-dreamers," but their opponents who have turned their backs to the facts or have shamelessly concealed them.

September, 1973

Friend Bookchin's stimulating remarks touch upon fundamental problems still being debated in the Anarchist movement. Regretably, adequate discussion of these questions are beyond the scope of this work.

While his views, in the main, parallel my own, I am sure that Comrade Bookchin himself, understands that some disagreement on such complex and controversial issues is inevitable. Not for a moment do I underestimate the very important things he has to say, nor, above all, the cordial libertarian spirit which animates him.—*Editor*

**THE ANARCHIST
COLLECTIVES**

The following map is intended to give a general picture of the areas of anarchist influence in Spain. Strongholds were in the areas of Andalusia (which was early in the war conquered by the fascists), Aragon, Catalonia, and sections of the Levant. There were isolated pockets elsewhere; particularly in Castile and Asturias.

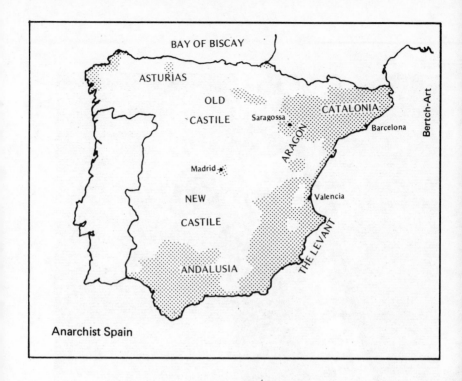

Anarchist Spain

Bertch-Art

part one:

background

Poster of the CNT-FAI. Caption reads "The Revolution and the War are inseparable."

chapter 1

The Spanish Revolution

The Two Revolutions
S.D.

The Spanish Revolution of 1936-1939 came closer to realizing the ideal of the free stateless society on a vast scale than any other revolution in history, including the aborted Russian Revolution of 1917.[1] In fact, they were two very different kinds of revolution. The Spanish Revolution is an example of a libertarian social revolution where genuine workers' self-management was successfully tried. It represents a way of organizing society that is increasingly important today. The Bolshevik Revolution, by contrast, was controlled by an elite party and was a political revolution. It set the doleful pattern for the authoritarian state capitalist revolutions in Eastern Europe, Asia (China, Korea, Vietnam), and Latin America (Cuba).

The Spanish Revolution thus marks a turning point in revolutionary history. Andrés Nin[2] conceded that it was "a proletarian revolution more profound even than the Russian Revolution itself." (Broué and Témime, p. 170) Yet it has been virtually ignored for over a quarter century: overshadowed by the Civil War or relegated to the "dustbin of history" as an "unsuccessful" revolution. Its significance is only now being adequately evaluated.

It is highly important for those interested in the study of modern revolutions to grasp the significance of social revolution in Spain. By

---

[1] See page 11 for the distinction between the terms "Russian Revolution" and "Bolshevik Revolution."

[2] With Joaquín Maurín, he founded the Spanish Communist Party, from which they split off to organize the dissident Marxist Party of Workers Unity—the POUM. He was murdered by the Stalinists in 1937.

comparing it with Marxist-Leninist doctrine and the Bolshevik example, certain themes will be introduced that will emphasize the Spanish Revolution's place as a libertarian revolution. These themes will point to the relevance of the Spanish Revolution to our own concerns with the movement for workers' self-management or workers' control. Gaston Leval, the French anarchist who participated in and studied the social revolution at first hand, admirably summarizes the achievements of the Spanish workers:

> Persuaded that we were fated to lose the war unleashed by Franco Fascism, I was determined to make a detailed study of the Revolution and record for future generations the results of this unique experience: to study on the spot, in the village collectives, in the factories, and in the socialized industries, the constructive work of the Spanish Revolution. . . . In Spain during almost three years, despite a civil war that took a million lives, despite the opposition of the political parties (republicans, left and right Catalan separatists, socialists, Communists, Basque and Valencian regionalists, petty bourgeoisie, etc.), this idea of libertarian communism was put into effect. Very quickly more than 60% of the land was collectively cultivated by the peasants themselves, without landlords, without bosses, and without instituting capitalist competition to spur production. In almost all the industries, factories, mills, workshops, transportation services, public services, and utilities, the rank and file workers, their revolutionary committees, and their syndicates reorganized and administered production, distribution, and public services without capitalists, high salaried managers, or the authority of the state.
>
> Even more: the various agrarian and industrial collectives immediately instituted economic equality in accordance with the essential principle of communism, "From each according to his ability and to each according to his needs." They coordinated their efforts through free association in whole regions, created new wealth, increased production (especially in agriculture), built more schools, and bettered public services. They instituted not bourgeois formal democracy but genuine grass roots functional libertarian democracy, where each individual participated directly in the revolutionary reorganization of social life. They replaced the war between men, "survival of the fittest," by the universal practice of mutual aid, and replaced rivalry by the principle of solidarity. . . .
>
> This experience, in which about eight million people directly or indirectly participated, opened a new way of life to those who sought an alternative to anti-social capitalism on the one hand, and

totalitarian state bogus socialism on the other. . . .(*Espagne Libertaire*, p. 11)

This experience in revolution explodes a number of widely held Marxian myths. For instance, that a social revolution could come only when the right stage of economic development prevailed (and then only with the help of a very centralized party dominated by a political elite). In Spain, however, the revolution immediately manifested the very different character anticipated by Bakunin:

The constructive tasks of the Social Revolution, the creation of new forms of social life, can emerge only from the living practical experiences of the grass roots organizations which will build the new society according to their manifold needs and aspirations. (Dolgoff, p. 180)

But spontaneity is not enough. The Spanish revolutionaries (as Bakunin himself repeatedly stressed) realized that it takes time for the "new forms of social life" to emerge, and to establish "grass roots organizations." To survive in a hostile atmosphere, to incarnate themselves into the revolutionary process, the new forms of organization must be prepared long before the outbreak of the revolution. And so they were. Seventy-five years of militant struggles and intense anarchist educational work prepared the Spanish industrial and land workers to meet the problems of the Social Revolution. (See "The Libertarian Tradition" below)

Trotsky himself conceded the potency of this revolutionary approach by comparing Spain in 1936 to Russia in 1917:

The Spanish proletariat displayed fighting qualities of the highest order . . . economically, politically and culturally, the Spanish workers from the very beginning of the Revolution showed themselves to be not inferior, but superior to the Russian proletariat at the beginning of the October Revolution in 1917. (Broué and Témime, p. 131 in the French edition)[3]

As indicated by Leval, the scope of the Spanish Revolution embraced the economic and political life of millions in the most populous and strategic areas of Republican Spain. About 75% of Spanish industry was

---

[3]I was impelled to translate this myself due to the distortion of Trotsky's remark (p. 170 in the English edition) by using the word "military" in place of the word "fighting"!

concentrated in Catalonia, the stronghold of the anarchist labor movement. This refutes decisively the allegation that anarchist organizational principles are not applicable to industrial areas, and if at all, only in primitive agrarian societies or in isolated experimental communities ' (See chapters 6 and 7 below on urban industrial collectivization).

The libertarian revolution was even more far reaching in the rural areas. This experience explodes the hoary Marxist dogma that only highly industrialized countries are ripe for communism. Augustin Souchy concludes in one of his many books on the Spanish Revolution that:

> The Marxist theory that Socialism will first be realized by the masses of the industrialized proletariat, next by the petty bourgeoisie, and last by the peasants is false. . . . The Aragon peasants have proven that industrialization is not the indispensable prerequisite for the establishment of libertarian communism. . . . libertarian communism was almost entirely realized in the smaller rural areas. . . . (*De Julio a Julio*, p. 172)

Nor are the peasants an inherently backward class as the Marxists would have us believe. All observers agree that:

> In the work of creation, transportation, and socialization, the peasants demonstrated a degree of social consciousness much superior to that of the city worker. (Leval, *Né Franco né Stalin*, p. 320)

This is quite different from the usual view of the revolutionary role of the peasants. A unique characteristic of the Spanish Revolution was the achievement of close cooperation between rural and urban workers. Years of agitation and education by the anarchists were very effective in dealing with what is one of the most crucial problems of every revolution: the relations between the industrial proletariat and the agricultural workers, between the anarchist and anarcho-syndicalist movements and the peasants. The intermeshing of local, regional, and national federations of peasant collectives (which included 90% of the poorest peasants) with the federations of urban socialized enterprises was the culmination of a process which traces back to the latter half of the 19th century.

The impression that Spanish anarchism was largely a rural movement, though exaggerated, is by no means unfounded. The terms "rural anarchism" and "rural anarcho-syndicalism" have often, and rightfully, been used to designate Spanish peasant rebellions. A few examples:

In 1881, farm workers ... constituted the largest single occupational grouping in the new Anarchist Federation. ... By September 1882, 20,915 of the 57,934 members were agrarian workers. ... The reemergence of rural anarchism in 1903 brought with it more continuous and widespread labor agitation than any previously recorded in Andalusia. The most serious outbreaks occurred in the traditional anarchist strongholds of Seville and Cadiz. ... From 1913 to 1917 ... anarcho-syndicalist locals sprang up both in the Levant and Aragon. In 1919 there were at least thirty-three such locals in Valencia alone. ... In Cordova [1920], for example, workers' organizations existed in 61 of the 75 townships and claimed a membership of 55,382 out of a total active rural population of 130,000. (Malefakis, pp. 139, 140, 148)

During this whole period while "the anarchists had awakened the peasantry," the Spanish socialists, like their prophet Marx, "largely ignored the existence of the agrarian problem." (Malefakis, p. 290) Marx placed all his hopes for revolution upon the industrial proletariat. He had no confidence in the creative revolutionary capacity of the agricultural workers. "Rural idiocy" was one of his favorite expressions.

From the experience of the Bolshevik Revolution it should by now be axiomatic that a revolution which provokes the resistance of the peasants, that cannot or will not establish solidarity between land and city workers, must inevitably degenerate into a counter-revolutionary dictatorship. The disastrous consequences of Lenin's forced requisition of peasant crops and livestock precluded such solidarity. The peasants retaliated by starving the cities, planting only enough for their needs, slaughtering livestock sorely needed by the cities, and finally forcing Lenin to reverse himself and institute his semi-capitalistic "New Economic Policy." Stalin's forced "collectivization" of land and the liquidation of millions of "Kulaks" (which all but crippled the economy for many years) proceeded along the same authoritarian lines and are too well documented to need further comment. The "Kholkhozes" (collectives) established by Stalin are not genuine collectives, that is, created and managed by the workers themselves. In the tradition of Lenin and Stalin, they are, like all the other "soviet" social and economic institutions, simply creatures of the state.

The pattern is all too familiar. The workers must obey the orders of the bureaucrats appointed by the state, who are in turn obliged to carry out the instructions of the political commissars. Payment is arbitrarily fixed according to norms (production goals, the speedup system) determined by the state planners. (See the selection below on "The Political and Economic

Organization of Society" in which a Spanish anarchist contrasts this authoritarian approach with the libertarian approach actually put into practice in Spain)

The Spanish Revolution shattered yet another Marxist dogma, that of the "transition period." During the first stage in the transition to full communism, so the doctrine goes, means can be separated from ends. Under "socialism," it is necessary to retain some of the main evils of capitalism. Thus workers will be paid not according to their needs but according to how much they produce. In line with this theory the Bolsheviks made no serious attempt to abolish the wage system or even to equalize wages.

In less than three years the libertarian collectives did away with the wage system. Where this was not possible because of the sabotage of the Republican government, the bourgeoisie and their socialist and Communist allies, they equalized income to the greatest possible extent (this was true of most of the socialized urban enterprises). The Revolution instituted the "family wage," under which commodities were distributed and services rendered not according to the amount of labor performed, but according to the number and needs of the family members. Similar arrangements were made for individuals living alone.

More than half a century after the October Revolution the piecework system still prevails. One need only compare the much higher earnings of a "Stakhanovite" (piecework "hero of labor") as against the low wages of the less "heroic" average worker. Or better yet, compare the privileges enjoyed by the not so new class of high ranking party officials, bureaucrats, technocrats, military officers, and the prostituted "intelligentsia," with their apartments in town, their "dachas" in the country, their domestic servants (and the rest), with the low living standards of ordinary Soviet families.

Evils "temporarily" tolerated become permanently encrusted and institutionalized into the totalitarian state apparatus, administered by a self-perpetuating ruling class which can be dislodged only by another revolution.

Contrary to Marxist-Leninist doctrine, the experience of the Spanish Revolution clearly demonstrated (even during this famous transitional period from capitalism to socialism) the practical superiority of libertarian organizational procedures to authoritarian dictatorial methods. Cooperation and free agreement from below get better results than rule by decree from the top down. The Marxist-Leninists did not even begin to grasp the most elementary principles of social reconstruction, of how to get things moving again. Adept as they were at political chicanery and seizing power, these "builders of socialism" had not the foggiest notion of how to organize even

THE BOLSHEVIK REVOLUTION
VS THE RUSSIAN SOCIAL REVOLUTION

In the course of the crises and failures which followed one another up to the revolution of 1917, Bolshevism was not the only conception of how the Social Revolution should be accomplished. . . . [A] second fundamental ideal, likewise envisaging a full and integral social revolution, took shape and spread among the revolutionary circles and also among the working masses: this was the Anarchist idea.

The Bolshevik idea was to build, on the ruins of the bourgeois state, a new *"Workers' State" to constitute a "workers' and peasants' government," and to establish a "dictatorship of the proletariat".* . . . In the contention of the Bolsheviki, it was the elite—their elite—which, forming a "workers' government" and establishing a so-called "dictatorship of the proletariat," would carry out the social transformation and solve its prodigious problems. The masses should aid this elite (the opposite of the libertarian belief that the elite should aid the masses) by faithfully, blindly, mechanically carrying out its plans, decisions, orders, and "laws." And the armed forces, also in imitation of those of the capitalist countries, like wise should blindly obey the "elites."

The Anarchist idea [was and] is to transform the economic and social bases of society *without having recourse to a political state,* to a government, or to a dictatorship of any sort. That is, to achieve the Revolution and resolve its problems not by *political or statist means,* . . . by means of natural and free activity, *economic and social, of the associations of the workers themselves,* after having overthrown the last capitalist government. . . . The libertarians hold that a favourable solution of the problems of the Revolution can result only from the freely and consciously collective and united work of millions of men and women who bring to it and harmonize in it all the variety of their needs and interests, their strength and capacities. . . . By the natural interplay of their economic, technical, and social organizations, with the help of the "elite" and, in case of need, under the protection of their freely organized armed forces, the labouring masses should, in the view of the libertarians, be able to carry the Revolution effectively forward.

VOLINE, from *Nineteen-Seventeen: The Russian Revolution Betrayed* (London, 1954)

Such is, and remains, the essential difference between the two ideas. Such also were the two opposed conceptions of the Social Revolution at the moment of the Russian upheaval in 1917.

a village collective, much less to restore the economic life of the great Russian nation. For example:

> Andrés Nin liked to tell his companions that the return of public services to normal working order had been incomparably faster in Barcelona in 1936 than in Moscow in 1917. (Broué and Témime, p. 170)

The purged Bolshevik "left oppositionist" Victor Serge (an ex-anarchist who had not entirely rejected all he had learned) criticized the criminal inefficiency of the Bolshevik administrators in dealing with the economic crisis. In seeking another resolution to the economic problems, he illustrated the relevance of libertarian organizational principles:

> Through its intolerance and its arrogation of an absolute monopoly of power and initiative in all fields, the Bolshevik regime was floundering in its own toils. . . . Certain industries could have been revived merely by appealing to the initiative of groups of producers and consumers, by freeing the State-strangled cooperatives, and inviting various associations to take over the management of different branches of economic activity. . . . In a word, I was arguing for a "Communism of associations"—in contrast to Communism of the State variety. . . . I thought of the total plan not as something to be dictated by the State from on high but rather as resulting from the harmonizing, by congresses and specialized assemblies, of initiatives from below. (pp. 147-148)

Unfortunately, these creative forms of social life (unions, soviets, factory committees, workers' councils, cooperatives, and other grass roots organizations), exhausted by years of war and privation, were not able to withstand the onslaughts of the well-organized Communist Party dictatorship. Valiant attempts—which took such forms as the Kronstadt rebellion, peasant uprisings, strikes, and passive resistance—to save the real Russian Revolution from its Bolshevik usurpers, were crushed.

The practical application of the libertarian principles that Serge talks about is precisely the achievement of the Spanish Revolution, in stark contrast to the Bolshevik experience (and the experience of most revolutions in this century). In Spain collectives were formed spontaneously according to Spain's historic traditions and anarchist-federalist principles.

The Spanish Revolution demonstrated in practice that libertarian communist measures could be introduced at once. The Revolution must simultaneously destroy the old order and immediately take on a federalistic and anarchistic direction. Revolutionaries exploring new roads to freedom are increasingly inclined to take these factors into account.

These collectives were not conceived according to any single plan or forced to conform to a particular framework. Freedom implies variety, and the reader will see in the selections that follow, the great variety of ways the workers devised to meet their everyday problems. From his observations made during his visits to rural collectives and urban socialized enterprises, Souchy concluded that:

> Economic variety, i.e., the coexistence of collective and privately conducted enterprises,[4] will not adversely affect the economy. But economic variety is, on the contrary, the true manifestation and indispensable precondition for a free society. Regimentation, the imposition of a uniform economic system by and for the benefit of the state, works out inevitably to the detriment of the people. . . . [5] (*Nacht über Spanien*, pp. 151-152)

The anarchist Diego Abad de Santillan is somewhat more explicit:

> In each locality the degree of communism, collectivism, or mutualism[6] will depend upon the conditions prevailing. Why dictate rules? We who make freedom our banner cannot deny it in the economy. Therefore there must be free experimentation, free show of initiative and suggestions, as well as freedom of organization. . . . We are not interested in how the workers, employees, and technicians of a factory will organize themselves. That is their affair. But what is fundamental is that from the first moment of Revolution there exist a proper cohesion (coordination) of all the productive and distributive forces. (*After the Revolution*, pp. 97, 98, 99)

More than any other revolution, the Spanish Revolution succeeded in effectively coordinating just such a mixed economy under conditions of freedom and a minimum of friction. Many individuals, petty peasant proprietors, were induced to join the collectives, not by force, but by witnessing the advantages of cooperation. The realistic policies and the

[4] Souchy is referring to enterprises that did not employ wage labor.

[5] Economic variety in a free society is not to be equated with the greater or lesser measure of private enterprise which peasants in "communist" countries forced their rulers to grant on threat of starving the cities. Nor for that matter is it to be equated with the "variety" claimed in capitalist countries.

[6] Mutualism is the economic doctrine of Proudhon and his followers.

humanitarian spirit of the Spanish libertarian collectives also earned the cooperation of technical, professional, and scientific workers in reorganizing economic life. Friendly relations were established with those who preferred to remain outside of the collectives.

It is a twofold historic tragedy that the Communist Party, which aborted the Russian Revolution of 1917, also crushed the Spanish Revolution of 1936-1939. But this takes us away from the very real accomplishments and lessons of the Spanish Revolution.

The Trend Towards Workers' Self-Management
S.D.

The social revolution in Spain was a libertarian revolution in many aspects, from its voluntaristic methods to its anti-bureaucratic principles. But perhaps the most important was the practice of workers' self-management, manifested in the freely formed collectives of urban and rural workers and their federalist form of coordination.

Frank Mintz writes in the foreword to his *La Collectivization en Espagne de 1936 à 1939* that the study of Spanish collectives is relevant because:

> The problem of collective management . . . collectivization in line with federalist theories, "self-government," "workers' control" . . . is even more applicable than before. . . . In advanced industrial countries, political and economic centralization leads to irrational concentration of industries. . . . To defrost the economy certain social groups (economists, politicians, the clergy) are advocating various forms of workers' participation in industry. . . . (pp. 2-3)

Economists, sociologists, politicians, administrators, and statesmen in both East and West now favor a measure of workers' control (decentralization, collectivization, co-management), not because they have suddenly become anarchists, but primarily because technology has rendered such forms of organization operational necessities. But as long as these forms are tied to capitalism or the state, these various forms of self- or

In a mass demonstration in Barcelona, workers hold a banner reading, "*Solidaridad Obrera*, the daily newspaper of the Revolution." The banner is inscribed with the initials CNT, FAI, and AIT (the International Workingman's Association).

co-management in both industrial and rural areas will remain a fraud, a more efficient device to enlist the cooperation of the masses in their own servitude.

For example, the Yugoslavian experiments (which have been variously called "workers' control," "self-management," "co-management," "collectives," or "communes ") have been hailed as a radical, even libertarian, departure from Soviet-style rural collectivization and industrial co-management. Yugoslavian Communists claim that these measures are in line with Marx's and Engels' prediction that the "state will wither away." In their acrimonious factional disputes, the Russians have accused their Yugoslavian comrades of flirting with the "old discredited utopian visions of Proudhon, Bakunin, Kropotkin, and the Anarcho-Syndicalists," allegedly imported by the Yugoslavian members of the International Brigade from Spain (thus implying a connection with Spanish anarchism). But upon closer examination the Yugoslavian system of "workers' control" turns out to be a brazen fraud, differing in no essential respect from the Russian totalitarian pattern. Daniel Guérin, a keen student of the subject, sums up the facts:

> Both in Yugoslavia and in Algeria . . . self-management is coming into being in the framework of a dictatorial, military, police state whose skeleton is formed by a single party . . . a small minority. . . . The real managers of the enterprises . . . perpetuate themselves in dictatorial positions, cutting themselves off from the rank and file workers whom they treat with arrogance and contempt. . . . The party cells in most enterprises falsify elections . . . pressure workers' councils to ratify decisions taken in advance, and manipulate the national congresses of the workers. . . . (pp. 145, 146, 147)

In this connection it is worth noting that the Yugoslavian Communists never intended to hand over control of the economy to the workers. As far back as 1952, they made sure that their party would remain in the saddle. According to *Borba*, the official organ of the party, of the 763 directors of enterprises, 763 were active party members: "all directors understand that their main obligation is to be faithful to the party and the state which named them to their posts in reward for their zealous service to the party. . . . " (*Borba*, Feb. 13, 1952, quoted in *Noir et Rouge*, Paris, 1966, p. 18)

Another more recent example of a "revolutionary" *and* totalitarian economy is Cuba. Guérin quotes (on p. 152) from *Cuba: Socialism and Development* (New York, 1970) by René Dumont, an economic specialist and sympathetic consultant to Castro. Dumont deplores the "hypercentralization" of the economy and "authoritarian" approach to managing industry. A knowledgeable Polish friend voiced Dumont's views when he said, "Cuba is beginning all over again the useless cycle of economic errors of the socialist countries." Dumont's recommendations closely resemble the organizational principles instituted by the Spanish libertarian collectives: genuine self-management including autonomous production units in factories and federations of small production cooperatives in agriculture. On page 148 Guerin points to "Spanish Anarcho-Syndicalism" as the model for the regeneration of the Cuban labor movement, crushed by Castro. To have genuine self-management there must be "an authentic trade-union movement, independent of authority and of the single party, springing from the workers themselves and at the same time organizing them..."

Dumont has since written another book with the revealing title *Is Cuba a Socialist Country?*, denouncing the Castro regime for the further degeneration and militarization of the Cuban economy and social life. He proceeds to answer the question (in his title) in the negative. Paul Zorkine, an expert who made an exhaustive study of the subject, states that:

> On the basis of the facts, *the idea of workers' councils is incompatible with the existence of the state*, and whenever these two (the state and the councils) tried to coexist, it was not the state that "withered away" but, on the contrary, the state absorbed the councils.... (*Noir et Rouge*, April, 1966, Zorkine's emphasis)

The idea of self-management of industry, urban and rural, not as a "partnership between management and labor" or between the state and its subjects but as the cornerstone of a libertarian society, is increasingly evident in the changing attitudes of the most advanced elements in the modern labor and socialist movements. Although (as is to be expected) there are all sorts of differing viewpoints, the libertarian trend of thought, too often clouded by authoritarian overtones, is unmistakable even among professed Marxists. A good example is an interview with Michel Pablo, formerly secretary of the Trotskyist "Fourth International" and a former member of the defunct Algerian Ben Bella government.

Question: [The] struggle for workers' control and self-management suggest a different type of "socialism" to what we have known. We have been used to revolutions... followed by the setting up of a centralized state apparatus which plans and directly manages an almost wholly nationalised economy. It is popularly held that . . . while it means that bureaucracy proliferates and the workers have less rights than in many advanced capitalist countries, it is the best way to quickly develop. . . . Is this "economic" justification valid?

Answer: I don't think so at all. . . . The basis of their [the "underdeveloped" countries] sustained, continuous economic development must, in my opinion, be the formation of the self-managed commune. These countries must be looked upon as a collection of communes, each commune representing not only an administrative unit but an economic unit which carries out its own plan of economic and social development . . . (*Bulletin of the Institute for Workers' Control*, Vol. 2, No. 5, 1970)

There is a growing disillusionment with nationalization of industry in both capitalist democracies and totalitarian "socialist" countries. Although not yet prepared to call for the total abolition of the state, the realization that the powers of the state must be curbed spurs the search for practical alternatives to authoritarianism. And this search is taking on an increasingly libertarian direction.

Truly, as so aptly put by Geoffrey Ostergaard, workers' control is "an idea on the wing."[7] This renewed interest spurs intensive research on the history and significance of the workers' control tendency from the days of Robert Owen up to the present. A vast recent literature on the subject piles up. But this research will remain woefully inadequate until such time as the movement is enriched by indispensable and adequate literature on the unparalleled constructive achievements of the Spanish Revolution.

It is hoped that the primary source documents of various eyewitnesses and activists assembled here will, in their own modest way, help fill the need for such vital information and inspire others.

---

[7] In this work we have generally chosen to use the term "workers' self-management" instead of "workers' control." Since Geoffrey Ostergaard wrote these words in *Anarchy* in the early 1960's, the concept of workers' control has been co-opted. See page 81 for a short discussion of the current differences between these concepts.

chapter 2
The Libertarian Tradition

Introduction

A social revolution is neither an accidental happening nor a *coup d'état* artificially engineered from above.

It is the culmination of a long period of gestation. Nurtured on the one hand by negative forces, there is rebellion against oppression springing from the inability of the old order to cope with acute economic and social problems. On the other hand there are the positive, contructive forces. The long submerged elements of the new society, freed by the Revolution, emerge as the old society decays and collapses. We are here primarily concerned with these positive constructive tendencies and traditions which will shape the character of the free society.

Spanish anarchism springs from two sources: the inherent libertarian tradition of rural collectives, and the deeply rooted and militantly federalist tendencies which found expression in Bakunin's anarcho-syndicalist organizational principles. We briefly trace these two sources below.

We conclude this chapter with the summation of an article by the anarchist theoretician Isaac Puente.[1] It is an example of how these two foundations of Spanish anarchism intermesh. He contrasts the state and authoritarian organization with the free association of individuals through libertarian urban industrial and agrarian organization. As he wrote in CNT (October 24, 1933), "We are not interested in changing governments. What we want is to suppress them. . . . " Here, Puente outlines alternatives to the authoritarian organization of society.

---

[1] A medical doctor, he was an important anarchist militant. He was imprisoned and murdered by the fascists while fighting on the Saragossa front during the Civil War.

The Rural Collectivist Tradition
S.D.

Gerald Brenan has written that "in its roots Spanish Anarchism is rural." (p. 199) There is indeed a strong agricultural and pastoral tradition in Spain that *is* anarchistic. This is not, however, all there is to Spanish anarchism, as we shall see in the next section of this chapter. But it is from rural roots that the first libertarian collectives sprang. They were not invented by the anarchists but date back to mediaeval times.

Agrarian collectivism is traditional in the Iberian Peninsula, as it is among the Berbers and in the ancient Russian *mir*. The historians Costa and Reparez trace the origins of a great many Iberian collectives. . . . A form of rural libertarian-communism existed in the Iberian Peninsula before the Roman invasion. Not even five centuries of oppression by Catholic kings, the State and the Church have been able to eradicate the spontaneous tendency to establish libertarian communistic communities. . . . (*Campo Libre*, anarchist magazine, 1936, quoted in Mintz, pp. 34, 35)

The beginnings of collective land tenure are obscure but probably come from many sources—such as the working of land that would only yield to collective efforts, and grants of land to communities of liberated serfs designed to populate certain areas. By the 18th century there were a great many villages in northern Spain that owned the surrounding land and the villagers would periodically divide it up among themselves. In the Pyrenees there were shepherd communities that had communal pastures.

Rural collectivism was not limited to land tenure alone, as in many other parts of the world. In fact an amazing strength of Spanish collectivism was the tendency of the people to introduce collectivist or cooperative ways of doing things into other aspects of their daily life.

What is, however, remarkable is that in Spain the village communities spontaneously developed on this basis an extensive system of municipal services, to the point of their sometimes reaching an advanced stage of communism. (Brenan, p. 339)

Municipal cooperatives often provided for the needs of village inhabitants: anything from the surgeon to papal indulgences. Guilds provided sickness and old age insurance for their members. Some fishing communities became collectivized as early as the 16th century. Even early industrial undertakings, like net-making, were collectivized.

Brenan gives impressive examples of these collectives from the investigations of J. Langdon Davies and Joaquin Costa, the greatest historian of agrarian collectivism in Spain. We can do no better than to quote from his example of the village of Port de la Selva in Catalonia. Brenan draws on Davies' description made shortly before the Civil War and then adds his own historical context:

> The village was run by a fishermen's cooperative. They owned the nets, the boats, the curing factory, the store house, the refrigerating plant, all the shops, the transport lorries, the olive groves and the oil refinery, the café, the theater, and the assembly rooms. They had developed the *pósito*, or municipal credit fund possessed by every village in Spain, into an insurance against death, accident, and loss of boats. They coined their own money.... Port de la Selva was in short a libertarian republic and had achieved the ideal of all those villages of Catalonia, Andalusia and even Castile which at different times during the past century have declared themselves independent and have proceeded to divide up lands and issue their own coinage....[2]
>
> What is interesting is to see how naturally these cooperatives have fitted into the Spanish scene. For Port de la Selva is one of the old fishermen's communes of Catalonia which have existed from time immemorial.... Here then we have a modern productive cooperative grafted on to an ancient communal organization and functioning perfectly. (pp. 337, 338)

There were, of course, other forces at work. Through the years many municipalities lost their democratic qualities as the king, nobles, and rich merchants intervened. The municipality often became an instrument of coercion and state power.

After 1868, anarchist thought began to influence popular dissent. (See

---

[2] Brenan, however, does not make a very important distinction between Port de la Selva and the libertarian collectives established during the revolution, where the land was *not divided* but *collectively owned.* —Ed.

"The Anarchist Influence" below) The workers organized themselves into local federations or syndicates. These syndicates provided the organizational basis for revolutionary pressure, and they portended the organizational form of the collectives during the social revolution. They were also identical in every way to the village assembly in many early municipalities.

An important period of revolutionary action in 1918 gives a flavor of the role (as a new form and an old form) that the syndicate played:

> That autumn saw therefore the immense majority of agricultural workers of the south and east of Spain, together with the tradesmen and the workers in small local industries, organized in one vast though loose syndicate. The beginning of a peasants' confederation that would cover the whole of Spain seemed to be in sight. During these years the local syndicates everywhere acquired immense prestige and authority. Their leading men, who sat on the committees, were the real rulers of the districts. The municipality kept only a nominal power. Every Sunday the syndicate would meet in full assembly to discuss local affairs. The whole village attended and anyone who wished to had the right to speak. Resolutions were passed and voting took place by a show of hands. During the rest of the week the committee enforced its will by a system of fines against which an appeal could always be made to the village assembly. What one was witnessing was really the rebirth of the municipality of the early Middle Ages. (Brenan, pp. 180, 181) .

Peasant movements on as great or greater a scale launched in the years immediately preceding the Spanish Civil War of 1936 are better known. Franz Mintz cites frustrated peasant rebellions to institute *Comunismo Libertario* in 43 villages in Granada, Malaga, Almeria, and Jaen.

> In January, 1932, the FAI launched an insurrectional movement in the mining region of Upper Llobregat and Cordona. . . . In the Levant at the end of 1932, Bétera, Bugarra, Pedralba, and Ribaroja proclaimed libertarian communism, hoisted the red and black flag, burnt records, and announced the abolition of money, private property, and the 'exploitation of man by man.' (Mintz, pp. 11-12, 40-41, 45. He also cites other examples.)

The nature of the Spanish rural collectivist tradition goes well beyond peculiar agrarian conditions, as we have suggested. It was all encompassing, tenacious, and clear about its goals:

There has not been a peasant rising in Andalusia in the last hundred years when the villages did not form communes, divide up the land, abolish money, and declare themselves independent—free, that is, from the interference of "foreign" landlords and police. (Brenan, p. 196)

Similarly, as peasants came to the cities to work in factories, etc., they brought this collectivist tradition with them.

[Industrial workers] ask, first of all, for self-government for their industrial village or syndicate, and then for a shortening of the hours, a reduction in the quantity of the work. They ask for more liberty and more leisure and above all more respect for human dignity, but not necessarily a higher standard of living. (Brenan, p. 196)

We conclude by quoting Brenan once more: "Again one finds the anarchists hastening to restore the groundwork of local life from which Spain in the days of her greatness had sprung." (p. 202, note N)

The Anarchist Influence

S.D.

The rural collectivist tradition in Spain laid the groundwork for Spanish anarchism. But it was the fundamental principles of anarchism worked out by Bakunin and the libertarian wing of the First International that decisively determined the orientation of the Spanish anarchist movement. The "Declaration of Principles" written by Bakunin on the founding of the International Alliance of Socialist Democracy on Sept. 25, 1868, provides an intellectual basis similar to this rural tradition we have already talked about:

The Alliance declares itself atheist; it seeks the complete and definitive abolition of classes and the political, economic, and social equality of both sexes. It wants the land and the instruments of labor (production), like all other property [not personal belongings], to be converted into the collective property of the whole society for utilization [not ownership] by the workers: that is, by agricultural and industrial federations. It affirms that all existing political and authoritarian states, which are to be reduced to simple administrative functions dealing with public utilities in their respective countries, must eventually be replaced by the worldwide union of free association, agricultural and industrial. (Dolgoff, p. 35)

Later that year, the Alliance was introduced into Spain by Bakunin's emissary, the Italian revolutionist Giuseppe Fanelli. Though knowing no Spanish, Fanelli was still able in a matter of weeks to lay a firm foundation for the acceptance of Bakunin's anarchism.

The founders of the International in Spain—men like Farga y Pellicer, Gaspar Sentiñon, Anselmo Lorenzo, Francisco Mora, Gonzalez Morago, and José Garcia Viñas—were all members of the Bakuninist Alliance. By the middle of 1870 the Spanish Federation of the International had over 20,000 members:

a new organization based solely upon the interests, the needs and the natural preferences of the populations—having no other principle but the free federation of individuals into communes, of communes into provinces, of provinces into nations, and finally of the nations into the United States of Europe first, and of the entire world eventually. ("Federalism, Socialism, Anti-Theologism", in Dolgoff, pp. 104, 105)

The resolutions of the libertarian sections of the International constituted the "Magna Carta" of Spanish anarcho-syndicalism. The important "Program of the Alliance," for instance, differentiated the organization of the masses from the state and emphasized the need for these organizational forms to be consonant with the daily life of the worker. Bakunin summarized this important point:

The organization of the International . . . will take on an essentially different character from the organization of the state. Just as the state is authoritarian, artificial, violent, foreign, and hostile to the natural development of the popular instincts, so must the organization of the International conform in all respects to these instincts and these interests. But what is the organization of the masses? It is an organization based on the various functions of daily life and of different kinds of labor. It is the organization by professions and trades. Once all the different industries are represented in the

Newspapers and magazines had long been important in the work of communicating libertarian ideas in Spain. This is a sample of publications associated with the CNT and FAI from many cities and towns in Spain.

International, including the cultivation of the land, its organization, the organization of the mass of the people, will have been achieved.

The organization of the trade sections and their representation in the Chambers of Labor [federations of unions] creates a great academy in which all the workers can and must study economic science; these sections also bear in themselves the living seeds of the new society which is to replace the old world. They are creating not only the ideas, but also the facts of the future itself. (Dolgoff, p. 255)

In the Spanish case these 'seeds' did allow for the intense learning and popular intelligence that actually produced a social revolution.

At the notorious Hague Congress of the International in 1872, these libertarian principles were repudiated by the Marxist faction and Bakunin, Guillaume, and the libertarian Jura Federation were expelled. The "Resolutions of the Congress of Saint-Imier" a few days later reconstituted the libertarian International. The Spanish Federations of the International endorsed these resolutions during Christmas week in Cordova, thereby aligning themselves with the libertarians and re-emphasizing their anti-authoritarian direction. The third resolution reads:

The economic aspiration of the proletariat can have no other aim than the establishment of absolutely free organizations and federations, based on the labor equally of all and absolutely separate and independent from every political state government; and that these organizations and federations can be created only by the spontaneous action of the proletariat itself, that is, by the trade bodies and the autonomous communes . . .

For these reasons, the Congress of Saint-Imier declares:
1)That the destruction of all political power is the first task of the proletariat;
2)That the establishment of a so-called "provisional" (temporary) revolutionary authority to achieve this destruction can be nothing but a new deception and would be just as dangerous for the proletariat as any existing government. (Dolgoff, pp. 390, 391)

The last resolution under the heading "Organization of Labor Statistics" recommends the naming of a commission which would present to the Congress "a plan for the universal resistance of labor against capitalism and the state" and complete statistics on work to "expedite this struggle and guide labor" in social reconstruction. In this connection, the resolution praised the efforts of the "Spanish section as up to now the best . . . "

Our purpose here has been to give a feel for the content of anarchist thought, especially Bakunin's, and a sense of its influence on Spain. These two elements, Bakunin's anarchist influence and the native Spanish collectivist tradition spoken of before, set the stage for the Spanish anarchists to actually "expedite this struggle and guide labor" in social reconstruction.

A word needs to be said about the intense preoccupation of the Spanish anarchists with libertarian reconstruction of society. It has been called an "obsession" and not altogether without reason. For example, under the following headings the Saragossa Congress in May, 1936 defined in considerable detail the organization and structure of *Comunismo Libertario* and the necessary initial steps leading toward the full realization of the new society: "Constructive Conception of the Revolution," "The Establishment of Communes, Their Function and Structure," "Plan of Economic Organization," "Coordination and Exchange," "Economic Conception of the Revolution," "Federation of Industrial and Agricultural Associations," "Art, Culture and Education." In short, practically the whole range of problems likely to affect the Revolution were discussed including relations with non-libertarian individuals and groupings, crime, delinquency, equality of sexes, individual rights, etc.

However, it was this very "obsession" that produced these resolutions and others dealing with the organization of the new society that were worked out by the various congresses of the Spanish sections of the International (in 1870, 1871, 1872, 1882, and up to and including the Saragossa Congress in May, 1936, only two months before the Civil War): resolutions that were, without major modifications put into effect by the agrarian collectives and socialized industries during the Spanish Revolution.

In a largely illiterate country, tremendous quantities of literature on social revolution were disseminated and read many times over. The resolutions mentioned above were more than just show pieces; they were widely discussed. There were tens of thousands of books, pamphlets and tracts, vast and daring cultural and popular educational experiments (the Ferrer schools) that reached into almost every village and hamlet throughout Spain.

The proclamation of the Spanish Republic in 1931, led to an outburst of "anticipatory" writings: Peirats lists about fifty titles, stressing that there were many more. . . . a proliferation of writings which contributed greatly to preparing the people for a revolutionary road. (Guérin, p. 121)

Newspapers and periodicals were of enormous importance also. "By the end of 1918 more than fifty towns in Andalusia had libertarian newspapers of their own. (Brenan, p. 179) By 1934 the CNT attained a membership of 1,500,000 and the anarchist press blanketed Spain. In Barcelona the CNT published a daily, *Solidaridad Obrera,* with a circulation of 30,000. *Tierra y Libertad* of Barcelona (a magazine) reached a circulation of 20,000; *Vida Obrera* of Gijon, *El Productor* of Seville, and *Acción y Cultura* of Saragossa had large circulations. The magazines *La Revista Blanca, Tiempos Nuevos,* and *Estudios* reached circulations of 5000, 15,000, and 75,000 respectively. This has not even begun to exhaust the list.[3]

Seventy-five years of such persistent agitation and unflinching revolutionary struggle not only inspired the workers and peasants to repulse the fascists but also prepared them for the great constructive work of the Spanish libertarian revolution.

The Political and Economic Organization of Society [4]
by Isaac Puente

Libertarian communism is based upon the economic organization of society, the economic interests being the only kind of social link upon which the interests of all individuals converge. The social organization has no other goal but to *place in common possession* whatever constitutes social wealth (the means of production and the distribution of goods and services) and to make the obligation to contribute to production a common obligation from everyone according to his ability. All *non-economic* affairs and functions will be left to the private initiative and activity of the individuals and their voluntary groupings without outside interference.

Libertarian communism is the organization of society without the State and without capitalist property relations. To establish libertarian communism it will not be necessary to invent artificial forms of social

---

[3] Statistics were derived from Gaston Leval's *Espagne Libertaire.*
[4] From *El Comunismo Anarquico,* by Isaac Puente.

We are communists. But our communism is not that of the authoritarian school: it is anarchist communism, communism without government, free communism. It is a synthesis of the two chief aims pursued by humanity since the dawn of its history—economic freedom and political freedom. . .

The means of production and of satisfaction of all needs of society have been created by the common efforts of all, must be at the disposal of all. The private appropriation of requisites for production is neither just nor beneficial. All must be placed on the same footing as producers and consumers of wealth. . . . Common possession of the necessities of production implies the common enjoyment of the fruits of the common production; and we consider that an equitable organization of society can only arise when every wage-system is abandoned, and when everybody, contributing for the common well-being to the full extent of his capacities, shall enjoy also from the common stock of society to the fullest possible extent of his needs. . . .

Each economic phase of life implies its own political phase; and it is impossible to touch the very basis of the present economic life—private property—without a corresponding change in the very basis of the political organization. Life already shows in which direction the change will be made. Not in increasing the powers of the State, but in resorting to free organization and free federation in all those branches which are now considered as attributes of the State.

—KROPOTKIN, from "Anarchist Communism" in *Kropotkin's Revolutionary Pamphlets* (New York, 1927)

Modern Anarcho-Syndicalism is a direct continuation of those social aspirations which took shape in the bosom of the First International and which were best understood and most strongly held by the libertarian wing of the great workers' alliance. . . .

Only in the realm of economy are the workers able to display their full social strength, for it is their activity as producers which holds together the whole social structure, and guarantees the existence of society at all. . . . For the Anarcho-Syndicalist the trade union is . . . the seed of the Socialist economy of the future, the elementary school of Socialism in general . . . The trade union, the syndicate, is the unified organization of labour and has for its purpose the defence of the interests of the producers within existing society and the preparing for and the practical carrying out of the reconstruction of social life after the pattern of Socialism. . . .

The organization of Anarcho-Syndicalism is based on the principles of Federalism, on free combination from below upward, putting the right of self-determination of every member above everything else and recognizing only the organic agreement of all on the basis of like interests and common convictions. . . .

Anarcho-Syndicalists are convinced that a Socialist economic order cannot be created by the decrees and statutes of a government, but only by the solidaric collaboration of the workers with hand or brain in each special branch of production; that is, through the taking over of the management of all plants by the producers themselves under such form that the separate groups . . . carry on production and the distribution of the products in the interest of the community on the basis of free mutual agreement.

—RUDOLF ROCKER, from *Anarcho-Syndicalism* (London, 1938)

organization. The new society will emerge "from the shell of the old." The elements of the future society are already planted in the existing order. They are the Syndicate and the Free Commune (sometimes called "Free Municipality") which are old, deeply rooted non-statist popular institutions spontaneously organized, and embracing all towns and villages in both urban and rural areas. The Free Commune is also ideally suited to cope successfully with the problems of social and economic life in libertarian rural communities. Within the Free Commune there is also room for cooperative associations of artisans, farmers and other groups or individuals who prefer to remain independent or form their own associations to meet their own needs (providing of course that they do not exploit hired labor for wages).

Both the Syndicates and the Free Communes, in accordance with federative and democratic procedures, will, by mutual agreement, be free to conduct their own affairs within their own spheres, without interference from any outside authority. This will not be necessary because the workers will, from sheer necessity, (if for no other reason) be obliged to establish their own Federations of Industries to coordinate their multiform economic activities.

Through their syndicates, their Free Communes and their subsidiary coordinating agencies, the workers will take collective possession of all private (not personal) property and collectively administer production and consumption of goods and public services locally, regionally and nationally.

The terms "Libertarian" and "Communism" denote the fusion of two inseparable concepts, the indispensable prerequisites for the free society: collectivism and individual freedom.

The contrast between statist authoritarian political organization and a free social order based upon anarchist communist economic principles cannot be more complete. In order to clarify and illustrate these diametrically opposed conceptions we make the following comparisons:

The Political State
1. It treats the people as minors, altogether incapable of self-government.

The Industrial Organization
1. The workers in each branch of production are fully able to administer their particular functions without the interference of the State or the employing classes.

The Political State

2. All powers reside in the State: economic life, education, the administration of justice, and the enactment and enforcement of laws involving all individual and social life.

3. Even in a democratic State, not the people but the *State* is sovereign. The State centralizes all armed forces (army, police, prisons, and courts), while the people are left defenceless to resist the agression of the State.

4. In the State and its authoritarian institutions the people are divided by their necessarily varied and often conflicting political, religious, and social ideas and interests. It is precisely in these areas where people unavoidably differ most and in a free society should differ.

5. Although the State represents a minority, it still claims to have more knowledge and more ability than the combined collective wisdom and experience of all mankind. "One knows all."

6. The State, in imposing a fixed norm to be followed at all times (a constitution or code), forfeits the

The Industrial Organization

2. Initiative and control passes to the workers' organizations: the control of education to teachers; health to medical workers; and communications to technicians and workers. The control of production belongs to the workers and their Federation of Unions.

3. Power is returned to and exercised by those directly affected. It is not monopolized. Every individual has his corresponding share thereof, leaving to the collective what everyone concedes to it. There is autonomy of individuals and coordination of groups through free agreement.

4. Men group into unions according to their needs and occupations, and into free Communes according to locality and common interests. This is the area in which the common interests of all men are greatest.

5. In a free Collectivity each benefits from the accumulated knowledge and specialized experience of all, and vice-versa. There is a reciprocal relationship wherein information is in continuous circulation.

6. In the industrial organization, the norm of conduct is decided in accordance with the prevailing and

The Political State

future and constricts life, which is always mutable and multifarious.

7. The State monopolizes everything for its own benefit. The people have nothing to do but pay, obey, produce, and conform to the supreme will of those who command: "Give me full power and I will make you happy."

8. Society is divided into two classes: those who rule and those who must obey.

9. The State perpetuates and legalizes the fiction of liberty, democracy, and autonomy, only to deceive the people and render them obedient.

10. The State evolves in the direction of fascism or state socialism. It camouflages its prerogatives, but is bound to lose its privileges as class-consciousness grows, and as individuals grow in ethical-intellectual stature.

11. In an organization with a political base, power flows upward toward the hierarchical bureaucracy and away from the people.

The Industrial Organization

changing circumstances.

7. All who would be "redeemers" and meddlers are dispensed with. Everyone conducts his own affairs, and thus frees himself from an imposed political-economic routine and regimentation inculcated by centuries of false political indoctrination.

8. All people are equal partners in a cooperative association of producers.

9. Industrial administration realizes the democratic principle: government (self-administration) by the people. It realizes the principle of federation—the granting of maximum autonomy and communal organization to each and every unit of production.

10. Evolution elevates the workers to the greatest possible degree. To defend and promote the economic rights of each individual, the workers eventually establish organizations capable of fulfilling their ethical responsibilities and obligations towards their fellow human beings.

11. In an industrial organization, power flows downward towards the collective and the individual.

A mass demonstration of the CNT in 1931. The banner proclaims, "The unemployed are starving. Bread for our children!"

The Prologue to Revolution
S.D.

Like all great movements, the Revolution must be evaluated within the context of the conflicting forces that shaped its course. In particular let us review the relations between the CNT-FAI and the political parties during the crucial years between the proclamation of the Republic in April, 1931, and the outbreak of the Civil War on July 19, 1936.

After the great strikes which precipitated the collapse of the monarchy, the Republic was formed by a coalition of bourgeois republicans and socialists. In the general elections to the Cortes (the Spanish parliament), 115 Socialist Party candidates, backed by the bourgeois parties, were elected. Largo Caballero, the socialist leader, became the powerful Minister of Labor. During his term of office (1931-33) the socialist dominated labor organization, the UGT, became the unofficial labor front of the government and thousands of socialists appointed to government posts reinforced the bureaucratic apparatus of the Republic.[1]

The 600,000 members of the CNT represented at its first open congress (1931) refused to collaborate with this new government. In Barcelona, a mass meeting of 100,000 workers took up the slogan: *As against the ballot box—the social revolution!* One of the posters read: *The Cortes is a barrel of rotten apples. If we send our deputies there, they too will become rotten. Don't vote!*

---

[1] It is no mere coincidence that during the monarchy, under the dictatorship of Primo de Rivera (1923-1929), Caballero had also served as the Minister of State for Labor. The UGT became the unofficial labor front of the government, while the CNT was outlawed.

As Minister of Labor, Caballero introduced a series of laws regulating relations between workers and employers. These severely limited the right to strike by instituting compulsory arbitration of all disputes. All contracts between workers and employers had to conform to government laws and the government enforced the fulfillment of contracts. A whole army of newly appointed government officials (mostly socialists) enforced these laws to favor the UGT. As intended, they were used *against* the CNT. Thus under Caballero the membership of the UGT jumped from 300,000 when he took office to 1,250,000 in 1933.[2] Another law, ostensibly against "socially dangerous elements," was the pretext for interning CNT militants in concentration camps. Persecution and intermittent periods of legality and illegality made it impossible, for instance, for them to hold another congress until 1936.

As noted by Santillan, the immense majority of the military and civilian office holders who had faithfully served the monarchy continued to serve the interests of the Army, the Church, and the wealthy landholders and capitalists under the Republic. They continued to sabotage the enforcement of every progressive measure. Worse yet, the new socialist and republican officials soon acquired all the vices of the old monarchical administration.

It soon became plain that the Republic represented nothing fundamentally new for the Spanish people. The coming of the Republic did not signal the dawning of a new and better social order truly capable of satisfying the pressing needs and the aspirations of the urban and rural workers. Rather, the Republican government, from the beginning and throughout its existence, was determined to crush the revolutionary movement.

Then began the prologue to the Revolution: that period of partial and general strikes and insurrections involving hundreds of thousands of workers which, in spite of setbacks, gradually enveloped all of Spain and directly involved the masses in the social revolutionary process.

In January, 1933, for instance, there took place the revolt of Casas Viejas which aroused all Spain. This little Andalusian village proclaimed *Comunismo Libertario*. The revolt was drowned in blood. Troops were ordered to kill, not to spare the wounded, and to take no prisoners. "Shoot

---

[2] This phenomenal increase was attained by enrolling hundreds of thousands of anti-revolutionary, bourgeois, non-proletarian elements into the UGT, such as municipal, provincial and national bureaucrats, petty-bourgeois employers, landlords, reactionary Catholic republicans and separatists, frightened liberals, etc. These same elements were later recruited during the Civil War by the Communist Party to crush the CNT-FAI.

them in the belly." Twenty-five dwellings were destroyed and thirty peasants were burned alive when the soldiers set fire to their homes. One of the leaders of the revolt, the 70 year old anarchist nicknamed *Seisdedos* (Sixfingers), together with his children and grandchildren, perished in the flames. These and other atrocities aroused a great storm of protest both within Spain and internationally and finally brought down the government. The Minister of the Interior, Casares Quiroga, and the President of the Republic, Manuel Azaña, were forced to resign.

On the eve of the national elections to the Cortes in December, 1933, the CNT proclaimed another general strike in Catalonia, Aragon, Andalusia, and Coruña. Hospitalet and Villanueva de la Serena in Catalonia proclaimed libertarian communism, as did villages in Aragon. The movement was suppressed after four days. The members of the Revolutionary Committee of Saragossa as well as the National Committee of the CNT were arrested. In Barcelona, militants imprisoned during the insurrection as well as some imprisoned earlier effected a sensational escape by digging a tunnel out of the prison.

Also in December, 1933, the CNT-FAI issued a manifesto warning of a possible rightist putsch, against which voting and parliamentary procedures would prove futile. They urged the workers not to vote but to "prepare for the social revolution." Even the left-wing section of the Socialist Party declared that in the event of a rightist electoral victory the decisive battle would have to be decided by armed forces in the streets. There were solid grounds for these fears. The right-wing forces were led by the fascist Gil Robles. Robles spent his honeymoon in Germany, where he enthusiastically soaked up the political ideas of Hitler and the Austrian fascist Dollfuss. Both he and the other right-wing leaders had long admired Mussolini.

The 1934 election of the reactionary Lerroux-Gil Robles government precipitated a wave of strikes and insurrections against the new regime. Even the meager reforms enacted by the liberal government were annulled. The government, determined to turn Spain into a fascist-style state, perpetrated wholesale arrests, including the imprisonment of 30,000 CNT members. Ironically enough, under this notorious *Bieno Negro* (accursed two year rule of the Gil Robles regime) the same atrocities committed by the preceding Republican government against the CNT were now also directed against the socialists. Once out of power the left-wing socialists began to talk about revolution. Caballero, now exalted as "the blue-eyed Lenin of the Spanish Revolution," proclaimed the necessity for the dictatorship of the proletariat during the transition period from capitalism to socialism.

Late in 1934 the strike of UGT and CNT workers in Asturias rapidly took on the proportions of a full-scale insurrectionary movement—a dress rehearsal for the Social Revolution. The revolutionary movement for workers' and peasants' councils spread throughout the whole region. The police barracks at Suma were attacked with sticks of dynamite. The small arms factory of La Turbia was stormed. Over 30,000 rifles and huge quantities of machine guns, hand grenades, and ammunition were taken. In the CNT strongholds in the port cities of Gijon and La Figuera, and in other towns, libertarian communism was being put into effect. Even the big city of Oviedo was occupied by the strikers. Imported Moorish and Foreign Legion troops under the overall command of Francisco Franco crushed the insurrection after three days of bloody battles, leaving 3,000 dead and 7,000 wounded. Tens of thousands (including Caballero) were jailed and large parts of Spain were placed under martial law. In the Cortes, Gil Robles, in the style of Hitler and Mussolini, demanded unlimited power to obliterate the revolutionary movement.

Under these circumstances, the right-wing government lost the February, 1936, elections. This time the CNT had not urged the workers not to vote. It had been tacitly understood that the CNT members and their friends would vote for the liberal-leftist parties because they were pledged to release the political prisoners. Santillan, who lived through these tragic events, indicates what a limited "victory" this was:

> The Left, who, thanks to us, had been returned to power by a narrow margin, still remained blind to the fascist menace. Neither the workers nor the peasants had gained anything but the release of the prisoners. The real power remained in the hands of the fascist capitalists, the Church, and the military caste who were openly and feverishly preparing a coup to unseat by force the republican and socialist politicians who had legally come to power in the February, 1936, elections. . . . (*Por Que Perdimos La Guerra,* p. 38)

The fascists, of course, would not accept the "verdict of the people." While they knew that the republican reformers were just as anxious to avoid social revolution as they were, they had no confidence in the ability of the "leftist" government to do so. It was primarily for this reason that the fascists were determined to unseat them. So, long before the elections and while still in power, the fascists had already plotted and organized a massive military assault to depose the Republican government and impose a military dictatorship. The takeover was launched July 19th, 1936.

Why had the Republican government ignored the fascist threat for so long? And why, once the threat became a reality, did the Republican government act so feebly in its defense and in the defense of the people? César M. Lorenzo (the son of a prominent CNT militant, his book is a gold mine of information) answers this question clearly:

> The Republic was in reality overwhelmed by events. Pulled between fear of a Social Revolution and Fascism, it unconsciously expedited both Fascism and the Social Revolution. The Republicans in power . . . were the only ones in Spain who could not or would not see the imminence of a national catastrophe. They allowed themselves to be fooled by the sermons of the generals. After the announcement of the military uprising they refused to distribute arms to the workers and hoped to arrange everything by negotiating with the fascist plotters. In fact they feared, above all, the coming of the proletarian society and committed themselves to the wrecking of the organizations established by the extreme left [the CNT-FAI] whom they hated. But the formidable reaction of the masses wiped out the fascists in over half of Spain and reduced to bits republican legality. On the one hand the triumph of the reaction, on the other, the triumph of socialism. . . . (p. 241)

The Revolution of July 19, 1936, thus marked the culmination of a double process. On the one hand, there was the economic and political degeneration of Spain due to the impotence of first the monarchy and then the Republic to effect fundamental changes, changes impossible without destroying the very privileges for which the Republic stood. On the other hand, there was the ceaseless, increasingly effective revolutionary activity of the powerful anarcho-syndicalist movement. The spirit of popular discontent, crystallized by the persistent agitation of the CNT, found expression in the increasing tempo and scope of the insurrections which shook the foundations of the exploitative society.

The Counter-Revolution and the Destruction of
the Collectives
S.D.

Both before and after July 19th, an unwavering determination to crush the revolutionary movement was the *leitmotiv* behind the policies of the Republican government, irrespective of the party in power. On this one point, at least, all the rival factions agreed.

> The government and the parties began their great offensive against the CNT. With patience they reconstituted the State, reorganized the regular police, and equipped an army of the classical type. At the same time they gave no financial aid to the industrial and agricultural collectives, leaving them to wither away for lack of capital. . . . They tried to return the goods and land to their former owners, to sabotage by all means the transformation of the economy. At the same time they systematically refused to arm the CNT columns, while by intensive propaganda they turned public opinion against "the irresponsible, uncontrollable groups of the CNT-FAI." (Lorenzo, p. 244)

The coalition of parties against the social revolution was not improvised on the spur of the moment. It had been long in the making. The inclusion of the anarchists in the anti-fascist front and the organization of the libertarian collectives had been very reluctantly tolerated by these elements. They saw no other alternative. At heart many of them would have preferred the victory of Franco to the social revolution. But they could not, in view of the situation and the power of the CNT-FAI, risk a premature frontal attack.

The Counter-Revolution in Catalonia

The first treacherous moves to undermine the position of the CNT-FAI were initiated by the *Generalidad* (the semi-autonomous government of Catalonia, the anarchist stronghold) during the crucial period *before* the fascist attack on July 19th. Luís Companys, President of the *Generalidad*, knew that his government could not defeat the fascists without the help of the CNT. The CNT-FAI pledged itself to cooperate in a united front with all anti-fascist forces against the common foe. But when asked to supply the necessary arms to the workers, the *Generalidad* refused on the pretext that it had none. When the workers helped themselves as best they could and took over 200 rifles and other materiel from the battleships *Marques de Camillas* and *Magallenes*, the chief of police brazenly demanded that the workers return the weapons to the government. The *Generalidad*, while lavishly supplying arms to its own police force and the Civil Guards, repeatedly refused to give any to the workers. The mood of desperation and the sense of impending tragedy are graphically portrayed by Santillan:

> Even our modest requests for a thousand rifles were refused.... Around midnight the day before the attack, General Aranguen, the commander of the Civil Guards, arrived at the President's reception room and found Companys arguing with a CNT delegation, who were demanding that at least half the arms of the Assault Guards should be given to the workers who had none. Companys again promised vaguely that he would "soon distribute arms at the right time." Durruti interrupted: *"We must act. This is no time for empty talk. We are not going to be slaughtered by the fascists for lack of arms just to satisfy a stubborn politician. From now on the CNT and FAI will conduct the fight! ..."*
>
> We had fully organized the defence of Barcelona. The armed workers' militias of the CNT-FAI patrolled the streets and manned all strategic points. The barricades were ready ... but the police of the *Generalidad* attacked our patrols. Repeated telephone calls for information about the fate of this or that comrade arrested for carrying arms were ignored.... It is no exaggeration to say that we had to concentrate all our efforts to defend ourselves from the police, who tried to confiscate even the few arms that we did have.... (quoted in Abel Paz, pp. 281, 282, 283)

Santillan reports that:

> The rifles we took from the ships, revolvers and other arms that we had managed to collect or requisition, and the hundred old small arms grudgingly given us by the *Generalidad* were all we had to combat the 35,000 well-armed fascists ....[3] (*Por Que Perdimos La Guerra*, p. 43)

---

[3] For fear of the revolution, it was the set policy of the Generalidad to arm its own forces (police, Civil Guards) and deprive the CNT-FAI of arms. Sufficient arms to put

On July 17th, two days before the Franco troops stormed Barcelona, the government censor prohibited the publication in *Solidaridad Obrera* of a manifesto detailing vital last minute arrangements for the defense of Barcelona and encouraging the workers. That afternoon the *Regional Committee of the FAI* was forced to print the manifesto on a handbill which was distributed all over the city and in the suburbs.

Two days after the workers crushed the fascists (July 21), Companys suddenly became very friendly and invited the CNT-FAI delegation to confer with him about the changed situation. He acknowledged that the CNT was the master of Catalonia and that his government was impotent, and he offered to resign. If the CNT so desired he would remain in office as the servant of the workers and the united front of the anti-fascist parties. His offer to continue in office was naively accepted. The offer turned out to be part of a scheme to get back into power. Companys was a conniver.

> He manipulated things with such skill that little by little he reconstituted the legal organs and the power of the state and reduced the revolutionary workers' organizations to *de facto* puppets of his government. (Paz, p. 183)

The formation on September 26th of the new *Council of the Generalidad* meant in effect the usurpation of the revolutionary workers' organizations by the Companys government. The famous Collectivization Decree (October 24, 1936) ostensibly legalizing the conquests of the Revolution actually established the power of the *Generalidad* to regulate and eventually to liquidate the collectivized industries and rural collectives of Catalonia.

The Caballero-Communist Coalition of Republican Spain Liquidates the Revolution

The counter-revolutionary treachery of the Communists during the Spanish Civil War has been rightfully stressed and can not be exaggerated. But the collusion of the Communists with the socialists and their leader, Francisco Largo Caballero (also an architect of the counter-revolution), has been rarely mentioned.

The Caballero government came to power September 8, 1936, and was deposed May 15, 1937, to be succeeded by the Communist Negrín.[4] When Caballero finally broke with the Communists he did so not because he

---

down the fascist uprising were finally obtained only after the CNT-FAI militants captured the San Andres artillery barracks and other depots.

[4] Negrin was a member of Caballero's cabinet.

objected to their counter-revolutionary program or to their atrocities against the anarchists and other dissident groups. He was primarily motivated by the well-founded fear that the Communists would finally dominate the socialist parties. During his administration Caballero and his allies presided over the liquidation of the Spanish libertarian collectives. One of the very best studies devoted to this aspect of the Spanish tragedy is Burnett Bolloten's pioneering work *The Grand Camouflage* (London, 1961). The following paragraphs summarize the salient point.

Caballero's relations with the CNT-FAI before the Civil War were marked by almost constant friction. Just before the Civil War, on April 24, 1936, *Solidaridad Obrera* (the anarcho-syndicalist organ) called Caballero "a dictator in embryo" who favored "the absolute hegemony of the Socialist Party on the morrow of the triumphant insurrection of the working classes." (Bolloten, p. 154)

In contrast, in the months before the Civil War the official relations between the left-wing socialists and the Communist Party had been most friendly. So much so that Caballero, then the General Secretary of the UGT and virtual leader of the *Socialist Youth Movement*, endorsed the fusion of the socialist and Communist trade union federations as well as the merging of the two youth organizations. In March, 1936, the Madrid section of the Socialist Party, headed by Caballero, proposed a fusion of the socialist and Communist parties. And in August, 1936, Caballero invited the socialists and Communists to join his government, which they did. He had earlier been warmly praised by the Communist Party leader Jose Diaz as "one that approaches most the revolutionary path, the path of the Communist Party and the Communist International." (Bolloten, p. 105)

On July 19th, 1936, the police powers of the Republic had crumbled under the dual impact of the military rebellion and the social revolution. The fascists' attempted coup d'état had been put down principally as a result of the skillful and intelligent work of the militants. Slowly the state moved to eliminate the working class militants. On this point the Communists, socialists, and republicans were of one mind. Recalcitrant militiamen were disarmed and arrested. The government took over the administration of public order in one locality after another. Under the Caballero government thousands of new members were added to the Civil Guards. When the Caballero cabinet was formed in September, 1936, there were 15,600 *Carabineros* in *all* of Spain. By April, 1937, there were 40,000 in Loyalist Spain alone (which was about half the area of Spain). (Bolloten, p. 170)

In December, 1936, the Caballero government, with the agreement of the Communist Party, decreed the dissolution of the spontaneous revolutionary committees and their replacement by governmental municipal and provincial councils in which all the popular front parties and trade unions would be represented. The Caballero administration was determined to dissolve the revolutionary organs that had assumed state functions. Both the Socialist Party paper *Claridad* (Feb. 19, 1937) and the Communist Party organ *Mundo Obrera* (Dec. 25, 1936) spoke out against the committees as impediments to state power. The latter commented:

> There can be no doubt that at the present time they ["the numerous bodies created at the beginning of the Civil War in the towns and villages"] ... greatly hinder the work of the government. (Bolloten, p. 167)

It was also necessary, in the opinion of the Communists as well as the socialists and the republicans, to break the power of the revolutionary committees in the collectivized factories, particularly in the basic industries, and the agricultural collectives. Nationalization would weaken the left-wing of the revolution at one of the principal sources of its power while putting agricultural and industrial enterprises under state control. *Solidaridad Obrera* (March 3rd, 1937) protested that:

> These reactionaries, ... enjoying unheard of official aid, are endeavoring to take over by assault the collectivized estates with the object of putting an end to the agrarian revolution. (p. 175)

The counter-revolutionary campaign initiated in the weeks preceding the revolutionary events of July 19th, 1936, gathered momentum during the months of December, 1936, and the spring of 1937. In preparation for the inevitable showdown, they had done all they could to undermine the prestige of the CNT-FAI and to sabotage the revolutionary achievements.

The first big attack on the agricultural collectives (March, 1937) was launched in the Levant region between Alicante and Murcia.[5] It was spearheaded by *Carabineros,* Civil Guards, Assault Guards, and other police forces militarized into artillery sections and equipped by the government with numerous guns and tanks (18 tanks in Gandia and 13 in Alfora). The Republic, so incapable of effectively fighting the fascists at the front, compensated for its impotence with cowardly attacks on the collectives on

---

[5] The destruction of the agricultural collectives is graphically depicted by Leval (*Espagne Libertaire*, pp. 367-377). See also Peirats (*Los Anarquistas en la Crisis Politica Espanola*, Chapters XV and XVI.

July of 1936. The people of Barcelona take up arms against the fascist uprising.

the home front.

The peasant comrades, who expected this assault, prepared to resist as best they could. They had no tanks, and fought with outdated pistols and two old cannons. The government planned to first storm the strategic villages of Tullera and Alfara. But almost the whole region was alerted and the neighboring villagers armed with hunting rifles rushed to repulse the attackers. The District Federations of Jativa, Carcagente, Gandia, and Sueca pooled their strength and organized the "Gandia Front." The villagers of Catarroja, Liria, Moncada, Paterna, and Burriana established the "Vilanesa Front." The tide of battle turned in favor of the collectivists when the peasants were reinforced by two libertarian battalions from the "Iron Front" as well as two battalions from the "Confederal Column" of the CNT who rushed from the Teruel-Segorbe front to reinforce the peasants.

The fighting in the Callera district of the Levant raged for four days, at the end of which the government, unable to break through, attacked in a different direction: towards Sella. Finally through the intervention of the CNT a cease-fire was arranged. Captured prisoners and arms on both sides were returned. But in violation of the truce, a number of our prisoners (mostly younger men) were released only much later. Although our comrades suffered casualties, dead and wounded, the collectives were far from being destroyed. On the contrary, they emerged from the conflict stronger than ever. All the evidence indicates that the whole operation was secretly launched by the right-wing socialists (specifically the Minister of War in the cabinet, Indelicio Prieto) together with the Communist enemies, who on this issue were temporarily reconciled.

As the war against the fascists and the counter-revolution against the collectives proceeded, Catalonia became a focal point. Here the revolutionary gains survived and the workers remained in armed opposition to the restoration of the state. Here too the PSUC was determined to end the revolution. The showdown came in the May Days of 1937. The coalition launched its all-out offensive in Barcelona, the anarchist stronghold, on the pretext that the CNT must be dislodged from control of the central telephone exchange. It could have been any other reason.

In the wake of the May Days, the systematic persecution of our comrades on a massive scale began and we lost positions on all fronts. The political parties, in league with Luís Companys, president of the Catalonian government (who turned against the anarchists when he no longer needed their support), evicted all our comrades from the most important posts. The Stalinists took over control of the police force.

The Communist leader Comorera became the Minister of the Economy of Catalonia. Not being able to altogether undermine the preponderant influence of the CNT syndicates, Comorera misused his immense power (in league with the Central Government) to sabotage production and then blame the CNT. He infiltrated strategic union locals and shops with Communists and even tried to return the control of the Barcelona transportation system and other enterprises to the capitalists. The list of sabotage and atrocities against our comrades is endless as the state reinstituted its control.

Following the 1937 May Days putsch in Barcelona, the newly appointed Communist Minister of Agriculture, Vincente Uribe, surprised everyone by publishing a decree legalizing the agrarian collectives in all of Spain, irrespective of the circumstances under which they were organized. It turned out that this decree was a fraud meant to camouflage the sinister plans of the counter-revolutionary coalition to destroy the collectives and to hand over the land to the former bourgeois landlords. Uribe's actions made clear his real intentions. In his radio broadcasts, Uribe repeatedly urged the peasants not to join the collectives. He guaranteed the restoration of holdings to the small and middle-class property owners. He reorganized the counter-revolutionary Peasant Landlords' Federation of Levant and created a counter-revolutionary united front. Under the pretext of helping the peasant collectives with the harvest (there was an acute shortage of manpower), young Communist "shock-brigades" spread themselves throughout the Levant and Catalonia, only to infiltrate and destroy the collectives.

The major offensive to destroy the collectives (staged June, 1937) was launched against the Aragon collectives. It was harvest time. The *Carabineros*, commanded by Communists, requisitioned trucks transporting produce from various collectives and confiscated the shipments. A little later, on orders from their commanders in Barbastro, *Carabineros* raided the collectives (under the authority of the Ministry of War), smashing everything and confiscating anything of value.

On the pretext that they were needed for an offensive, young men sorely needed to gather in the harvest were mobilized. The same held true for other villages. And while these young men were being sent to the front, idle troops from other regions who were never sent to the front were being quartered in strategic villages from which offensives could be mounted. These parasites gorged themselves with food and delicacies and played *pelote* (a Basque game) all day long while wheat lay rotting in the fields for lack of manpower!

But this was not all. The worst was yet to come. In July, 1937, the collectives were brutally attacked by mobile brigades of regular army troops commanded by the notorious Communist officer Enrique Lister. These same troops who so "valiantly" attacked the collectives, when facing the fascists at Belchite fled in panic like scared rabbits!!

Thirty percent of the collectives were completely destroyed. At Alcora de Cinco, the Municipal Council that administrated the collective was arrested. The aged pensioners in the old folks home were driven out. Wholesale arrests were made in other collectives: Mas de las Matas, Monzon, and Barbastro. Warehouses, stores, cooperative markets, and installations were pillaged and wrecked. At the October, 1937, National Plenum of Peasants in Valencia, the Aragon delegates made this report (which we summarize):

More than 600 organizers of collectives have been imprisoned. The government-appointed committees seized the food markets, the land, livestock, and tools, and returned them to members of fascist families or fascist suspects whom the revolution refrained from prosecuting. The harvest was expropriated and distributed in the same way, including even livestock raised by the collectives. In certain villages like Bordon and Calaciete they even confiscated seeds.

So great was the destruction that Republican Spain was threatened with starvation. The counter-revolutionists proved incapable of resuming production and, much against their will, they were forced to halt their depredations and permit the reestablishment of collectives. Although some collectives were reconstituted, this noble movement was irretrievably crushed (disbanded, nationalized or restored to private monopoly)—a great historic atrocity which the bogus "anti-fascist counter-revolutionaries will never live down.

chapter 4
The Limitations of the Revolution

Introduction

In this selection *Gaston Leval sketches the frame of reference for an intelligent assessment of the Spanish Revolution: the prevailing circumstances; the specific obstacles that limited its scope; as well as the extent to which other important factors shaped its character. Leval reminds all of us never to lose sight of the fact that the unfinished libertarian social revolution (aborted by our "friendly" enemies), was—to use his own expression—actually a "semi-revolution"; that this fact, far from detracting, only enhances its spectacular achievements.*

Like other responsible historians, Leval graphically portrays the tragic dilemma of the Spanish anarchists. The libertarian movement was hopelessly trapped between the cruel choice of collaborating with its anti-fascist enemies or of accepting—at least partially—the awesome historic responsibility for the fascist victory.

More than thirty years after the tragedy of Spain, what the anarchists should have done under these conditions is still being debated. So far, the so-called "collaborationists" who approved the participation of the anarchists in the Republican government, or the "hard-shell" anarchists who still condemn the CNT-FAI leadership for doing so, have not been able to suggest a satisfactory practical alternative. Irrespective of what the anarchists should or should not have done, one fact is clear: the war against fascism and with it the Spanish Revolution was doomed to certain defeat, as Leval himself foresaw.

But on the constructive achievements of the libertarian agrarian collectives and urban socialization under workers' self-management, there is no controversy. *The lessons to be learned from the mistakes and the triumphs of the Spanish Revolution are of permanent value to new generations seeking new ways to rejuvenate society.*

The Limitations of the Revolution [1]
by Gaston Leval

If the constructive achievements of the Spanish Revolution passed almost unnoticed, it was not only because of the tacit conspiracy of silence of our enemies, but even more because it was at one and the same time a civil and international war on the territory of Spain. Everyone was preoccupied with the main overriding problem—the war.

But we must not forget that this was also the attitude of both the revolutionists and the Spanish people. For the workers, the peasants, the petty bourgeoisie—in short, everybody—the principal thing was to prevent the victory of Franco. The *anarchists*, too, faced with the fascist peril, the suppression of free speech and the right to organize, faced with the inevitable persecutions of all those who would not submit to dictatorship, realized that everyone must unite against fascism. Problem Number One was to fight the fascists, to whom even the meager reforms of the Republic were monstrous and not to be tolerated.

Durruti's celebrated phrase, "We renounce all except victory," summed up the sentiment of a great many militants. The victory he sought was the victory over fascism. But unfortunately the *all* was the Revolution itself. . . . The Spanish anarchists had suffered many long years of repression. Persecuted, exiled, outlawed under the dictatorship of Primo de Rivera as well as under the monarchy and under the Republic, they knew that under fascism it would be even worse. Their movement, which even in the dark years was at least to some extent able to function, would be altogether suppressed. The syndicates would be obliterated and the anarchists would at best be forced to cling to the slim possibility of coming

---

[1] From Leval, *Né Franco, né Stalin*, pp. 76-94.

to life under a liberal or monarchical government. In short, the acute problems of the anarchist movement would be worsened a hundredfold in case of a fascist military victory.

And it was partly, but only partly, for this reason that Garcia Oliver (spokesman for the CNT delegation) on July 20, 1936, accepted (in my opinion a little too eagerly) the offer of the head of the Catalan government, Companys, to organize a solid anti-fascist front. Oliver argued that this was not the time for revolution and that the prime concern of the anarchists was to halt the advance of the fascist troops toward Catalonia by freeing Aragon.

Many Spanish anarchists had a distorted idea of the situation of that time. They said that it was not the "people" of Barcelona who defeated the fascists. More than any other city in Spain, they said, it was primarily the anarchists and with them the Assault Guards. It is true that numerically, and by their example of initiative and daring, the anarchists—politically speaking—were from the beginning masters of Barcelona. They seemed to have the support of the people. Everywhere we heard the cry: *Viva la CNT! Viva la FAI!* But to what extent did the bourgeoisie, the merchants, the bureaucrats, the employees of the banks and commercial houses, and the whole of the parasitic and semi-parasitic classes (as numerous as the workers) *really* support the CNT-FAI? It is this question that must be answered.

Their support was purely fictitious and superficial. Most of these elements applauded the CNT-FAI for its great exploits. But this did not mean or even imply that they also accepted the principles, aims, and social conceptions of the anarchist organizations. There was a sentiment of gratitude. But the Republican remained a Republican; the Catalan, a separatist; the liberal, a bourgeois; the Socialist remained a Socialist; and the anti-fascist monarchist continued to hope for a king.

This is a perplexing situation which seems much more complicated than it actually is. At the end of 1936, all those among the anarchists who were preoccupied primarily with the revolutionary question oversimplified and underestimated the political problem. The Social Revolution would sweep away the entrenched powers and institutions. The political parties would disappear. The parasitic classes, no longer able to count on the support of the state, would disintegrate. And all that would remain to be done would be to organize the new anarchist society.

But the necessity of fighting the war against fascism completely upset these expectations. The state continued to exist: the Central Government, the regional government in Catalonia, and another in the Basque provinces.

Each of these governments still had its own police and a certain number of military units. The municipalities, together with their local police forces and legal authority, remained. The political parties were still firmly rooted. And the middle classes were still a power to be reckoned with. All these people were more or less anti-fascist. Taken together they added up to most of the population. As compared to any single grouping, the CNT and the anarchist movement were the most powerful in Spain. Yet all these other elements, taken together, constituted an incomparably greater force.

Furthermore, a very important segment of the public was inclined to be indifferent to politics, but being progressive and liberal-minded they supported the government. To them the government was the symbol and guarantee of liberty—the only force capable of creating a solid fighting bloc against fascism. The anarchists could not therefore sweep away the political parties controlling the municipalities, who with equal fervor were fighting with them against fascism. They could not attack the power of the police, who as far as the people were concerned were just as anti-fascist as the militiamen fighting at the front. The general preoccupation being to defeat the fascists, . . . the anarchists would, if they came out against the state, provoke the antagonism not only of the political parties and other more or less organized forces, but even of the majority of the people, who would accuse them of collaborating with Franco.[2]

The anarchists were therefore obliged to tolerate the bourgeoisie, the small capitalists, the merchants, the generally reactionary landlords, and all the Catalan bourgeois parties because all these elements were opposing fascism.

Another serious problem was that in all of Eastern Spain (Catalonia, the Levant, Aragon, half of Castile, and part of Andalusia) there were no arms factories. There was no iron, no coal, no raw materials, and no machinery necessary for the making of rifles, machine guns, tanks, and artillery. The principal arms factories were in Asturias or separated from the main part of Republican Spain by the fascist armies. . . .

Now suppose that the anarchists could have succeeded in overthrowing the Central, the Catalan, and the Biscay (Basque) governments (which would have been most unlikely because the Basque government was

[2] The great majority of the people living in Republican Spain were above all dominated by the fear of a Franco victory, and they could not understand why the anti-fascist political and social movements and groups should not constitute a united front. The people were not committeed to a set of political-philosophical theories. They demanded that the CNT and the infinitely less powerful FAI enter and collaborate with the government to ensure the unity of action and coordination which they deemed indispensable . . . [This paragraph from Leval's Espagne Libertaire, p. 360, has been added to better clarify this important point.—Ed.]

completely dominated by the Catholics and anti-anarchist monarchical anti-fascists). Suppose the anarchists could have, against the will of the majority, imposed an anarchist dictatorship. The result would have been the instant closing of the frontier and the blockade by sea by both the fascist and the democratic countries. The supply of arms would be completely cut off, and the anarchists would rightfully be held responsible for the disasterous consequences. It is obvious that it would have been extremely difficult, if not altogether impossible, to make the social revolution under these circumstances.

In the beginning, not to antagonize the political parties, only foreign property was expropriated.... If libertarian agrarian collectives were successfully established all over anti-fascist Aragon, it was only because the anarchist militias (most numerous in Aragon) protected them from the political parties. Even then the threat was not wholly removed, and it was still necessary to create a semblance of government, *The Council of Aragon,* headed by our comrades. Aragon was the only area in which the revolutionary situation corresponded to the expectations of the anarchists as formulated in the 1870s. But Aragon was only a small part of Spain. In the rest of Spain it became necessary to collaborate loyally with our anti-fascist enemies against the much more dangerous common enemy.

After the Caballero government rejected the proposal of the CNT to establish a joint defense committee to conduct the war, to be composed of a majority of delegates representing the UGT (socialist) and CNT (anarcho-syndicalist) labor unions and a minority of political party representatives, the CNT in accord with the FAI decided to reinforce the coalition (on the basis of Caballero's false promises, skillful cajolery, and blackmail) and to enter the government headed by him. On becoming government Ministers or officials in various government departments, certain anarchists soon became infected and succumbed to the virus of power.

Fortunately the strength of the Spanish anarchist movement did not depend upon its officials. The Spanish anarchist movement was saved by the rank and file, the thousands and thousands of seasoned militants. In all or almost all the villages of Aragon, the Levant, and Andalusia our CNT militants proved to be experienced and capable organizers within their own syndicates or in the conduct of village affairs. Their initiative and exemplary conduct earned them the unquestioned confidence of the people. These comrades had for many years been promoting the Revolution, suffered prison, deportation, torture.... Now, despite the war and the sabotage of the politicians, they still continued to work for the Revolution and did the best they could.

But other members of the anti-Franco coalition were in effect representing the interests of property owners and employers and posing as anti-fascists. Be it deliberately or because they were incapable, they turned out to be very unreliable and very poor partners in the anti-fascist struggle. Industry in Barcelona was paralyzed, but the owners were not in the least interested in restoring the economy.

Through their syndicates the CNT and anarchist militants reorganized the economy and got things going again. In the metallurgical workshops it was they who built the first auto tanks. It was the CNT who, to step up production, refused to accept a reduction in working hours ordered by the Catalan government. In a system so disorganized by the Civil War, which paralyzed activity, disoriented the people, and, at first, produced so much chaos, one could not expect perfect results. Certainly mistakes were made—what revolution did not do so? Be that as it may, the fact is that only the CNT had from the very beginning taken upon itself full responsibility to restore services and resume production and all other economic activities.

Where the CNT could not immediately expropriate a firm, it exercised a certain amount of control over the conduct of the employers. Willingly or not, the employers accepted the situation. Industries and other establishments which were not immediately expropriated were then operated by control committees. They forced the employer himself to work and to pay his workers. But when the establishment went bankrupt, which happened often, the business was expropriated under the full control of the workers.

In other cases expropriation took place more rapidly. On various pretexts the workers, inspired and guided by our comrades, expropriated industries from the bosses before they went bankrupt. So vast was this movement for expropriation that the Catalan government (in which we had four ministers, called "councillors") noted in 1936 *The Decree of Collectivization* legalizing the expropriations of those factories, offices, yards, and docks employing more than 100 workers that were abandoned by the fascists or other employers. This decree legalizing an already accomplished fact stabilized the situation.

The decree had the baneful effect of preventing the workers' syndicates from extending their gains. It set back the revolution in industry. The CNT was further curbed. Being by force of circumstances compelled to enter into a sacred anti-fascist union with the bourgeoisie, it had to repress its anger and tolerate the outrageous maneuvers of our unfriendly collaborators.

The necessity of taking into account the owners, the petty bourgeoisie, and the political parties led to a paradoxical situation. Because the workers expropriated and fully controlled the various enterprises, they came to look upon the plants as their private property. They began to think and act like their ousted former employers. The factory committees even went so far as to go into business for themselves, often in competition with similar committees. To some extent the war situation contributed to this situation. (This practice was quickly stopped and the whole system drastically reorganized.)

In many cases our syndicates succeeded in getting control by applying double-play tactics. On the one hand the CNT seemed to collaborate with the non-proletarian groupings to win the war, but on the other hand, on the pretext that war production must be increased (it was already stretched to the limit), the CNT moved into and exercised *de facto* control over many other industries.

This control became more and more necessary as the employers became more and more passive. Faced with a semi-revolution, they would have preferred the victory of fascism. And at the same time the UGT became increasingly unfriendly in their relations with us. For example, the Republican government decreed obligatory unionization. All those living on wages, salaries, or other remuneration had to join either the CNT or the UGT. All the counter- and anti-revolutionary elements rushed to join the UGT only because it was against the revolution: small Catalan peasant proprietors, state bureaucrats (employees), prison guards, the police, unexpropriated shopkeepers, professionals, and reformist or conservative-minded manual workers. And all these elements allowed themselves to be taken in by the growing Stalinist propaganda.[3]

The Stalinists in Catalonia organized the PSUC (Catalan Party of Socialist Unity). Many workers and others who did not know its true nature joined the party in good faith. And most of them were induced to join the UGT of Catalonia (which the Stalinists succeeded in colonizing).

On the other hand, those socialists who still controlled their unions were inveterate reformists who opposed the revolutionary aims and measures of the CNT. Many of the union leaders preferred a Franco victory to the triumph of the semi-revolution. Many rank and file UGT workers continued, as always, to cooperate with us. Others would have liked to do so but lacked the courage to antagonize their leaders. They were immobilized by their leaders.

This became all too evident in the "unionization of production" decree—particularly in the textile industry (the most important in Spain and

---

[3] This propaganda was specifically designed to cater to their counter-revolutionary sentiments.—*Ed.*

in Catalonia where it was centered). The decree stipulated that collectivization, expropriation, and control of an enterprise by the workers must be *unanimously* approved by the union members. The textile industry was partly organized by the UGT. While in such cases the UGT almost always voted for joint UGT-CNT control and socialization, at the general membership meeting of the unions called to decide on socialization of the textile industry the UGT workers reversed themselves. This time the membership, under pressure from their leaders, voted against socialization. Although most of the members favored partnership with the CNT, they were too fainthearted and could not overcome the habit of obedience to the commands of their phony leaders. The pretext for this betrayal? "The time was not ripe for socialization," "It might provoke foreign intervention to protect the investments of foreign capitalists," and similar excuses. In industries where UGT, socialist, and Communist influence was weak, it was easier to carry through anarchist measures. . . .

While the state was severely crippled immediately after the fascist attack of July 19 (1936) it was by no means as impotent as is generally assumed. All the machinery of the state was still intact; ministries and their officials, a police force in all its ramifications, an army, though weakened, and an entrenched bureaucracy still survived. Notwithstanding the over optimism of the revolutionaries, the state still constituted an effective force in many provinces and cities. It was only in three or four cities (Barcelona was the most important) that the anarchists dominated the situation, and then only for three or four weeks. Even in Barcelona, where our situation was particularly favorable, the support of the public (aside from our members and sympathizers) went no further than a vague sentiment of gratitude.

In three other provincial capitals in Catalonia, namely Tarragona, Gerona, and Lerida, (although our forces patrolled the streets) we were not in control. And in Castellon de la Plana, Valencia, and Murcia the republican authorities, supported by the municipal police and a part of the Civil Guards, together with agencies of the National Valencia government, were firmly in control and accepted the collaboration of our comrades only because it was not to their advantage to refuse it.[4] This was also the case in Albacete, Almeria, and in all eastern and northeastern provincial capitals (San Sebastian, Bilbao, and Santander) and in the cities of the Asturias.

It is therefore altogether fallacious to assume that the anarchists were masters of the situation. When some of our comrades still insist that we were in full control, they base themselves only on the euphoric atmosphere

---

[4] Valencia became the seat of the "Central" or National government when it evacuated the Capital in Madrid.—*Ed.*

that prevailed for a few weeks in Barcelona and two or three smaller cities. However, under more peaceful circumstances we exercised considerable influence. In the streets patrolled by us traffic flowed smoothly. The red and black flag flew from many buildings, installations, and public places. We occupied the factories and the offices. Although hampered by insufficient preparation and the necessity of coexisting with our unfriendly allies who did everything they could to sabotage our efforts, we succeeded in administrating and coordinating economic and commercial operations and benefiting from the advice of experienced former administrators who cooperated and joined the committees that managed our commercial enterprises.

The political parties, men of the state who could not tolerate so bold a violation of their cherished conceptions and principles, could only look with disfavor on what to us was an insufficient and uncompleted revolution. They could not bear to see their authority questioned and their institutions flouted, reduced to inferior status.

But our enemies could not at that time come out prematurely against the CNT-FAI. It was the hour of sacred union and concentration against fascism. Neither we nor they could risk a civil war between anti-fascists which could benefit only Franco, who in repressing and obliterating all opposition would make no distinction between republican or anarchist "leaders." To regain lost ground, such an offensive against the revolution needed time for the secret reorganization of the counter-revolutionary forces. It had to be done carefully and skillfully. While we could not be altogether certain if the collectivization decree of the Catalonian government was deliberately enacted for that purpose, it nevertheless constituted a first step in the campaign to crush the revolution. The fact is that in the process of legalizing collectivization (which was already an accomplished fact that the government could not hope to reverse) the state, in arrogating to itself the exclusive right to enforce the decree, would sooner or later inevitably abuse and broaden its powers for its own sinister purposes.

As usual, the government began by reorganizing and augmenting as much as possible its police force. Four months after the 19th of July, mounted municipal guards patrolled the streets, ostensibly to help our comrades of the CNT-FAI, but gradually to retake from our comrades—who kept perfect order—the control of the streets. It was the Minister of the Interior of the Central Government in Valencia (moved from Madrid) who came to Barcelona purposely to re-establish the police and increase the number of Assault and Civil Guards. These forces were supposed to reinforce the fighting troops at the front, but actually they remained in the rear. In addition to the police, and Assault and Civil Guards, the best armed and disciplined rearguard élite military corps was the *Carabineros.* And this force, often in collusion with unscrupulous individuals and political parties, manifested a growing hostility towards us.

In January, 1937, while on a trip to France, I was amazed to see the road from Barcelona to the frontier crowded with long lines of ambulances and small cars bearing in big letters the insignia *Carabineros:* eight months after the Revolution, there were already twenty thousand *Carabineros* in Catalonia, testimony to the growing power of the state.

But Catalonia was much less statified than was central Spain. And while our comrades were battling without arms on the Aragon front, the twenty thousand arms and rifles of the *Carabineros* would have been sufficient to disrupt and pierce the fascist front. At the same time the Central Government continued to consolidate its power for a twofold purpose: fight at the front against Franco, and in the rear against the Revolution (doubtlessly more to crush the Revolution than to defeat Franco). Carefully weighing every word, I am convinced that if half the intelligence used to combat the Revolution had been turned against Franco, the *Caudillo* would never have triumphed.[5]

But it is necessary to stress this conclusion: not only was the power of the state and authoritarian institutions restored through the initiative of the government (made easier by war circumstances), but also by the pressure of the propertied classes and the political parties (both reformist and conservative), who could under no circumstances accept the idea of economic equality, as well as those who for other reasons feared the Social Revolution.

On the other hand, many individuals cooperated with us even though they did not agree with our ideas. We mean not only manual workers but even professionals, intellectuals, and small land owners. For example, almost

---

[5] We cite a few examples from Guérin of the economic sabotage of the Central Government to throttle the libertarian revolution:

The Central Government had a stranglehold over the collectives; the nationalization of transport made it possible for it to supply some and cut off all deliveries to others. ... It imported Republican army uniforms instead of turning to the Catalonian textile collectives. ... The Republican Central Government refused to grant any credit to Catalonian self-management even when the libertarian Minister of the Catalonian economy, Fabregas, offered the billion pesetas of savings bank deposits as security. In June, 1937, the Stalinist Comorera took over the portfolio of the economy and deprived the self-managed factories of raw materials which he lavished on the private sector. ... (pp. 141, 142)—*Ed.*

all the doctors in Barcelona saw in the CNT the only organization seriously concerned with creating new and better health services. Almost all non-exploiting professionals refused to join the UGT, which was the refuge for all the conservatives and those more or less sympathetic to fascism. There are many other examples. But there were also others, among them not only those who had always been anti-anarchists, but ostensibly "radical" neutrals who, when faced with new events, became virulent outright counter-revolutionists.

As a concession to the progressive revolutionary sentiments of a section of their membership, the political parties modified their policies to some extent. But they did all they could to save the state. Others, because it could supply arms and aid from Russia, worked with or joined the Communist Party. To fight the CNT on the labor front they joined the counter-revolutionary UGT.

If the government of Catalonia (embracing four of the most industrialized provinces in Spain) against its own principles was forced to legalize the collectivization of industry, it did so only because it was already a fact and the government had at that time no other alternative. But the Central Valencia government did not do so. It refused to make concessions because it was confident that the government would eventually legally intervene and restore the collectivized property to the former owners. If the Valencia government was for the time being obliged to tolerate collectivization, it did so only because the employers, who secretly admired Franco, were not at all inclined to cooperate in the anti-fascist war against Franco.

There was yet another statist opposition to the Revolution: the Communist Party. This party, at the beginning of the Revolution, had very little influence. Afterwards, in some cities in the war zone, the Communists exerted a preponderant influence. The arrival of Russian arms earned the sympathy of the people, who saw Franco troops at the gates of Madrid. The Communists skillfully exploited this favorable situation to the limit. Intelligently directed by a select general staff of skilled and unscrupulous connivers, they constituted a major political power which no other party could rival. They actually commanded all military operations (to his credit General Miaja, a brave but incapable officer, refused to knuckle under). The prestige of the International Brigade, whose members were ignobly sacrificed to the propaganda line of the party, heightened their popularity. These skillful tactics succeeded. . . . [6]

---

[6] Leval's description of the counter-revolutionary role and betrayals of the Communist Party during the Civil War and their campaign to destroy the collectives (especially in

Even the POUM (Workers' Party of Marxist Unification), whom the Stalinists hated even more than they did the anarchists, opposed our constructive revolutionary achievements (in Aragon I saw and read their publications against collectives), not on principled grounds . . . but that the time was not ripe for socialization. In respect to the necessity for a party and the state they did not differ fundamentally from the other authoritarian political parties. The POUM could not understand how socialization was possible without the exclusive or preponderent direction of the state. In different ways the state always interfered. The political parties and grouplets (bourgeois, proletarian, dictatorial, and democratic), in spite of all their quarrels and their differing ideas, all agreed on one thing: the necessity for the state. For that reason alone they opposed libertarian socialization.

Even some of our own comrades, bewildered by the complexity of the situation as well as the paucity of their constructive ideas, lost their bearings and, seeing no other alternative, joined the government. And once again history has decisively demonstrated the pernicious influence that the exercise of power (particularly the power of the state) exerts to alter the character of men. Most of our comrades occupying official positions came to see our problems only from the angle of the state and lost sight of the anti- or non-state organizational alternatives and measures. And often the spirit of governmental collaboration and compromise proved to be stronger than the need for common, direct action, leading them to act like opponents of libertarian socialization. Finally in Catalonia the about-face of Companys[7] indicated that the long brewing showdown between the Catalonian government and the anarchists was imminent. The government could no longer tolerate a situation in which it had to share power with anyone. The anarchists had to be dumped and conflict was inevitable. The decisive struggle took place during the tragic days of May, 1937, after which we were practically excluded from power. The pretext? The Catalan government wanted to take possession of the Central Telephone Exchange which had been in the hands of our comrades since the end of July, 1936.

Aragon) and the anarchist movement are well documented in English and need not be repeated here. Leval concludes that the Communists did everything in their power and used the most reprehensible tactics to "provoke the hatred and hostility of the civil and military population against the anarchists and their revolutionary innovations. . . . " —Ed.

[7] Betraying his anarchist allies who collaborated in his government, the Generalidad of Catalonia, Companys joined the counter-revolutionary alliance. During the tragic May Days of 1937 Companys aided and abetted the assault to dislodge the CNT from its stronghold in Barcelona collaborating with the Communists, the bourgeoisie and the C.P. dominated UGT to destroy the Catalonian collectives. —Ed.

But the conflict would have broken out anyhow, whatever the pretext. Although our comrades, aided by the POUM, in three days of fighting completely controlled four-fifths of Barcelona, the conflict was halted by the stupid intervention of our government ministers, Garcia Oliver and Federica Montseny.

But fortunately the anarchist movement was very strong. It had a sense of reality, excellent organizational ability, and, despite severe setbacks, the movement continued to function. An orator could stampede a plenum into accepting collaboration with the state, but after thinking it over the rank and file CNT and FAI members would reaffirm their deeply felt convictions and continue to work for the Revolution. These militants were able to administer a collective, work on the land, use a hammer, or guide a local assembly or syndicate with their sensible ideas on how to solve practical problems.

It is because the Spanish libertarian movement was based on this kind of concrete practical activity (particularly the militants who had acquired in the CNT through long years of struggle the experience and know-how) that the libertarian organizations were able to flourish in spite of the increasing power of the state and the growth of governmental political parties. Even when Camorera, the Communist economic minister of Catalonia, sabotaged industrial collectivization . . . our influence continued to grow. It grew because the bourgeois-capitalist machine was half paralyzed, the state proved incapable of administering production, and the UGT syndicates lacked audacity and initiative.

The following map locates a number of
areas, cities, and villages mentioned in
this book. A complete listing is not
intended. "The Levant" refers to the
eastern coast of Spain from Murcia to
Valencia.

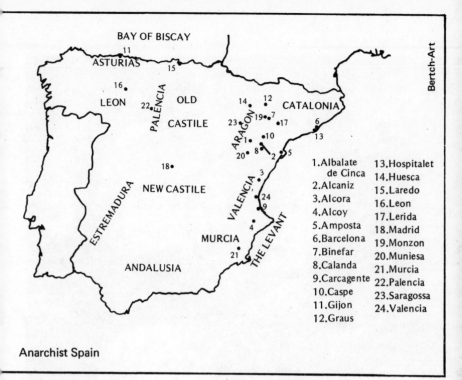

Anarchist Spain

Bertch-Art

part two:
the social revolution

Anarchist peasants in rural Spain.

chapter 5
The Economics of Revolution

Introduction

The social revolution in Spain was faced with basic economic problems under conditions of unusual difficulty. How were commodities to be produced, distributed and public services rendered? How and by whom were economic decisions to be made? To the greatest possible extent, these problems were tackled in a libertarian communist manner—without the capitalist profit system and without the "top-down" authoritarian bureaucratic system of state-capitalist "socialism." The Spanish libertarian collectives developed practical alternatives to both the "democratic" and state-capitalist systems.

In this chapter, Santillan illustrates with examples the problem of scarcity of resources as well as economic sabotage by anti-libertarians. Augustin Souchy outlines how the workers' collectives organized federations to successfully coordinate the libertarian economy. The final selection in this chapter deals with the necessity for some medium of exchange, demonstrating that the revolutionary economy must also revolutionize the form of exchange. It explains how the workers' collectives worked out new and ingenious forms of exchange—local currency, vouchers, tokens, ration cards—without introducing profit, interest, or rent. Thus, as much as possible, they did away with the monopoly of money and credit of the capitalist banking system, which would otherwise perpetuate the exploitation of the people.

Economic Structure and Coordination[1]
by Augustin Souchy

Iwo great industrial systems, private capitalism and state capitalism, dominate economic society. The notion that state ownership or control of production is preferable to private capitalism is a widespread falsehood. . . . This, however, does not mean that capitalism is in itself a good economic system. Even without its endemic economic imperialism and imperialistic wars, capitalism would still be a social disaster. Nor is the fundamental evil of exploitation automatically abolished under state capitalism.

The alternative economic system is collectivism—or a socialism established by the people themselves without state interference. To an astonishing degree this ideal was being realized in Spain. Within a few years, during the Spanish Civil War, the Spanish workers and peasants were establishing what could be loosely called libertarian syndicalist socialism, a system without exploitation and injustice. In this type of libertarian collectivist economy, wage slavery is replaced by the equitable and just sharing of labor. Private capitalism or state capitalism is replaced by the workers' factory council, the union, and the industrial association of unions up to the national federation of industrial unions.[2]

[1] From Augustin Souchy, *Nacht über Spanien*, pp. 164-167.
[2] It is essentially a system of workers' control at all levels, each unit exercising autonomy within its own sphere. Santillan's formulation is more explicit:

> The structure of the new economy was simple: Each factory organized a new administration manned by its own technical and administrative workers. Factories in the same industry in each locality organized themselves into the Local Federation of their particular industry. The total of all the Local Federations organized themselves into the Local Economic Council in which all the centers of production and services were represented: coordination, exchange, sanitation and health, culture, transportation, etc. Both the Local Federations of each industry and the Local Economic Councils were organized regionally and nationally into parallel National Federations of Industry and National Economic Federations. . . . (*Por Que Perdimos la Guerra*, Buenos Aires, 1940, p. 82)—*Ed.*

The Spanish syndicalists demonstrated that such a system is practical. Libertarian collectivism preserves and widens freedom, stimulates and encourages initiative, and smooths the way for progress. A syndicalist collective economy is not state planned or state dominated. Planning is directed to satisfy the consumer. The syndicalist collective is for the producer what the consumer's cooperative association is for the consumer.

The collectives organized during the Spanish Civil War were workers' economic associations without private property. The fact that collective plants were managed by those who worked in them did not mean that these establishments became their private property. The collective had no right to sell or rent all or any part of the collectivised factory or workshop. The rightful custodian was the CNT, the National Confederation of Workers Associations. But not even the CNT had the right to do as it pleased. Everything had to be decided and ratified by the workers themselves through conferences and congresses.

The new order was flexible. The factory or plant was operated by the workers, but they did not resemble Fourier's "Phalansteries" or the "national workshops" in Louis Blanc's sense. The collectives were an attempt to organize work on the basis of solidarity and mutual aid: to organize the economy through the organization of mutual credit without interest in a manner somewhat similar to Proudhon's Mutual Credit Banks. Nor did the syndicalist collective economy resemble the "free enterprise" system. There is no connection whatever between an economy based on workers' control, mutual aid, and self-management and a capitalist economy with its unrestrained exploitation and cutthroat competition.

The syndicalist economic structure was firmly established in a few years. The plants were managed by the workers themselves through managers chosen by them. Problems beyond the capacity of the single plant were tackled by the local Economic Council. . . . On August 28, 1937, one year after the beginning of collectivization, an economic congress of the Catalonian collectives was held in Barcelona. Shortly after, a national economic congress embracing all urban and agrarian collectives and all socialized industry was held in Valencia. How the Barcelona Congress dealt with problems illustrates the character of the new economic structure. Several examples:

1) The collectivized shoe factories need credit of 2,000,000 pesetas. They have always paid the workers full wages, but because of a leather shortage they have been forced to cut down working time. In spite of this, they are paying 500 workers full weekly wages without deductions for lost time. The Economic Council studied the condition of the shoe industry. It

reports that there is no surplus of shoes. Granting of credit will enable the purchase of leather and the modernization of a number of outdated factories which will result in lower costs and lower prices, and with it increased consumption. The reorganized and rehabilitated industry will then be able to help other industries in need of assistance. Acting on this favorable report, credit is granted.

2) There are no aluminum factories in Catalonia. The aluminum factory located in Huesca is in fascist hands. To carry on the war, aluminum is crucially needed. The Economic Council, with the cooperation of chemists, engineers, and technicians, work out plans to build a new aluminum factory. Water power, electricity, coal, and bauxite are available. The Economic Council also submits a plan to finance the installation. Money is to be raised through the collectivized plants, the socialized industries, and from the union. The issuing of stocks and bonds is not recommended because it would lead to the restoration of capitalism. Capitalism, ejected from the door, would climb back in through the window. . . .

3) The Barcelona Economic Council, to mitigate unemployment in the cities, worked out a plan with the cooperation of the agricultural workers union to bring new areas into cultivation (irrigation, fertilizers, new installations, etc.). Unemployment in the cities was appreciably reduced, while needed labor from the cities was supplied to modernize agriculture. Russian state capitalism solved such problems by forced labor, herding many workers (at least 2,000,000) into concentration camps. Libertarians viewed such means with repugnance. The Spanish libertarian collectives have proven that compulsory labor is counterproductive and totally unnecessary. The unemployed worker did not have to be forced to work in the country. He was, on the contrary, welcomed on equal terms as a brother worker engaged in a common cooperative enterprise, sharing both the burdens and rewards of his fellow workers.

4) How were such vast, complex, and costly operations financed and coordinated? The workers helped each other. Isolated enterprises were financial pygmies. With all the collectivized factories and establishments working and pooling their resources together, they were giants. The finances of all the collectivized plants, the socialized industries, and the unions were deposited in the Central Labor Bank in Barcelona, with branches everywhere. The bank channelled funds from more prosperous collectives to less prosperous collectives in need of credit. Cash transactions were reduced to an absolute minimum. Credit was not given in cash. The bank balanced accounts between collectives and arranged credit where needed not in cash but in exchange for products or services.

The Bank of Labor also arranged foreign exchange and importation and purchase of raw materials and other products. As in domestic transactions, payment was made (where possible) in commodities, not in cash. All important operations of the Labor Bank were reviewed, and policies set, at union congresses. Finally, the Labor Bank was not a capitalist bank in business to make money by usury. It served as a coordinating agency and charged only 1% interest to defray expenses.

A Note on the Difficult Problems of Reconstruction[3]
by Diego Abad de Santillan

It is hard to imagine the complexity of the problems which this convulsion, war and revolution, created: the rupture of the old relations and the creation of new forms of social life. And all this simultaneously with carrying on the anti-fascist war, to which we sent 30,000 men to the Aragon front, not counting auxilliary forces. It takes the labor of 200,000 industrial and agricultural workers to supply an army of 30,000. All this had to be built up from scratch, lacking indispensable resources and under the worst possible conditions.

If on the day following the victory over the fascists the railroad system did not function smoothly at full capacity under the new management of the revolutionary workers, it was not for lack of ability, but because coal was in short supply, and priority had to be given to war transportation. From the very beginning we suffered from an alarming lack of indispensable war materials in a region naturally poor in minerals, textile fibers, and coal. Barcelona normally consumed 56,000 tons of coal daily. And we extracted from the poor mines in the region, after exceedingly hard labor, only 300 tons daily. We were able in a few months to increase output to 1,000 tons. Despite all our efforts, the scarcity of coal was a constant tragedy, particularly coal for the metal industry (foundries, etc.). Asturias could have

---

[3] From Diego Abad de Santillan, *Por Que Perdimos la Guerra*, p. 81

helped greatly,[4] but in response to our requests one of its top officials, Amador Fernandez, preferred to ship coal to others or to keep it unused rather than to supply Catalonia. This in spite of the fact that we offered to exchange scarce products badly needed in Asturias (especially cloth and other materials) in exchange for the coal. . . .

Money and Exchange
S.D.

One of the most vexing problems of the Spanish Revolution, as in every revolution, was exchange. The whole question of the "abolition of money" particularly provoked considerable controversy. This problem had a great bearing on the Revolution, especially the rural collectives. The views outlined here of the workers of the CNT textile workers union (the industry was collectivized a few months after July 19th) are especially cogent:

> In a viable social order, money only as a symbol to facilitate exchange of goods and services will have to be adapted to the revolutionary economy, preserving all its invaluable advantages (the product of the economic experience of generations). It is to be used solely as the most efficient means of conducting transactions yet developed.[5]

Some form of money, a uniform standard for the exchange of the *infinite variety of dissimilar goods and services,* is indispensable in a complex organized society. Thus viewed, "money" is a standard for measuring the value of goods and services just as the metric system is used

---

[4]Santillan refers to the period before the fascists took over the region.—*Ed.*

[5]Incidentally, this opinion is in harmony with Malatesta's statement that after the abolition of the state and capitalism, with the coming of abundance, and pending the full realization of an anarchist society, money will still remain "the only means (apart from the most tyrannical dictatorship or the most idyllic accord) so far devised by human intelligence to regulate production and distribution automatically." (*Life and Ideas,* p. 101)

STATISTICAL INFORMATION ON AGRARIAN AND INDUSTRIAL SOCIALIZATION

Adequate statistical information on this subject has not yet been compiled and is very difficult to obtain, but the following data should give a general idea of the extent of the libertarian revolution on the land and in the cities.

Pierre Broué and Emile Témime state that in Aragon, "under the control of the anarchists, the collectivization movement embraced more than three-quarters of the land, almost exclusively in communities affiliated to the CNT." (p. 159)

"Over half the land in the Republican zone was collectivized." (Souchy) Leval talks about "revolutionary experience involving, directly or indirectly, 7 to 8 million people."

Peirats is more specific on the number of hectares cultivated by the collectives and makes a revealing comparison with the land "legally distributed during the five years of agrarian reform by the Republican government"—876,327 hectares—while only "in a *few weeks* the Revolution expropriated 5,692,202 hectares directly occupied by the peasants. . . ." (*Los Anarquistas en la Crisis Politica Española*, Buenos Aires, 1964, p. 145—italics ours).

Frank Mintz estimates 1,265 to 1,865 collectives, "embracing 610,000 to 800,000 workers. With their families, they involve a population of 3,200,000. . . ." (p. 149)

Leval lists 1,700 agrarian collectives, broken down as follows: Aragon, 400 (for Aragon Souchy estimates 510); Levant, 900; Castile, 300; Estrémadura, 30; Catalonia, 40; Andalusia, unknown. For the collectivized urban industries he estimates: Catalonia, all the industries and all transportation; Levant, 70% of all the industries; Castile, part of the industries—he gives no figures. (*Espagne Libertaire*, p. 80)

While some anarchist collectives abolished the use of money altogether, others issued their own local currency coupons and ration cards for limited use within the collective.

to measure distances or the dimensions and weight of objects. Just as the metric system replaced other systems of measurement, the monetary system can also be altered. Ninety-nine percent of the world's transactions are conducted not in hard cash but by vouchers in the form of checks, notes, credit cards, trading stamps, etc. But this does not mean that "money is abolished." It simply means the substitution of one symbol of exchange for another.

When talking about the Spanish Revolution, the confusion stems from the failure to stipulate that "abolishing money" refers to the *official national money of Spain as distinct from the local money issued by the collectives.* Only the *local* use of this national currency was abolished or, most often, in varying degrees curtailed. (The value of goods and the balancing of accounts was still calculated in terms of the peseta.) It would be more correct to say that the libertarian collectives in each locality (to assure just and equitable sharing of goods and services, and prevent hoarding and speculation) worked out their own systems of exchange. They issued their own local money in the form of vouchers, tokens, rationing booklets, certificates, coupons, etc., which carried no interest and were not negotiable outside of the issuing collective.

Aside from the loose use of the term "money," Burnett Bolloten gives a fair general idea of the exchange system in typical libertarian communities:

> In those libertarian communities where money was suppressed, wages were paid in coupons, the scale being determined by the size of the family. Locally produced goods, if abundant, such as bread, wine, and olive oil, were distributed freely, while other articles could be obtained by means of coupons at the communal depot. Surplus goods were exchanged with other anarchist towns and villages, money [the legal national currency] being used only for transactions with those communities that had not yet adopted the new system. (pp. 61, 62)

Some collectives did in fact abolish money. They had no system of exchange, not even coupons. For example, a resident of Magdalena de Pulpis, when asked, "How do you organize without money? Do you use barter, a coupon book, or anything else?," replied, "Nothing. Everyone works and everyone has the right to what he needs free of charge. He simply goes to the store where provisions and all other necessities are supplied. Everything is distributed free with only a notation of what he took."

However, these attempts to really abolish money were not generally successful. Peirats recalls that:

Under the constant pressure of political-military circumstances, the first attempts to abolish money and wages had to be abandoned and replaced by the family wage. (*Los Anarquistas en la Crisis Politica Española*, p. 131)

Some kind of family wage became quite common in the Spanish collectives. This wage was assigned to families and varied according to the number of members in a family. It was based on the needs of the family rather than on the product of the family members. The exact nature of a particular family wage system depended on numerous things (like the relative abundance or scarcity of necessities for a collective or region). This led to a wide variety of "monetary" experiments. Leval comments that:

In regions like Castile, Catalonia, or in the Levant, where the republican state was more entrenched, the "peseta," official national currency based on the gold standard, was retained. Although obliged to use the "peseta" as the standard of value and unit of distribution, the libertarian communist collectives adopted the family wage. . . . Where the state was weaker, each village tackled exchange in its own fashion. In such localities, above all Aragon, local collectives issued as many as 250 and even 300 different kinds of local money, vouchers, coupons, ration booklets, metal tokens, cards, etc.[6] (*Espagne Libertaire*, pp. 203, 208)

This chaotic situation could not be tolerated for long. The Congress of the Aragon Federation of Peasant Collectives, for instance, unanimously agreed to replace local currencies with a uniform ration booklet for all the Aragon collectives, leaving it for each collective to stipulate the quantity of items available to each family or individual living alone.

The family ration booklet, dated April 23, 1937, (when the new system went into effect) to December 31, 1937, was divided into weekly columns enumerating 21 articles more or less in the following order: bread, wine, oil, rice, chick peas, green beans, flour, sausage and smoked sausage, lard, sugar, pudding, various preserves, canned tomatoes, potatoes, milk, lentils, olives, chocolate, footwear, household articles, hardware, haberdashery. . . . (Gaston Leval, *Espagne Libertaire*, p. 210)

---

[6] See Mintz, appendix, pp. 36-37.

A uniform ration booklet was one attempt to refine a chaotic situation. Another problem was how to cope with the complex transactions necessary in the economic world without falling back to old statist and capitalist ways of doing things. Gaston Leval reports the decision of the Peasant Federation of Levant:

> to establish a bank of our own . . . to keep things moving between our collectivized villages, and for trade with other towns . . . instead of helping the government cut the ground from under us. (*Né Franco né Stalin*, p. 310)

And Mintz points out that:

> [the] anarchists abandoned the idea of a substitute for national money. The agrarian collectives decided to abolish money, only to adopt other systems of exchange. . . . The difficulties created by local money and the lack of a unified currency soon became evident. Very soon the collectivists of Aragon saw the advantages of a kind of national bank. (p. 168)[7]

Diego Abad de Santillan (Minister of the Economy in the Catalonian government in 1936) formulated an approach to this problem. In outlining his conception of the future new revolutionary economy, he suggests that foreign and domestic transactions would be conducted by federations of coordinative "Councils of Credit and Exchange," sort of clearing houses whose "personnel would be selected from the present banking institutions."

> Credit will be a social function and not a private speculation or usury. . . . Credit will be based on the economic possibilities of society and not on interests or profit. . . . Should it be necessary, as it probably will, to create a symbol of exchange [money] in response to the necessities of circulation and exchange of products, the Council will create a unit for this purpose exclusively as a facility and not as a money power. . . . The Council of Credit and Exchange will be like a thermometer of the products and needs of the country. (*After the Revolution*, pp. 87, 88, 89)

Santillan anticipated the exchange measures adopted by the libertarian

---

[7]It cannot be overemphasized that these were *not capitalist banks*, i.e., loan sharks accumulating wealth by usury, investment, control of property, and exploitation of labor. Mintz does not make this crucial distinction.—*Ed.*

Levant Federation of Peasant Collectives. Souchy points out that:

> Widespread and complex transactions made it necessary for the Federation to establish its own bank. . . . The bank, through its federated branches, coordinated the exchange and sale of products within Republican Spain and regulated all matters pertaining to foreign trade. The Federation's bank was of course administered by the Bank Workers Union. . . . In the Central Labor Bank of Catalonia, organized in August, 1937, cash transactions were reduced to a minimum. Credit was not given in cash. The bank balanced accounts between collectives and arranged credit when needed, not in cash, but in exchange of goods or services. . . . It served as a coordinating agency. (Souchy, pp. 156, 157)

Bolloten illustrates Souchy's reference to the kind of "complex transactions" necessitating the bank:

> In the region of Valencia, the center of the great orange industry, . . . the CNT set up an organization for purchasing, packing, and exporting the orange crop[8] with a network of 270 committees in different towns and villages, elbowing out of this important trade several thousand middlemen. (p. 49)

Leval concludes that the collectives tackled the problem of distribution, which is, after all, a problem of money and exchange

> with an originality, initiative, and practical sense which can only call forth universal admiration. . . . The collective genius of the rank and file agricultural workers resolved, by trial and error, problems which the Central Government would never have been able to solve. . . In the Republican zones dominated by the state the incapacity of the government to halt the rise in prices and speculation brought ruinous inflation and with it the devaluation of the peseta. . . . (*Espagne Libertaire*, p. 211)

That the collectives were able to solve the problem of distribution in accord with the spirit and principles of libertarian communism under such circumstances and on so vast a scale is a feat never equaled by the French, Russian, or any other revolution.

---

[8] Ninety percent of the crop was exported.

chapter 6
Worker's Self-Management in Industry

Introduction

Collectivization was a spontaneous outgrowth of the revolutionary situation. The industrial system had broken down and it became absolutely necessary to resume production. But the workers refused to go back to the old system of exploitation. They demanded the expropriation of the capitalists and full collective self-management by themselves.

Souchy points out that in many enterprises there was immediate and full collectivization. In many privately owned enterprises, as a prelude to full collectivization, workers' control committees assumed partial control and closely watched the operations of the enterprises. Under full collectivization genuine workers' self-management was instituted. From their own ranks the workers' elected technical/administrative committees to run the enterprise. The committees were responsible to the workers and carried out their instructions. Those failing to do so were immediately replaced.

Organizationally, too, the principles of anarchism which guided the coordination of the 2½ million workers of the CNT in the inner federalist structure of the organization, were applied to the structure of the collectivized enterprises. The principles of workers' self-management and federalism were tested successfully in undertaking the task of the immediate and efficient restoration of the everyday necessities of life—food, clothing, shelter and public services.

Workers' Self-Management in Industry[1]
by Augustin Souchy

With the repulse of the fascist assault on the 19th of July and the days following, the big commercial and industrial properties were abandoned by their owners. The big executives of the railroads, urban transport, the big metal and machinery plants, the textile industry, etc., disappeared. The revolutionary General Strike called by the workers as a measure against the fascist military putsch paralyzed the economic life of Barcelona and suburbs. With the victory over the fascists, the workers decided to go back to work. But the General Strike was not merely a strike for better working conditions. The bosses were gone. The bourgeois republicans did not know how to restore production. . . .

From being mere employees taking orders from their former bosses, it became incumbent on the workers to take over the control and management of the whole economy. In short, the workers had to henceforth be responsible for the efficient administration of the economic life of the country.

One cannot, however, conceive of socialization or collectivization in accordance with a detailed preconceived plan. In fact, practically nothing was prepared in advance, and in this emergency situation everything had to be improvised. As in all revolutions, practice takes precedence over theory. Theories were, in effect, altered and modified in accordance with the ever pressing realities. The partisans of the idea that it is possible to establish a new social organization gradually, by peaceful evolutionary means, are just as mistaken as those who believe that a new social order can be established easily if only the political power fell into the hands of the working class. . . .

Both of these views are erroneous and it would be more correct to

[1] From *Collectivisations: L'Oeuvre Constructive de la Révolution Espagnole (1936-1939)* (Collection of Documents) forward by Augustin Souchy, pp. 6, 7, 8 , and *Los Anarquistas en la Crisis Politica Española*, pp. 121-128, 133.

formulate them thus: the military, police, and public power of the capitalist state must be broken to leave the way free for the emergence and establishment of new social forms. And it must also be stressed that the creators of the new economic life must be theoretically and practically prepared with a clear conception of their organizational tasks, objectives, and tactics. In every social theory there is a good measure of utopia. And it is good that this is so, for without the element of utopia nothing new can be created. Precise ideas, notions, and interpretations on how to realize our aims must spring from our vision of the future. . . .

In Spain, particularly in Catalonia, socialization began with collectivization. . . . While the socialization was spontaneous, the influence of the anarchist doctrine is incontestable. . . . In their assemblies of unions and groups, in their pamphlets and books, the problems of the revolution were ceaselessly and systematically discussed. What must be done on the morrow of the victory of the proletariat? The governmental apparatus must be smashed. The workers must administer industry themselves. The syndicates must control all economic life. The associated branches of industry must manage production. The local federations must administer consumption and distribution.[2]

The immediate task of the revolutionaries on the day after the revolution is to feed the people. . . . In revolution a hungry people will inevitably be victimized by unscrupulous adventurers and demagogues. (See Kropotkin, *The Conquest of Bread*) While the streets still echoed with gunfire, the distribution of basic food supplies had already been undertaken by the *Comites de Asbastos.* [3] These committees originated in the neighborhoods and districts (*Barrios*).[4]

---

[2] Such were the ideas which the workers endeavored to put into practice immediately after they defeated the fascists. In this last section of the chapter, Jose Peirats graphically sums up how they began to do so.—*Ed.*

[3] More accurately called Workers' Committees of Control and Management—*Ed.*

[4] It was no small achievement to feed and restore the economic life of Barcelona, a city of 1,200,000 (the most populous in Spain). Souchy reports that the food unions, together with the hotel and restaurant workers, opened communal dining halls in each neighborhood. Broué and Témime state that in August the food committee "fed up to 120,000 people a day in open restaurants on presentation of a union card." (p. 166) The big food wholesale establishments were collectivized. Thirty unions organized themselves into a Food Workers' Industrial Union (the most important: bakers, butchers, dairy workers). The unions, in general membership meetings, fixed their own wages. The workers became their own bosses. The system embraced all of Catalonia, and five hundred workers coordinated the operations. Broué and Témime conclude that "essential food supplies for militiamen and for the inhabitants of the towns were guaranteed without an appreciable rise in prices." (p. 166)—*Ed.*

The Committees collected and stored provisions in big warehouses. Markets remained open under union control and the union committees were commissioned to supply them with merchandise. Mobile units of the Committees gathered food from the surrounding farms and villages, arranging for the exchange of products with the cities. The Committees set up a system of distribution and rationing of provisions in short supply. For example, articles like milk, chickens, and eggs were set aside for hospitals and other emergency cases. Wounded militiamen, children, women, and the aged came first. At the beginning a system of free exchange with the suppliers was established: industrial goods in exchange for farm products. In many cases vouchers or receipts in payment for foodstuffs and other necessities, guaranteed and redeemable at a later date by the unions and the *Generalidad* (government) of Catalonia, were instituted . . . .

On the insistence of the anarchists, the *Generalidad* expropriated banks and froze the accounts and resources of all those suspected and convicted of collaboration with the fascists. The anarchists, during these euphoric moments of the Revolution, attached no importance to money. Paper money expropriated from the churches, convents, or the mansions of the rich was not even counted, and freely handed over to the Committees or the *Generalidad*. Sometimes the paper money was burned together with religious images, property titles, industrial stocks and bonds, treasury notes, etc. Gold and silver currency was reserved for foreign exchange. The organizations soon realized that this money, instead of being wasted or destroyed, could and must be used to purchase arms and other supplies from abroad—something which the Central Government carelessly or deliberately ignored.

The collectivization of expropriated property by the workers of the CNT was spontaneous. After risking their lives on the barricades, the workers refused to return to the factories under the same conditions. The Red and Black flag of the CNT waved over the expropriated factories. To assure efficient production and services, the same workers and friendly technicians who previously worked in the same factories themselves took over the administration, control, and management of their respective enterprises.

Since 1931 the workers of the CNT had been organized into National Industrial Federations.[5] This preparation facilitated the necessary

---

[5] In 1919, at its Madrid Conference, the CNT decided to replace the outdated craft-union setup, and in conformity with the growth of modern industry, adopted the industrial union form of organization. Those opposed to this change objected that it would lead to excessive centralization and the various local trade unions would lose their autonomy. The resolution to adopt the industrial union form of organization was

WORKERS' CONTROL VS WORKERS' SELF-MANAGEMENT

Workers' control is a concept that is currently becoming popular among Western sociologists and industrial managers as well as social democratic union leaders. The concept is referred to by such terms as "participation," "democratization," and "co-determination." For those whose function it is solve the new problems of boredom and alienation in the workplace in advanced industrial capitalism, workers' control is seen as a hopeful solution. . . a solution in which workers are given a modicum of influence, a strictly limited area of decision-making power, a voice—at best secondary—in the control of conditions of the work place. Workers' control, in a limited form sanctioned by the capitalists, is held to be the answer to the growing non-economic demands of the workers.

Workers' self-management, the exercise of workers' power through collectivization and federation as in the social revolution in Spain, is very different. Self-management is not a new form of mediation between the workers and their capitalist bosses, but instead refers to the very process by which the workers themselves *overthrow* their managers and take on their own management and the management of production in their own work place. Self-management means the organization of all workers in the work place into a workers' council or factory committee (or agricultural collective), which makes all the decisions formerly made by the owners and managers. Nor does self-management allow the gravitation of power from the workers themselves to a bureacratic heirarchy. When power is delegated by the workers, it is for a specific purposed and it is delegated to other workers who are always recallable.

In Spain the social revolution did not meet with complete success: the revolution was often stopped short of full workers' self-management. But the ideal, the goal toward which the workers were striving, was clear enough.

revolutionary reorganization and coordination. . . . The production centers of an industry constituted interconnected units. Each expropriated bourgeois establishment was collectively worked and administered by the most capable workers and technicians, freely designated by the general assemblies of the workers at the point of production.

In some industries collectivization went far beyond local limits. It embraced whole regions and whole industries from raw materials to finished products. This type of collectivization was called "socialized industry." For example, the wood industry of Barcelona, from lumber camps in the forests to the manufacture and sale of finished wood products, constituted a single unbroken coordinated unit.

To get the maximum benefits from machines and efficient handwork, small workshops were consolidated into big, modern factories called *talleres confederales*. This procedure also insured maximum technical development.

Another example was the baking industry. As in the rest of Spain, Barcelona's bread and cakes were baked mostly at night in hundreds of small bakeries. Most of them were in damp, gloomy cellars infested with roaches and rodents. All these bakeries were shut down. More and better bread and cake were baked in new bakeries equipped with new modern ovens and other equipment.

Enterprises that could not yet be collectivized were placed under workers' control. The financial and other operations of the owners were closely watched. The control committees in these factories, were designated to watch over the administrative personnel, checked up on the economic condition of the company, and estimated the true value of its products. They collected information on orders, the cost of materials and all transactions, the conditions of machinery, and wages; and watched out for fiscal frauds (with special attention to counter-revolutionary sabotage by the owners and their stooges).

Workers' control was often the prelude to expropriation: a transition period during which the control committees were transformed into technical/administrative committees of the collectivized company. (In all cases both the control committees and the technical/administrative committees were elected by the general assembly of the workers on the

rescinded (1919), but was finally put into effect by the 1936 Congress of the CNT. The Congress divided industry in 18 industrial federations (later reduced to 15 by the 1938 Valencia economic plenum of the CNT). In no way did industrial unions curtail the freedom of the various crafts. The industrial union was essentially a federation of these interdependent crafts, each exercising full autonomy within its own sphere. The industrial union not only augmented the fighting capacity of the proletariat under capitalism but also constituted the basis for the new socialized economy.—*Ed.*

job.) These methods of revolutionary organization of production, distribution, and administration were adopted in all liberated regions or spontaneously developed, always under the influence of the anarchist activists. . . .

The fundamental difference between the UGT and CNT conceptions of workers' control was that the UGT collaborated with the employers in squeezing as much as they could out of the workers while the CNT exercised control to check up on the employer with a view to getting rid of him and taking over full management.

The collectivization of the fishing industry, the second most important industry in Asturias, also embraced the processing plants, fish canneries, and the processing of dried fish. Socialization was introduced on the initiative of the fish workers syndicates. In the cities and villages distribution was undertaken by cooperatives united in an organization called "The Council of Provincial Cooperative Federations." During the first months of the experiment money was abolished. Family supplies were procured upon showing a producer's and consumer's identification card in various denominations. The fishermen brought in their merchandise and received these cards in exchange. A similar system was tried in Santander (province of Laredo) by agreement between the CNT and the UGT.

A plenum of *Sindicatos Unicos* (Dec., 1936) formulated norms for socialization in which the absurd inefficiency of the petty bourgeois industrial system was analyzed. We quote:

> The major defect of most small manufacturing shops is fragmentation and lack of technical/commercial preparation. This prevents their modernization and consolidation into better and more efficient units of production, with better facilities and coordination. . . . For us, socialization must correct these deficiencies and systems of organization in every industry. . . . To socialize an industry, we must consolidate the different units of each branch of industry in accordance with a general and organic plan which will avoid competition and other difficulties impeding the good and efficient organization of production and distribution. . . .

This document is very important in the evolution of collectivization. The workers must take into account that partial collectivization will in time degenerate into a kind of bourgeois cooperativism. Encased in their respective competing collectives, the enterprises will have supplanted the classic compartmentalized monopolies only to degenerate inevitably into a bureaucracy: the first step leading to a new form of social inequality. The collectives will end up waging commercial wars with just as much ferocity as did the old bourgeois companies. It is therefore necessary to widen the base of the collectivist conception, to amplify and implement the organic solidarity of all industry into a harmonious community. This is the concept of socialization which was from the very beginning expounded by the most influential anarchists and syndicalists. . . .

chapter 7
Urban Collectivization

Introduction

Industrial collectivization was limited primarily to Barcelona and the province of Catalonia, where the anarcho-syndicalist influence was greatest. Soon after July 19th, the control of the industries of Catalonia passed into the hands of the workers of the CNT.

Rural collectivization of land was far more widespread and far more thorough than urban collectivization. The CNT—FAI was not able to carry out urban collectivization to the extent it desired or was possible because opposition was much greater in the industrialized areas than in the countryside. The UGT, republicans, liberals, socialists, communists, the former property owners and their allies, the Government of Catalonia and the Central Government in Valencia bitterly opposed and sabotaged not only full, but even partial collectivization.

However, as these selections show, to the limited extent that urban collectivization did prevail, it was successful. Collectivization was advanced not only in Catalonia, but in Alcoy (in Alicante province), where all industry was completely collectivized, and in the Bay of Biscay area where the fishing industry was partially collectivized.

The selections also show, the structure and the functioning of the urban collectives varied greatly. Collectivized enterprises embraced industries employing many thousands of workers as well as workshops employing less than a hundred workers. The extent of collectivization ranged from the consolidation of numerous small factories and workshops to the vast federative coordination of railway networks.

Finally, these selections again demonstrate the non-authoritarian rank and file democratic character of the collectives. The technical-administrative committees were composed of workers elected by and at all times responsible to their fellow workers. They served without pay, and generally transacted their affairs after working hours. They were elected for no fixed term, subject to recall at any time by the membership. One of the innovations was rotation of rank and file workers to these committees. There is of course, no form of organization which will unfailingly prevent abuse of power. But everything humanly possible was done to insure the maximum degree of grass roots democracy in industry.

Collectivizations in Catalonia [1]

by Augustin Souchy

The collectivization in Barcelona embraced construction, the metal industry, bakeries, slaughter houses, public utilities (gas, water, electricity, etc.), transportation, health services, theaters and cinemas, beauty parlors, hotels and boarding houses, etc. . . . Wages were equalized. The wages of lower paid workers were increased and high salaries in the upper income brackets reduced.

The takeover of industry was surprisingly quick. And the takeover proved beyond the slightest doubt that modern industry can be efficiently conducted without stock and bond holders and very highly placed executives. Wageworkers and salaried employees (engineers, technicians, etc.) can themselves operate the complicated machinery of modern industry. Examples are endless. Here are a few:

The Collectivization of Municipal Transportation

The first measure in the collectivization of the Barcelona street railways was to discharge the excessively paid directors and company stooges. The saving was considerable. A conductor averaged 250 to 300 pesetas a month,

---

[1] From Augustin Souchy, *Nacht über Spanien*, pp. 98-110.

while the general director (manager) was paid 5,000 and his three assistants 4,441, 2,384, and 2,000 pesetas respectively. The amount saved through the abolition of these posts went to increase the wages of the lowest paid workers 40% to 60%, and intermediate and higher brackets 10% to 20%. The next step was the reduction of working time to 40 hours per week (but for the war situation, it would have been cut to 36 hours weekly).

Another improvement was in the area of management. Before the Revolution, streetcars, buses, and subways were each privately owned by separate companies. The union decided to integrate and consolidate all transportation into an efficient system without waste. This improvement meant better facilities, rights of way, and incomparably better service for the riding public. Fares were reduced from 15 to 10 centimes, with free transportation for school children, wounded militiamen, those injured at work, other invalids, and the aged.

The repair shops worked extra shifts to repair damaged, and remodel old, conveyances. This proved better for all concerned: better service for the public, lower fares, and better wages and working conditions. Naturally the only ones who complained were the investors and high salaried bureaucrats. The Transportation and Communication Workers' Union became a collectivized transportation association. This report of the Expropriation Committee is an example of how this change was effected:

> On the morning of July 24th, while the people in arms were still fighting the fascists in the streets of Barcelona, . . . a number of armed comrades from the CNT, at the request of the Transportation Union, left the barricades and in armored cars drove to the head offices of the street railway transportation company to enforce and expedite the expropriation and collectivization of the street car system. The place was patrolled inside and out by Civil Guards. After a short consultation, the guards left and the CNT took possession. There was neither ready cash in the safe nor funds in the bank. The owners had absconded with the funds, and the workers had to resume operations without capital. . . .[2]

---

[2] The tramways serving Barcelona and suburbs covered 69 routes and constituted the mainstay of its transportation system (which also included busses and taxis). Of the 7,000 employees, 6,500 belonged to the CNT Transportation Workers Union.

During the fighting with the fascists, the streets were torn up and obstructed by barricades. After estimating the damage and specifying repairs, a commission representing different departments (electric power, cables, traffic signals, rolling stock, operating personnel, etc.) arranged to resume operations and radioed all personnel to return.

Working around the clock, service was restored only five days after fighting ceased.

The Socialization of Telephone Service

More than half the telephone lines were destroyed by grenades during the fighting. The restoration and repair of telephone connections was imperative. Without waiting for orders from anyone, the workers restored normal telephone service within three days. Thousands of new lines were installed in union locals, militia centers, and committee districts. Once this crucial emergency work was finished a general membership meeting of telephone workers decided to collectivize the telephone system. From within their own ranks the workers chose a management committee. Each district elected its own responsible director. Although very few telephone workers belonged to the UGT (most belonged to the CNT), the collectivization was conducted under the joint auspices of the UGT and CNT.

The subscribers declared that telephone service was better under collectivization than under private ownership. As in collectivized transportation, the wages of the lowest paid workers was significantly increased.

Seven hundred trolleys (instead of the former 600), newly painted in the red and black colors of the CNT-FAI, were placed in service. This miracle was achieved because the various trades coordinated and organized their work into one industrial union of all the transport workers. Each section was administered by an engineer designated by the union and a worker delegated by the general membership. The delegations of the various sections coordinated operations in a given area. While the sections met separately to conduct their own specific operations, decisions affecting the workers in general were made at general membership meetings.

The engineers and technicians did not (as in "socialist" and capitalist countries) constitute a separate privileged elite. The work of the technicians, engineers, and manual workers was permanently interwoven and integrated. The engineer, for example, could not undertake an important project without consulting the other workers, not only because responsibilities were to be shared but also because in practical problems the manual workers acquired practical experience which technicians often lacked. And the manual workers' committees could always advise the technicians on the feasibility of various plans and make suggestions.

Under socialized transportation better service was provided for more riders (an increase of 50 million trips in one year). Before the Revolution only 2% of supplies for maintenance and repairs were manufactured by the privately owned company. Under socialization, within only one year, 98% of the repair supplies were made in the socialized shops. The union also provided free medical services, including clinics and home nursing care, for the workers and their families.—Ed.

The Collectivization of the Railroads

Spanish railroads were privately owned. During the fascist military uprising and the general strike, rail service was halted. Pitched battles were fought near Barcelona's main terminal. On the third day of fighting the anarcho-syndicalist unions, certain of victory (though the fighting was still going on), organized a revolutionary railroad committee. This led to the occupation and expropriation of railroad stations, railroad rights of way, and the administrative headquarters. All important railroad junctions were guarded by workers' patrols. The executives fled abroad. The workers installed new administrative committees. Although the syndicalists constituted the overwhelming majority, they nevertheless accorded the social-democratic unions equal representation on the management committees: three members from each organization. The Spanish anarcho-syndicalists did not want to institute a Bolshevik-type dictatorship.[3]

In a few days all the Catalonian railroads were socialized. For lack of supplies, technical improvements could not be made. With the end of the fighting, railroad operations were resumed under the new union management. The railroads functioned normally without interruption. Fares and rates remained the same. The wages of the lowest paid workers were substantially increased. The sinecures of high salaried executives and useless bureaucrats were abolished. Obviously collectivization meant the end of private capitalist corporations. Stocks, bonds, and debts contracted by the old administration were repudiated.

The railway repair yards in Barcelona manufactured armored vehicles. Only a week after returning to work the first ambulances were built. The equipment elicited the praise of the medical profession. And the medical department of the Catalonian government officially congratulated the railroad metal workers for their excellent workmanship. The credit for these achievements belongs solely to the syndicalist workers. There were no high placed functionaries to give orders. The workers themselves designated their technicians and administrators from within their own ranks. And these achievements must to a very great extent be ascribed not to Stakhanovite competition between fellow workers, but to the spirit of good will and mutual aid that inspired the workers.[4]

[3] While conceding this point, the wisdom of such an arrangement has been contested on the grounds that justice would have been better served by proportional representation.—*Ed.*

[4] There were two big railway unions, the UGT National Railway Union and the CNT

The Collectivization of the Longshoremen

At the expense of the low wages and poor working conditions for longshoremen, the racketeers dominated the waterfront. The waterfront reeked with graft, waste, and stealing. The racketeers and the ship agents, ship captains, and the longshore bosses were all in collusion. These abuses provoked endless strikes, often accompanied by violence, not only against the employers but against the whole system.

After July 19th, the port and maritime unions got rid of the racketeers and their agents. They decided to deal directly, without go-betweens, with

---

National Industrial Federation of Railway Workers. In Catalonia, most of the railway workers adhered to the CNT. In the rest of Spain, before July 19th, the majority of the railway workers belonged to the UGT. But with the growth of the CNT unions after the Revolution, the CNT membership almost equalled that of the UGT.

Technicians who fled were replaced by capable, experienced workers chosen by their workmates. Although these workers had less formal technical schooling, they knew how to get things done properly. With the close cooperation of the workers possessing practical experience within their own special field, efficient railway service was quickly restored.

The cumbersome bureaucratic administration of the railways was dismantled and the new system decentralized to insure genuine and efficient rank and file workers' self-management at all levels: local, regional, and national. Each section and subsection designated its own technical/adminstrative committee. Each section also elected its own delegates to the coordinating commission in each locality. The general membership meetings of the various sections met twice monthly, in turn, to review the reports of the coordinating commission and issue new instructions.

This procedure was also applied to the reorganization of the railway system of Catalonia into a unified federation in which the local and regional operations were synchronized by the interlocking local and regional coordinating committee.

The Federation consisted of three main divisions: traffic, technical/engineering, and administration. The technical/engineering department was subdivided into three sections: material and traction, power, and right-of-way and construction. The first took care of the upkeep of locomotive depots, freight and passenger equipment, and repair shops. The second section took care of electricity, fuel (coal and oil) stations, trackage, and communications (telegraph, telephone signal system, etc.). The third section arranged to furnish provisions to all employees at cost price and also operated a school for technical and administrative training.

The administrative division was also divided into three sections. The first section dealt with safety, cleaning of cars and equipment, and first aid facilities in stations and workplaces. The second section took care of finances and accounting, kept daily records of revenue and expenditures, and compiled statistical information. The third section was concerned with providing for the general welfare of the workers and dependents (adequate medical service, home nursing, operation of clinics, etc.).

On November 5th, 1936, after the workers took over possession of the railways, the

the ship captains and the ship companies. This led to the takeover of harbor operations by the newly formed port workers' collective. While contracts already made between foreign ship companies and their agents could not be cancelled, the unions closely supervised the financial operations of the Spanish agents of foreign ship companies.

These changes brought much higher wages and better working conditions for the longshoremen. By setting aside a certain sum for each ton of cargo handled, unemployment, health and accident protection, and other benefits were provided.[5] The port of Barcelona was socialized.

The Collectivization of Gas, Water, and Electricity

Water, gas, and electric utilities in almost all Spanish cities were privately owned. The Barcelona Waterworks Company and its subsidiary, Llobregat Waterworks, owned gas and water utilities in many Spanish cities. It was a mammoth corporation capitalized at 275 million pesetas, with an average yearly profit of over 11 million pesetas.

The financiers left the country before July 19th to await the outcome of the fascist military offensive. The syndicates decided to take over and collectivize the properties. The managerial staff was selected from their own ranks by the workers. Under private ownership the workers were refused wage increases and other demands. Under collectivization, a minimum daily wage of 14 pesetas and the 36 hour week were instituted. Later, because of the war crisis and shortage of manpower, the work week was increased to 40 and still later to 48 hours, with equal wages for women, sick benefits, and old age pensions. The savings accruing from good management, and abolition of dividends, profits, interest on loans, etc., were diverted to

---

Federation circulated a questionnaire, explained that:

> In view of the profound socio-economic transformation in our country, we must work out new and better ways of improving our railway system. . . . We appeal to our comrades in general, and to all station committees in particular, to supply the following information . . . (About ten key questions relative to better coordination, services, and auxiliary transportation were listed.).

Among the achievements of the new administration was providing bus and truck service to remote areas in Catalonia (especially in the province of Lerida) previously deprived of adequate service. The deficit incurred was made up by better revenues from other lines.—Ed.

[5] Welfare, better known as "fringe benefits," is now taken for granted in industrialized countries. In the Spain of 1936, and in many countries even now, such "extreme" innovations were regarded as "revolutionary."—Ed.

lowering water rates by 50%. Above all, contributions to the anti-fascist military committee totaling over 100,000 pesetas were made during the first few months after the 19th of July.

Foreign observers were amazed to see how quickly and smoothly the changeover from private to collective management was achieved. The reason is not hard to find. The marvelous success of collectivization was to a very great extent due to the systematic preparation of the syndicalists to tackle just such problems of the Social Revolution. *The Bulletin of the Water, Gas, and Electric Collective* explains:

> During the revolutionary period we organized, within the unions, management commissions. These commissions prepared themselves for management by making themselves familiar with the particular problems in each district. The commission supervised production, calculated water needs—for summer and for winter, studied how to find the right personnel for the right jobs, observe safety measures, adequate dining facilities, etc.

Through these and other preparations, the workers were able to surmount difficult problems. The management procedures worked out by the workers themselves bear witness to the heightened feeling of responsibility of the workers fostered by the syndicalist organizations.

Plant councils, managers, and administrative boards at every level functioned according to instructions openly discussed and enacted by all the workers assembled in their general plant meetings. All persons in responsible posts were held strictly accountable by union control commissions. Only fully capable and qualified workers of proven personal integrity were deemed fit for responsible posts. It was considered a privilege and an honor to be entrusted with responsibilities by their fellow union members. . . . [6]

---

[6]The Federated Public Utility Workers Industrial Union of Catalonia, which from the beginning of the Revolution assured an adequate supply of water, gas, and electricity, was organized in 1927 (in spite of the opposition of the dictatorship of General Primo de Rivera). The union serviced all of Catalonia. Similar regional federations embracing all of Spain were affiliated to the National Federation of Public Utility Workers with headquarters in Madrid. CNT membership in Catalonia reached 8,000. A little less than half the utility workers throughout Spain belonged to the UGT.

Technicians and certain skilled workers belong neither to the UGT or the CNT, but formed an independent union. The necessity to restore and improve service, and the feeling of solidarity generated by the Revolution inspired them to closer unity with the manual workers. Consequently, the technicians, at a general membership meeting, voted by acclamation to dissolve the independent union and affilliate with the CNT (fifty technicians, solely for ideological reasons joined the UGT).

The Collectivization of Hairdressing Establishments

Collectivization also embraced smaller establishments: small factories, artisan workshops, service and repair shops, etc. The artisans and small workshop owners, together with their employees and apprentices, often joined the union of their trade. By consolidating their efforts and pooling their resources on a fraternal basis, the shops were able to undertake very big projects and provide services on a much wider scale. Independent artisans with their tools and workshops also joined the trade collectives. The collectivization of hairdressing shops provides an excellent example of how the transition of a small scale manufacturing and service industry from capitalism to socialism was achieved.

The hairdressers of Barcelona, Madrid, and other Spanish cities voluntarily and on their own initiative reorganized their industry. In Madrid the shops were collectivized even before July 19th. The purpose of the collectivization was to obliterate the difference between shopkeepers and their assistants. Hairdressing was not big business. For the Spanish syndicalists, however, socialism and collectivism could not be confined only

---

Important technical/administrative decisions were made at joint general membership meetings of both unions. In spite of the opposition of their leaders, the rank and file UGT workers cooperated in full solidarity with their fellow workers of the CNT. Water, gas, and electrical service continued to be furnished during the whole course of the Civil War, even when temporarily interrupted by the fascist bombardments.

Each installation was managed by a council elected by the workers of each department. To coordinate the work of the whole district, the general membership of each installation named two delegates to the District Industrial Council—one technical and the other administrative.

As in the local, district, and regional bodies, each industry (water, gas, and electricity) was composed of eight delegates, four from the UGT and four from the CNT. Half these delegates were named by the general assemblies of the unions. The other half were named by the general assemblies of the technical workers. This procedure was adopted to make sure that only the most qualified technicians would be chosen. For in general meetings the members might be persuaded by clever orators and politicians to choose less capable delegates for ideological and political reasons.

The General Council of all three industries was also composed of eight delegates, four from the UGT and four from the CNT. The General Council coordinated the joint activities of the three industries, harmonized production, procurement, and distribution of essential supplies, organized the overall general administration, fixed rates for services, and put forth other measures benefiting the consumers. It must be emphasized that the policies of the General Council (as well as the operations of the Industrial Councils) were at every level controlled by the membership.—*Ed.*

to the abolition of large scale capitalism. In the reorganization of labor according to the principles of freedom and cooperation there was room for everyone. Even the smallest enterprises employing one or several individuals were entitled to participate in the reorganization of society.

Before July 19th, 1936, there were 1,100 hairdressing parlors in Barcelona, most of them owned by poor wretches living from hand to mouth. The shops were often dirty and ill-maintained. The 5,000 hairdressing assistants were among the most poorly paid workers, earning about 40 pesetas per week while construction workers were paid 60 to 80 pesetas weekly. The 40 hour week and 15% wage increase instituted after July 19th spelled ruin for most hairdressing shops. Both owners and assistants therefore voluntarily decided to socialize all their shops.

How was this done? All the shops simply joined the union. At a general meeting they decided to shut down all the unprofitable shops. The 1,100 shops were reduced to 235 establishments, a saving of 135,000 pesetas per month in rent, lighting, and taxes. The remaining 235 shops were modernized and elegantly outfitted. From the money saved wages were increased by 40%. Everybody had the right to work and everybody received the same wages. The former owners were not adversely affected by socialization. They were employed at a steady income. All worked together under equal conditions and equal pay. The distinction between employers and employees was obliterated and they were tranformed into a working community of equals—socialism from the bottom up.

The Collectivization of the Textile Industry

It is no simple matter to collectivize and place on firm foundations an industry employing almost a quarter of a million textile workers in scores of factories scattered in numerous cities. But the Barcelona syndicalist textile union accomplished this feat in a short time. It was a tremendously significant experiment. The dictatorship of the bosses was toppled, and wages, working conditions and production were determined by the workers and their elected delegates. All functionaries had to carry out the instructions of the membership and report back directly to the men on the job and union meetings. The collectivization of the textile industry shatters once and for all the legend that the workers are incapable of administrating a great and complex corporation.

Upon building the collective, a management committee of 19 was chosen by the rank and file membership. After three months the management committee reported back to the membership on the condition of the collective and the progress made.[7]

With the crushing of the fascist putsch, the owners transferred themselves and the assets of the industry abroad. But by cutting off dividends and premiums and eliminating high salaried directors and other wasteful expenditures, the collectives were able to pay the increased costs for raw materials. Two new machines for the manufacture of artificial silk were purchased from abroad. The necessary foreign exchange was raised by the sale of finished products abroad.

Every factory elected its administrative committee composed of its most capable workers. Depending on the size of the factory, the function of these committees included inner plant organization, statistics, finance, correspondence, and relations with other factories and with the community. Particularly significant was the organization of a top flight technical commission staffed by the most intelligent technical and administrative experts in the entire industry. This commission of engineers, technicians, and commercial experts drafted plans to increase production, division of labor, installations, etc. Several months after collectivization the textile industry of Barcelona was in far better shape than under capitalist management. Here was yet another example to show that grass roots socialism from below does not destroy initiative. Greed is not the only motivation in human relations.

Collectivization brought better conditions for the workers. The 60 hour work week in some factories was cut to 40. Wages were more equalized. Overtime work was abolished, and weekly wages increased from 68 to 78 pesetas. Wage rates were fixed by the workers themselves at union meetings.

A great many troops from the textile industry manned the fighting fronts. From Barcelona alone more than 20,000 textile workers of the CNT joined the militia. Non-combatant workers contributed voluntarily 10% to 15% of their weekly wages to finance the war against fascism, and in the last

---

[7] In this connection, Section B of its report, headed *The Structure of the Collective Organization of the Textile Industry*, reads:

> When collectivization in each expropriated factory is put into effect, the Committee of Control [which kept tabs on the former owners] will become the Technical Advisory Committee ... which will be chosen by all the workers of the factory at a general assembly convoked by the Factory Council and the Union Local. ...

The heading *Departments—Organizing a Group of Factories* reads:

> The committees charged with the coordination and administration of all factories in a given city or county will be chosen by the technical committees of these factories subject to the approval of the general assembly of the Textile Workers Industrial Union of the given city or county. ... (*Collectivizations*, p. 50, 52)—*Ed.*

three months of 1937 contributed two and a half million pesetas to the anti-fascist militias. . . .

The Collectivization of the Metal and Munitions Industry[8]
by Augustin Souchy

One of the most impressive achievements of the Catalonian metal workers was to rebuild the industry from scratch. Toward the close of the Civil War, 80,000 workers were supplying the anti-fascist troops with war material. At the outbreak of the Civil War the Catalonian metal industry was very poorly developed. The largest installation, Hispano-Suiza Automobile Company, employed only 1,100 workers. A few days after July 19th this plant was already converted to the manufacture of armored cars, hand grenades, machine gun carriages, ambulances, etc., for the fighting front. The first war vehicle carried the CNT-FAI insignia for the two fighting organizations of the metal workers. In Barcelona during the Civil War, four hundred metal factories were built, most of them manufacturing war material.

Eighty percent of the munition workers adhered to the CNT. While the political parties were bickering and conniving to seize power, the syndicalists were working to rebuild the industry and defeat the fascists. The work began in August, 1936, under the direction of the energetic and capable technician Eugenio Vallejo, a dedicated anarcho-syndicalist. Experts were truly astounded at the expertise of the workers in building new machinery for the manufacture of arms and munitions. Very few machines were imported. In a short time, two hundred different hydraulic presses of up to 250 tons pressure, one hundred seventy-eight revolving lathes, and hundreds of milling machines and boring machines were built. A year after the beginning of the Civil War, production of ammunition increased to one million 155-millimeter projectiles, fifty thousand aerial bombs and millions of cartridges. In these last three months of 1937 alone, fifteen million cartridge cases, a million caps for hand grenades, and enormous quantities of other war materials were produced.

---

[8] From Augustin Souchy, *Nacht über Spanien*, pp. 111-112.

Above—Women working in a collectivized textile factory in Barcelona.
Below—Men operating sewing machines in a collectivized factory.

With the introduction of state control over the arms and munitions industry, the self-management of this industry by the workers was ended. But the tremendous accomplishments of the Spanish workers in their collectivized, metals industry bear permanent witness to the achievements of the anarcho-syndicalist movement.

The Collectivization of the Optical Industry [9]

If by industry is meant a group of manufacturing establishments making the same type of merchandise in a county, province, or region, then there was no optical industry in Spain before the 19th of July. With the end of the fighting (in which the optical workers took part), the workers rapidly began to collectivize the small workshops. The first step was to institute strict workers' surveillance to prevent the bosses from absconding with funds and merchandise. Owners who accepted collectivization were admitted to membership on equal terms with their former employees. The plants were converted into a production collective.... Methods of modernizing and rebuilding the industry were studied and put into effect.

Sexual discrimination was abolished—equal pay for both men and women and the family wage prevailed. Workers twenty-four years of age and over received 400 pesetas monthly, plus 50 pesetas for each of their dependents, even if they were not related and did not previously work in the same industry. The greatest innovation was the construction of a new factory for optical apparatuses and instruments. The whole operation was financed by the voluntary contributions of the workers. In a short time the factory turned out opera glasses, telemeters, binoculars, surveying instruments, industrial glassware in different colors, and certain scientific instruments. It also manufactured and repaired optical equipment for the fighting fronts. (The workers presented Buenaventura Durruti with a special set of field

[9] From *Collectivisations: L'Oeuvre Constructive de la Révolution Espagnole (1936-1939)*, pp. 72-74.

glasses.) Another achievement was the opening of a new, up-to-date optical school. . . . The workers had every reason to be proud of these achievements. What private capitalists failed to do was accomplished by the creative capacity of the members of the Optical Workers' Union of the CNT.

The Socialization of Health Services[10]

by Gaston Leval

The socialization of health services was one of the greatest achievements of the revolution. To appreciate the efforts of our comrades it must be borne in mind that they rehabilitated the health services in all of Catalonia in so short a time after July 19th. The revolution could count on the cooperation of a number of dedicated doctors whose ambition was not to accumulate wealth but to serve the afflicted and the underprivileged.

The Health Workers' Union was founded in September, 1936. In line with the tendency to unite all the different classifications, trades, and services serving a given industry, *all* health workers, from porters to doctors and administrators, were organized into the one big union of health workers. . . .

Five months after the Revolution, 8,000 health workers joined the union (excluding the masseurs and physical therapists for whom we have no figures). The UGT also organized a health union, but numerically very much inferior to ours—100 doctors to our 1,020 doctors. Here is a partial list: 1,020 doctors, 3,206 nurses, 133 dentists, 330 midwives, 203 practitioners (student doctors), 180 pharmacists and 66 apprentice pharmacists, 153 herbalists, 353 sterilizers, 71 radiologists, and 200 veterinaries.

But the syndicate did not confine itself solely to enrolling new members. The urge to recreate the health system was greatest among doctors who had never done a thing in this regard before the Revolution. Paradoxically enough, it was these very doctors who were, in this respect, the most audacious revolutionaries. I could cite many examples.

---

[10] From Gaston Leval, *Né Franco né Stalin*, pp. 122-127.

Although Spain has a healthful and generally dry climate, infant mortality was one of the highest in Europe. This was due not only to poverty, lack of hygienic facilities, etc., but also to a gang of racketeering doctors who took advantage of this situation and the incompetence of the government to enrich themselves.

Our comrades laid the foundations of a new health system. . . . The new medical service embraced all of Catalonia. It constituted a great apparatus whose parts were geographically distributed according to different needs, all in accord with an overall plan. Catalonia was divided into nine [sic] zones: Barcelona, Tarragona, Lerida, Reus, Borghida, Ripoll, and Haute Pyréenées. In turn, all the surrounding villages and towns were served from these centers.

Distributed throughout Catalonia were twenty-seven towns with a total of thirty-six health centers conducting services so thoroughly that every village, every hamlet, every isolated peasant in the mountains, every woman, every child, anywhere, received adequate, up-to-date medical care. In each of the nine zones there was a central syndicate and a Control Committee located in Barcelona. Every department was autonomous within its own sphere. But this autonomy was not synonymous with isolation. The Central Committee in Barcelona, chosen by all the sections, met once a week with one delegate from each section to deal with common problems and to implement the general plan. . . .

The people immediately benefited from the projects of the health syndicate. The syndicate managed all hospitals and clinics. Six hospitals were opened in Barcelona. . . . Eight new sanitariums were installed in converted luxurious homes ideally situated amidst mountains and pine forests. It was no easy task to convert these homes into efficient hospitals with all new facilities. One of them, for the treatment of tuberculosis, was considered among the best installations anywhere. . . .

To avoid excessive travelling of sick people to specialized centers, polyclinic hospitals where all these specialized treaments could be given in one place were organized. . . . Where there had been an artificially created surplus of doctors serving the wealthy under capitalism, there was now under the socialized medical system a shortage of doctors badly needed to serve the disadvantaged masses who never before received good medical care. . . .

When the inhabitants of a locality requested the services of a doctor, the syndicate analyzed their health needs and from a panel of doctors designated one whose training could best serve the needs of the patients. If he refused to go, he must have had very good reasons. If not, he may be suspended. The hospital expenses were paid by the *Generalidad* (Catalan government) and the municipality. Polyclinic hospitals were built under the auspices of the syndicates and the municipalities. Not all health services could be entirely socialized, but most of the dental clinics in Catalonia were controlled by the syndicate, as were all the hospitals, clinics, and sanitariums. The trend was to substitute the socialized organization of medicine for private practice. Private doctors still practiced, but the most prevalent abuses had been eliminated. The cost of operations was controlled. Payments for treatments were made through the syndicates, not directly to the physicians.[11]

In the new clinics, surgery and dental extractions were free. The number of mental patients admitted to asylums for treatment was much greater than before. The old privileged physicians fought these changes, but the younger, less favored doctors voluntarily cooperated with the new organization. Young doctors were enthusiastic. Under the old system they would have had to work for years with little or no payment and they would have had to wait for the death of the old doctor to take his place.

All the hospitals' doctors were paid 500 pesetas a month for three hours work per day. There was no private practice (for them). Since a skilled manual worker drew 350 to 400 pesetas a month for seven hours work per day, the reader can draw his own conclusions.[12]

The money saved through wage equalization was enough to pay all expenses. There were no longer doctors receiving enormous fees while others were in need. In a public establishment no one could have outside jobs. More than half the doctors, after working their regular hours, worked free of charge. No one pressured them to do this. They donated their time gladly and compulsion was not necessary.

"Everything is just fine," said the secretary of the medical department, a Basque for whom tireless dedication to his work was a moral imperative. "The famous doctor who condescends to visit the dispensary once a week is dethroned. The important personage who parades down the hospital aisles attended by a half-dozen subservient colleagues, hierarchically inferior, one holding a basin, the other his satchel, and the rest escorting his honor, humble and awed before so great an authority (not always deserved), is happily a thing of the past. *We* are now all equal comrades, working together, who esteem and respect each other."

---

[11] Thus eliminating the temptation of the physician to syphon off funds for himself.—*Ed.*

[12] On the extent to which wages were equalized, as against the previous great difference in earnings.—*Ed.*

Industrial Collectivization in Alcoy[13]

by Gaston Leval

Alcoy, the second largest city in the province of Alicante, has a population of 45,000 and is entirely devoted to industry and commerce. The textile industry was most important and included the manufacture of fabrics, lingerie, and hosiery. Next in importance is the manufacture of paper.

Our movement in Alcoy has a long tradition of struggle dating back to the First International (1869). . . . It had, in fact, a higher proportion of anarchists than any city in Spain. . . . In 1919 the movement was invigorated by the organization of *Sindicatos Unicos.*[14]

On my first visit in February, 1937, the UGT (Socialist Party union) had a membership of 3,000, mostly anti-revolutionary civil service employees, small tradesmen (who saw in the UGT the guarantee of their status), and the political parties (naturally hostile to the CNT). But the CNT controlled the essential economic functions necessary to social life.

The CNT industries organized in the CNT unions were: food; paper and cardboard manufacture; construction, including architects; hygiene (barbers, launderers, street cleaners); transport; public service workers; cobblers and bootblacks; technicians; linen and clothing workers; metal workers; dressmakers; professionals (school teachers, painters, writers); and, in the suburbs, horticulturists.

Their clarity of ideas enabled our comrades to act quickly and decisively. To reach collectivization Alcoy did not have to pass through the often prolonged phase of piecemeal collectivization of small shops or individual

---

[13] This section consists of two parts with material from Gaston Leval, *Né Franco né Stalin,* pp. 160-169; with additional material from his *Espagne Libertaire.* pp. 357, 369, 371

[14] Industrial instead of craft unions, which took in all the workers in a given industry irrespective of their occupation. —*Ed.*

Above—The first bus built in the workshops of the collectivized General Autobus Company.
Below—Workers in a collectivized aircraft engine plant in Barcelona.

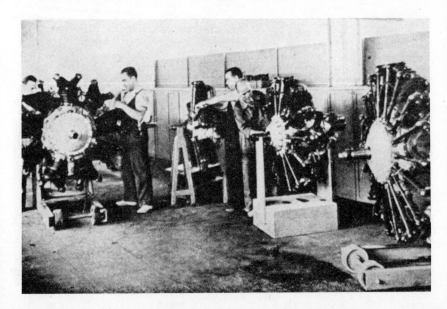

Above—Workers in a large collectivized factory shifted to the production of war materiel.
Below—Spanish men and women working side-by-side in a small, modern machine shop.

plants. From the very beginning, the syndicates took the initiative in organizing *all the industries*. It was, in fact, the most complete example of the "syndicalization of production". . . . The best example was in the textile industry, with a CNT membership of 6,500 workers.

As was to be expected, disputes with the textile employers became inevitable. The employers interpreted "workers' control" in an altogether different fashion than did the syndicates. For the employers "workers' control" meant (at most) allowing a committee to inspect the accounts of the company. But the demands of the workers went much further than that. They wanted the expropriation of the factories under the total control and administration of production by their syndicate, the CNT. . . .

The first step in this direction was the organization by the workers of a technical Commission of Control which from supervising the activities of the employers quickly transformed itself into the organ for the overall administration of the textile industry. The employers were eliminated and the workers took over. On September 14th, the syndicate officially took possession of 41 textile factories, 10 spinning mills, 4 dye works, 5 processing factories, 24 linen works, and 11 carding shops, all of which comprised the whole textile industry in Alcoy. Its day to day activities were determined on the one hand by the feelings (desires) of the workers, and on the other hand by the organization of the managing committees.

Everything was controlled by the syndicates. But it must not therefore be assumed that everything was decided by a few higher bureaucratic committees without consulting the rank and file members of the union. Here also libertarian democracy was practiced. As in the CNT there was a reciprocal double structure: from the grass roots at the base—the mass of unionists, workers, and militants—upwards, and in the other direction a reciprocal influence from the federations of these same local units at all levels downwards. From the source back to the source. "From the circumference to the center and from the center to the circumference," as formulated by Proudhon and stressed by Bakunin.

Every Sunday in each factory, designers, technicians, and production workers met in joint session, and examined the accounts, production reports, quality, and all other pertinent matters. These meetings made no decisions, but their findings were submitted to the sections of the syndicates involved for their consideration.

The technical organization of the factories was divided into five sections. Each of these nominated a delegate to the factory committee and these committees joined together to form the administrative committee of the syndicate. In this way each different working group in every department of the factory was represented and the coordinated organization thus reflected the internal structure of the industry. . . .

The representatives from each of these five technical divisions constituted only one half of the administrative commission. The other half consisted of the overall Commission of Control (mentioned above). It is nominated by the general assembly of syndicated workers and has delegates direct from the factories so as never to lose contact with the workers. In the factories and workshops, committees are elected by an assembly of workers gathered together on the spot. . . . We are not therefore facing an administrative dictatorship but rather a functional democracy, in which all the specialized workers play their roles which have been settled after general examination by the assembly. . . .

The other industries were organized along similar lines: complete organization in the hands of the syndicates. In the metallurgical works that I visited, work was proceeding vigorously under the direction of the workers' councils. In a few months a new armaments industry had been organized without competition, private profits, or capitalism. . . . The solidarity of libertarian organization made it possible to help weaker industries like printing and paper-making to overcome their difficulties (financial and otherwise). In fact the sixteen other syndicates that make up the local Industrial Federation of Alcoy help any of their affiliated unions whenever necessary.

Each industry is coordinated through the Syndical Administrative Committee. This committee is divided into as many sections as there are industries. When an order is received by the sales section it is passed on to the production section whose task it is to decide which workshops are best equipped to produce the desired articles. While settling this question, they order the required raw materials from the corresponding section. The latter gives instructions to the shops to supply the materials and finally the buying section receives details of the transaction so that it can replace the material used.

In spite of all the monumental difficulties, one big fact stands out: in Alcoy 20,000 workers organized in their syndicates administrated production, coordinated economic activities, and proved that industry can be operated better in every respect than under capitalism, while still assuring freedom and justice for all. . . .

Control of Industries in the North[15]

by Jose Peirats

Although reports about collectivization in the northern area are, in view of the situation, necessarily vague, the following three reports are more definite and reflect the revolutionary realizations spontaneously achieved despite monumental obstacles. The reports include the first joint Manifesto of the UGT and the CNT, of the fishing industry of Gijon and of Laredo.[16] The text of the Manifesto [summarized by us] reads as follows:

Manifesto on the Control of the Industries of Asturias, Leon, and Palencia

The Provincial Secretariat of the UGT and the Regional Committee of the CNT of Asturias have come to the following agreement:

1) Where one or the other syndicate represented in the Control Committee constitutes less than 10% of the workers, the majority syndicate shall assume direction of the Control Committee.

2) Elections to the Control Committee will be democratic. The syndicate should nominate only such candidates who by their exemplary conduct have earned the confidence of the membership, preferrably men who belonged to either union before July 19th, 1936. Both syndicates shall hold regular joint meetings to deal with common problems.

---

[15] From José Peirats, *La CNT en la Revolucion Espanola,* vol. I, pp. 356-359.

[16] The CNT, though strong, constituted a minority in the labor movement of the northern region (particularly Santander, Gijon, and Laredo), predominently influenced by the socialist UGT and in the Basque region by the Catholic Republican Separatists. The UGT leadership was, in the main, opposed to collectivization, and accepted it with great reluctance only when forced to do so by the rank and file. For this reason, collectivization in the UGT area was not as thorough as it would have been if the situation were reversed and the CNT unions would have controlled the fishing industry. Another and even more important factor was the early fascist occupation of the northern zone, which contributed so heavily to the defeat of the Republic and also cut short the unfolding of the Revolution.—*Ed.*

3) Control Committees shall be established in:
   a) factories and workshops
   b) mines and construction
   c) ports and seafaring
   d) railways
   e) agricultural producers' and consumers' cooperatives. . . .

4) The Control Committees shall in no way usurp the powers of management or of the technical administration and their functions. The principal functions of the Control Committees are to help management to carry out worthwhile plans, offer constructive suggestions, process workers' grievances, and improve working conditions and wages. . . .

5) A member elected to serve on the Control Committee should consider it an honor and a mark of confidence that he must not betray. To cut off the pernicious growth of bureaucracy at the source, Committee members shall voluntarily serve without pay, shall transact their business after working hours, and be required to report back to their membership at frequent regular meetings. . . .

7) Both the CNT and the UGT agree not to lure members away from each other nor prevent workers from joining the union of their choice. . . .

9) The sole and immediate objective of the UGT and the CNT is to *win the war and organize the revolution*, and all the efforts of both syndicates must be directed to that purpose. . . .

10) This agreement shall be published in the official journals of both syndicates for eight days. . . . Gijon, January, 1937.

Signed: for the Regional Committee of the CNT, Silverio Tuñon, Secretary. For the Provincial Federation of the UGT, Valdes, Secretary.

The Fishing Industry of Gijon[17]

At first the local Control Committee left the distribution of fish to the committees which spontaneously sprang up to supply necessary provisions to the people. These arrangements were worked out by the Fishing Workers' Industrial Union at the rank and file general membership meetings. As soon as the fishing fleet docked, the fish was first supplied to hospitals and then to the civilian population and the militias.

During the first few months after July 19th, the wage system in the fishing and other industries was abolished. Every worker carried a consumer's card listing the number of family members, their age, and

---

[17] Summarized by Peirats from an article by Solano Palacio in the magazine *Timon*, July, 1938.

occupation. The fishery workers simply deposited their merchandise in exchange for these cards, which entitled them to rationed supplies.

Later local cooperatives replaced the ad hoc Supply Committees. Through a Provincial Cooperative Council, the Department of Commerce supplied all the cooperatives. Nevertheless, the people were reluctant to accept this arrangement.[18] In November, 1936, Amador Fernandez published a series of articles in *Advance*,[19] defending the rights of the petty bourgeoisie and merchants, which provoked vehement polemics between the anarcho-syndicalists and the socialists. The fascist blockade was partly mitigated by the fishing fleets who braved seizure and sinking by the fascist patrol boats. Many boats were lost and their crews drowned or, if captured, taken to the fascist headquarters at El Ferrol to be tortured and shot.

Refrigerating plants and food canneries, the largest in Spain and the second most important industry in Asturias, were from the very beginning completely socialized (as were the markets). Everything was controlled by the syndicates who much later united into the Fisheries Council. This control was exercised through delegates in all ports of Asturias, wherever there were fisheries and canneries. . . .

The Fishing Industry in Laredo[20]

The fishing industry . . . , socialized by the CNT and UGT Seamen's Unions, was organized into an Economic Council made up of six UGT and six CNT representatives. The whole fishing fleet was expropriated. The shipowners fled. Economic inequalities were abolished. No longer did the shipowners and their agents appropriate the lion's share of the income. Now 45% of the profit from the sale of fish (after deducting expenses) went to improve and modernize the fishing industry and the remaining 55% was equally divided among the fishermen. Before, the middlemen sold the fish in Bibao, Santander, etc., and pocketed the profits. The middlemen were eliminated and the Economic Council carried on all transactions. This exploded the lie that the workers were unable to operate industry without their employers. . . . Soon the CNT and the UGT municipalized housing, the land, public services—in short, everything. And society was being transformed. The ideal which both Marxists and anarchists strove to bring about was being realized by the people of Laredo. . . .

---

[18] The report does not explain why.—*Ed.*

[19] Presumably a social democratic paper.—*Ed.*

[20] Quoted by Peirats from the Press Service of the Libertarian Youth of Bilbao, Jan. 1937.

os ha
nacido
una vida
que os
capacitará
para un
trabajo
digno y una
existencia
humana.

A libertarian poster reads, "Every person is born with the capacity for dignified work and a human existence."

chapter 8
The Revolution on the Land

Introduction

In our introduction we quoted Gaston Leval's conclusion that:

In the work of creation, transportation and socialization, the peasants demonstrated a degree of social consciousness much superior to that of the city worker.

In this chapter Jose Peirats tells how the land was expropriated and transformed into collectives; how the collectives were operated; how all the operations of the collectives (work-teams, distribution, social services, maintenance, housing, the administrative committees; relations with other collectives, etc.) were chosen by and were at all times responsible to the general assemblies of all the members of the collectives.

Particularly significant is the fact that collectivization was not (as in the Soviet Union or Cuba) imposed from above by decree, but achieved from below by the initiative of the peasants themselves. Nor did the libertarian collectives, like Stalin, adopt disastrous measures to force poor peasant proprietors to surrender their land and join the collectives. On the contrary, the collectives respected the rights of individual proprietors who worked their land themselves and did not employ wage labor: relying on persuasion and example to convince individual peasant owners to join the collectives. By and large this policy was remarkably effective. Underdeveloped areas seeking to collectivize the land could learn a great deal from the successful examples of the Spanish agricultural collectives.

The Revolution on the Land[1]
by Jose Peirats

On the 19th of July, 1936, in the villages and towns, the syndicates affiliated with the CNT and the UGT, together with the political parties, organized a coalition of revolutionary or anti-fascist committees. These committees were the first to expropriate the land and other property of landlords and fascists who fled. At first the committees replaced the municipal governments. Much later the committees transformed themselves into town councils, with proportional representation for all the affiliated units. The majority syndicate or party would designate one of its members as mayor or president of the newly organized council.

The expropriated lands were turned over to the peasant syndicates, and it was these syndicates that organized the first collectives. Generally the holdings of small property owners were respected, always on the condition that only they or their families would work the land, without employing wage labor. In areas like Catalonia, where the tradition of petty peasant ownership prevailed, the land holdings were scattered. There were no great estates. Many of these peasants, together with the CNT, organized collectives, pooling their land, animals, tools, chickens, grain, fertilizer, and even their harvested crops.

Privately owned farms located in the midst of collectives interfered with efficient cultivation by splitting up the collectives into disconnected parcels. To induce owners to move, they were given more or even better land located on the perimeter of the collective.

The collectivist who had nothing to contribute to the collective was admitted with the same rights and the same duties as the others. In some collectives, those joining had to contribute their money (Girondella in Catalonia, Lagunarrotta in Aragon, and Cervera del Maestra in Valencia).

Small landlords more or less opposed to collectivization, who were called

[1] From José Peirats, *Los Anarquistas en la Crisis Politica Española, pp. 149–168.*

"individualists," found the going tough, especially around harvest time, because they could not hire wage laborers, and because their holdings were too small to use machinery (which they couldn't afford anyhow). In some towns or villages the "individualists" would cooperate by helping each other with the work, but the crops were small and of poor quality. Most of the collectivists treated the "individualists" well. In Monzon the collective loaned them machinery and certain necessary supplies. Some "individualists" distributed their produce through the collective's cooperatives. And some finally joined the collective (Mas de las Matas).

In some places the revolutionary committees expropriated the landed estates of the big landlords. At an assembly of farm laborers, in which all the people participated, the land was parcelled out to the collectivists and to the "individualists." The collectivists drew up a general plan to guide the collective. If the CNT and UGT could not agree on how the collective should be organized, two separate collectives were established (often side by side). . . .

The area of the collective varied according to population and the political orientation of the collectivists. . . . In some areas the size of the collectives was reduced because of the misfortunes of war, the reactionary policies of the government, and the military assaults of communist troops. In Peñalba (Aragon) the collective embraced the whole town. . . . Many of the small proprietors, protected by the communist bayonets, demanded and received land belonging to the collectives. In Brihuega, after the disastrous defeat of the Italian fascists (March, 1937), many small proprietors abandoned their land and fled with the retreating troops. This is how almost all of Alcaria was collectivized.

The work of the collectives was conducted by teams of workers, headed by a delegate chosen by each team. The land was divided into cultivated zones. Team delegates worked like the others. There were no special privileges. After the day's work, delegates from all the work teams met on the job and made necessary technical arrangements for the next day's work All the work team delegates as well as the members of the administrative commission of the collective were elected by the general assembly of all the workers. The assembly made final decisions on all important questions and issued instructions to both the team delegates and the administrative commission.

Work age varied between a minimum of 14 years and a maximum of 60 years. Young single men usually worked in the collective's workshops or in the distribution cooperatives (stores). Housewives were not obliged to work outside the home except when absolutely necessary. Pregnant women were treated with special consideration. Everyone worked according to their physical capacity. Days lost because of illness were counted as days worked. In Cuenca, men 60 years or over could retire, but in Graus they chose to do useful work. . . .

Surplus commodities were sold or exchanged directly or through federated agencies created for that purpose. . . . In some Catalonian towns the old style bourgeois agricultural syndicates supplied needed commodities to peasant landlords and small businesses. The Montblanc syndicate distributed the collective's surplus wine and oil. Usually the bourgeois-oriented associations organized their own cooperatives. For example: in Barcelona the peasants' associations opened their own stores in different sections of the city, but the central fruit and vegetable market in the agricultural suburb of Barcelona remained collectivized. . . . In Aragon, commodities were distributed by the Regional Federation of Collectives (organized Feb., 1937).

The collectives were provisioned through their respective cooperatives from great storehouses frequently located in churches that had opposed the revolution. Payment for goods varied. In Lerida, peasant families were supplied with a Consumer Account Booklet in which the quantity of articles withdrawn from the collective's storehouse was marked. Every week the difference between the amount earned and the amount spent was also recorded. In Montblanc (pop. 6,000), purchases were made in local currency issued by the collectives. In some places during the first months of the Revolution a system of libertarian communism was instituted: "Take what you need!" In other places, non-negotiable vouchers were used. In Llombay (Castellón), distribution was based on a fixed amount for each family. Prices were fixed by an administrative council. In all cases scarce articles were rationed, with priority for children, invalids, the aged, and pregnant women. Non-essential rationed articles were distributed in rotation. . . . On the other hand, when there were abundant quantities of provisions (like fruits and vegetables) these items were distributed free, without restrictions of any kind.

In distribution the collective's cooperatives eliminated middlemen, small merchants, wholesalers, and profiteers, thus greatly reducing consumer prices. The collectives eliminated most of the parasitic elements from rural life, and would have wiped them out altogether if they were not protected by corrupt officials and by the political parties. Non-collectivized areas benefited indirectly from the lower prices as well as from free services often rendered by the collectives (laundries, cinemas, schools, barber and beauty parlors, etc.).

Transactions between collectives were conducted without money.[2] The Calanda collective, using the barter system, traded oil for Barcelona cloth. Adamuz (Valencia) used both barter and money exchange. At first the city merchants rejected interchange of goods. But as the prolonged war produced scarcity of necessary goods and even provisions, and inflation set in, they gladly accepted the interchange (barter system).

The agrarian collectives expanded their operations by developing supplementary industries: bakery, carpentry and cabinet making, blacksmith and iron works. Another area of expansion was farm installations and animal husbandry. Thus Vilaboi (pop. 500) installed an immense barn costing 30,000 pesetas which housed 20 milk cows, 200 sows, 27 calves, and a number of chicken houses. Amposta's installations were valued at 200,000 pesetas, and Graus was famous for its modern facilities (douches for the animals and scientific treatment of animal diseases). . . .

The collectives were well stocked with farm animals and necessary tools. Few lacked agricultural machinery. Hospitalet de Llobregat acquired machinery worth 180,000 pesetas, including new trucks. Amposta (pop. 10,000) had 14 tractors, 15 threshers, and 70 teams of work horses. Alcaniz had 9 oil presses, three flour mills, and an electric power plant. Calanda made good use of seeders, threshers and tractors. On March 27th, 1938, the Seros collective was occupied by the enemy. At that time the collective had very little money, but possessed 1,200 head of sheep, 100 sows, 30 cows, 36 horses and mules, a well-stocked chicken house, and a threshing machine. Between September, 1936 and August, 1937, Hospitalet de Llobregat took in more than 5 million pesetas. For this same period the expenses were 4,200,000 pesetas. The Sueca collective, in March, 1938, announced assets of 850,559 kilograms of rice, 140,000 pesetas worth of merchandise in its cooperative, and 3,300 25-pound cartons of oranges.

How did the collectives budget their income? Cuenca: 25% for education, 25% for machinery and tools, and the remaining 50% to be expended as the general assembly decides. Hospitalet de Llobregat budgeted 7,000 pesetas weekly to improve the flood control installations of the Llobregat river. Amposta built 14 new schools, a sanitarium, a hospital, and purified the supply of drinking water. In Montblanc the collective dug up the old useless vines and planted new vineyards. The land, improved by modern cultivation with tractors, yielded much bigger and better crops. . . . Many Aragon collectives built new roads and repaired old ones, installed modern flour mills, and processed agricultural and animal

---

[2] Exchanges between collectives and the "free market" or the government were conducted in the standard legal currency, the peseta.—*Ed.*

waste into useful industrial products. Many of these improvements were first initiated by the collectives. Some villages, like Calanda, built parks and baths. Almost all collectives established libraries, schools, and cultural centers. Some of the centers were housed in luxurious former bourgeois villas, and renamed "Villa Kropotkin," "Villa Montseny," "Villa Bakunin," etc.

Preoccupation with cultural and pedagogical innovations was an event without precedent in rural Spain. The Amposta collectivists organized classes for semi-literates, kindergartens, and even a school of arts and professions. The Seros schools were free to all neighbors, collectivists or not. Graus installed a school named after its most illustrious citizen, Joaquín Costa.[3] The Calanda collective (pop. only 4,500) schooled 1,233 children. The best students were sent to the Lyceum in Caspé, with all expenses paid by the collective. The Alcoriza (pop. 4,000) school was attended by 600 children. Many of the schools were installed in abandoned convents. In Granadella (pop. 2,000), classes were conducted in the abandoned barracks of the Civil Guards. Graus organized a print library and a school of arts and professions, attended by 60 pupils. The same building housed a school of fine arts and a high grade museum. In some villages a cinema was installed for the first time. The Peñalba cinema was installed in a church. Viladecana built an experimental agricultural laboratory. . . .

Some collectives were not solely manned by CNT members or sympathizers. Except for Catalonia, many rank and file UGT members were attracted to the libertarian experiments. The Catalonian UGT was colonized by the communists to contest the hegemony of the CNT. In the rest of Spain, the CNT and the UGT were on good terms, particularly during the first months, before they were brainwashed by the skillful Communist party propaganda machine.[4]

Either alone or in cooperation with revolutionary committees, the CNT carried through its expropriations. The land expropriated in this manner was given to the affiliated peasant sections of the CNT. These sections, under the guidance of the CNT, organized collectives. The CNT feared that the collectives, which by virtue of their economic importance exercised considerable political influence, would eventually become totally immersed

---

[3] Born in Graus, Sept. 14, 1846, Joaquin Costa died on Feb. 8, 1911, cursing governments and politics. He wrote about the tragedy of the Spanish peasantry and traced the history of grass roots agricultural collectivism by the peasants themselves. Costa, in no small measure, influenced the Spanish collectivist movement.—*Ed.*

[4] Peirats, we are sure, is referring to the rank and file UGT members, not to their leaders, who behaved abominably.—*Ed.*

Workers on a collectivized farm bring in the grain harvest.

in petty local politics, lose their revolutionary character, and gradually degenerate into puppets of the state and of the political parties. To prevent this, the CNT safeguarded its control by building a nexus of economic connections, relations, and syndicates, paralleling the federations of collectives at every level—local, regional, and national. Thus the district and regional federations took on a twofold character—economic and syndical.

In some places the expropriated land became public (municipal) property. The municipality allowed both the collectives and the "individualists" to use the land (as in Amposta). In other areas (Alcaniz, Montblanc) only urban property was municipalized. . . .

Wages varied according to the season and other circumstances. After the harvest in Vilaboi . . . the collectives increased their weekly wages to 85 pesetas. At the close of 1938, on account of inflation, weekly wages rose to 130 pesetas. . . . Some of the collectives adopted a libertarian communist or mixed system,[5] and, properly speaking, had no wage system. Everyone had only to work according to his ability and physical condition to use as much as was available. The communal dining halls were generally established in the cities. But the desire for more privacy, a more intimate way of life, was met by switching to the "family wage." This, of course, raised the problem of what is to be done about single people with no homes. In Lerida, a single person was allowed 50 pesetas weekly for himself and the other 25 pesetas for the collective dining hall. A married man without children was allowed 60 pesetas and 70 if he had children. In Plá de Cabra, 5 pesetas per day and 2 pesetas more for each additional family member was allowed. Oriols changed from the "communal bin" (take what you need) to the family wage: husband, 5 pesetas; wife, 3 pesetas; single men over 15 years of age, 3 pesetas. In Monzon, the arrangement was: married men, 9 pesetas plus 3½ pesetas for each additional minor child. In all collectives full wages were paid during periods of unemployment, disability, accidents, etc.

In Seros single men living alone took their meals in the collective's dining hall, and also used its laundry service. Homes of newly married couples were paid for by the collective. . . . In Peñalba, newly marrieds' homes were completely outfitted: furniture, linens, cooking utensils—everything free of charge. In San Mateo, cooking and cleaning services for single people living alone were in certain cases provided by the collectives.

Many collectives issued their own currency. Others, for a certain time, used no money. Many substituted certificates and vouchers for official

---

[5] A mixed system in relation to libertarian communism means that there is a token of exchange (voucher, ration card, etc.) for some articles and free distribution for necessities and surplus articles.—Ed .

currency. In Peñalba, drastic measures were taken to prevent hoarding of money. A system was worked out which obliged the collectivist to spend his money immediately. In any case, because of inflation, the value of money depreciated to the point where all confidence in the stability of the peseta evaporated.

In conducting their internal affairs, democratic procedures were scrupulously and zealously observed in all the collectives. Hospitalet de Llobregat held regular general membership meetings every three months to review production and attend to new business. The administrative council, and all other committees, submitted full reports on all matters. The meeting approved, disapproved, made corrections, issued instructions, etc.[6]

In all collectives, admission and expulsion of collectivists was decided by the general assembly of all the collectivists. If a member violated the rules of the collective for the first time he was reprimanded. If the offense was repeated his case was referred to the general assembly. Only the assembly, after weighing all the evidence, could expel a member. In Cuenca, delegates of work groups could not apply sanctions for violations of work rules. Such cases were referred to the Administrative Commission, which in turn brought the case before the general assembly for final decision. Work delegates or council members who exceeded their authority or failed to carry out the instructions of the members were suspended or removed by the General Assembly. . . .

The collectives paid special attention to health, medical care, and sanitation—all provided free of charge. The Masroig collective paid the doctor a yearly salary to take care of the collectivists. In Peñalba, the doctor, his unlicensed assistant, and the veterinarian belonged to the collective. All treatment of Aragon collectivists in the General Hospital was paid for by the Aragon Federation of Peasant Collectives. Granadella made the same arrangements with the Barcelona People's Hospital.

As the war neared its disastrous conclusion, refugees from the fascist

---

[6]Supreme power was vested in, and actually exercised by, the membership in general assemblies, and all power derived from, and flowed back to, the grass roots organizations of the people. Leval remarks in *Espagne Libertaire*, (p. 219) that:

Regular general membership meetings were convoked weekly, bi-weekly, or monthly . . . and these meetings were completely free of the tensions and recriminations which inevitably emerge when the power of decision is vested in a few individuals—even if democratically elected. The Assemblies were open to the public, objections and proposals were discussed openly, and everyone could participate in the proceedings. Democracy embraced all social life. In most cases, even the "individualists" who were not members of the collective could participate in the discussions, and they were listened to by the collectivists. . . .—*Ed.*

occupied areas were evacuated to the Republican zone in the rear. Many thousands of these refugees were welcomed in full solidarity. The agricultural collective of the Barcelona area welcomed 600 refugees; Vilaboi, 100 families; Amposta in Aragon harbored 162 families; Graus, 50 families; and Utiel sheltered 600 families evacuated from the Central (Madrid) front.

The collectives voluntarily contributed enormous stocks of provisions and other supplies to the fighting troops. Utiel sent 1,490 litres of oil and 300 bushels of potatoes to the Madrid front (in addition to huge stocks of beans, rice, buckwheat, etc.). Porales de Tujana sent great quantities of bread, oil, flour, and potatoes to the front, and eggs, meat, and milk to the military hospital.

The efforts of the collectives take on added significance when we take into account that their youngest and most vigorous workers were fighting in the trenches. 200 members of the little collective of Vilaboi were at the front; from Viledecans, 60; Amposta, 300; and Calanda, 500.

chapter 9

The Coordination of Collectives

Introduction

The perennial problem of how effectively and harmoniously to coordinate the operations of local agricultural units into collectives and the collectives into district, regional and national federations without stifling local initiative and freedom of action at all levels was surmounted by the peasant masses who organized themselves into collectives in accordance with libertarian principles.

This chapter documents the two most successful examples: a report by Leval on how the landworkers organized the Peasant Federation of Levant embracing 900 collectives, and excerpts from the resolutions adopted by the founding Congress of the Aragon Federation of Collectives embracing approximately 500 collectives. The scope of these efforts and above all the spirit of solidarity and the creative capacity of the "ordinary," the much snubbed peasant masses are here amply demonstrated.

The Peasant Federation of Levant[1]
by Gaston Leval

The Regional Federation of Levant, organized by our comrades of the CNT, was an agrarian federation embracing 5 provinces with a total population of 1,650,000 at the outbreak of the Civil War, with 78% of the most fertile land in Spain. It is in the Levant where, thanks to the creative spirit of our comrades, the most and best developed collectives were organized. (The number of collectives grew from 340 in 1937 to 900 at the end of 1938, and 40% of the total population of these provinces lived in collectives. . . .)

These achievements will not surprise those acquainted with the social history of the region. Since 1870 the libertarian peasants were among the most determined and persistent militants. While at certain times the movement in the cities (particularly Valencia) was altogether suppressed, the movement remained alive in the countryside. The peasants carried on. For them the Revolution was not confined only to fighting on the barricades. For them the Revolution meant taking possession of the land and building libertarian communism. . . .

In general, the character of the Levant collectives differed from those in Aragon. In Aragon the predominence of the CNT-FAI militias for a long time protected the collectives from the police, the state, and the political parties. In Levant, as in the rest of Republican Spain, Assault Guards, Carbineros, and troops commanded by officers totally devoid of revolutionary spirit constituted a constant threat to the development and even the very existence of the libertarian collectives.

In the Levant, the collectives were almost always organized by the peasant syndicates on the grass roots level, the "point of production." But they remained as autonomous organizations. They were not dominated by the syndicates, with whom they maintained only formal relations. The

[1] From Gaston Leval, *Né Franco né Stalin*, pp.143–152.

syndicates constituted the necessary intermediary connection between the "individualists" (petty peasant landlords) and the collectivists. The "individualists," in fact, conducted their transactions through the syndicates. Their isolationism was dissipated by their dependence on the syndicates. The peasant syndicates organized their own administrative commissions for agricultural production: one for rice, another for oranges, a third for truck farming, etc. The collectives duplicated the work of the syndicates. They too had their separate stores and their own administrative commissions. Much later this wasteful duplication was done away with. The stores were unified and the commissions now included both the collectivist and "individualist" members of the syndicates. These mixed commissions now did the purchasing for the collectives as well as for the individual farmers (machines, fertilizers, insecticides, seeds, etc.). They used the same trucks and wagons. This practical demonstration of solidarity brought many formerly recalcitrant "individualists" into the collectives. This method of organization served a double function: it encompassed everything that could be usefully coordinated, and, thanks to the syndicates, succeeded in spreading the spirit of the collectives among new layers of the population rendered receptive to our influence.

Revolutionary changes were being rapidly introduced—revolutionary order out of capitalist chaos. Rationing of goods in short supply and the family wage were established in all districts. The wealthier villages helped the poorer villages through district committees set up for that purpose. Every district or local center organized a panel of technicians, accountants, and bookkeepers, as well as an agronomist, a veterinarian, a specialist on plant diseases, an engineer, an architect, and an expert on commerce. This setup assured efficient distribution and coordination of services. By far most of the engineers and veterinarians belonged to the CNT unions, as did a great many agronomists. All but six specialists in wine culture (grape growing) and wine making also belonged to the CNT union. Even privately employed engineers and veterinarians, not members of the collective, selflessly cooperated in planning and carrying out various projects.

The agronomists recommended essential and practical projects such as planning agricultural improvements, transplanting, and crossbreeding of plants in accordance with geologic and climatic conditions (which private property owners would rarely permit on their land). The veterinarians instituted scientific stock breeding. Instead of working at cross purposes, the technicians and scientists cooperated, consulting each other on the feasibility as well as the coordination of all projects. For example: the veterinarians consulted the architect and the engineer on the construction of piggeries, stables, and poultry houses. . . .

The engineers introduced the very latest irrigation construction—on a big scale, particularly in the Murcia and Cartagena regions. In Villajoyosa, the construction of a huge dam brought water to more than a million parched almond trees. Throughout the region, the architects designed construction. A center for the study of plant diseases and tree culture, schools of agriculture, new housing, and new roads were all improvements made in accordance with general plans embracing the whole region. They were worked out through the cooperative efforts of the workers, the technicians, and the collectives at general assemblies and administrative technical councils.[2]

The 900 collectives of the Levant were subdivided into 54 local or district federations which were reassembled into 5 provincial federations. The operations of the federations were coordinated by regional administrative commissions. The administrative commission consisted of 26 technical sections. The agrarian section included: fruit growing, vegetables, grape vines, olives, truck farming, rice, and livestock (cows, swine and goats, etc.). The industrial sections included: wine making, liquors, brandy and whiskey, preserves, oil, sugar, fruits, essential oils and spirits, perfumes and other agricultural derivatives, machinery, fertilizers, building construction, transportation, import-export trade, hygiene, education, etc.

An example of the large-scale operations of the Peasant Federation of Levant is shown by the fact that it produced more than half of the total orange crop in Spain: almost four million kilos (1 kilo equals about 2 and one-fourth pounds). It then transported and sold through its own commercial organization (no middlemen) more than 70% of the crop. (The Federation's commercial organization included its own warehouses, trucks, and boats. Early in 1938 the export section established its own agencies in France: Marseilles, Perpignan, Bordeaux, Cherbourg, and Paris.) Out of a total of, 47,000 hectares in all Spain devoted to rice production, the collectives in the Province of Valencia cultivated 30,000 hectares. (1 hectare

---

[2] The libertarian movement has always been extremely sensitive to the dangers of bureaucratic organization, particularly when it involves the work of specialists, scientists, and administrators (to say nothing of politicians). In this regard, Souchy reports that the libertarian collectives took measures:

... to nip in the bud every manifestation of bureaucracy. Every work-group had its delegate. To be well-informed on what was being done, the collectives arranged regular meetings of the administrative commissions. A general congress of all the collectives was convoked every six months. At the congress the plans and projects of the collectives were scrupulously reviewed; detailed instructions on all important matters were given to the administrative commission. Incapable administrators were removed. The congress controlled all operations of the Federation. . . . (*Nacht über Spanien*, p. 155)—*Ed.*

equals about 2½ acres.)

It is worth calling attention to another innovation: the large-scale manufacturing of agricultural by-products with the substantial help of the peasants themselves. The peasant federations built and operated fruit and vegetable canneries, and other processing plants (the most important were located in Burriana, Murcia, Alfassar, Castillan, Oliva, and Paterna). . . .

To facilitate the transfer of merchandise, the distribution points and warehouses in the District Federations were located near main highways and railroad depots. Each collective in the district sent its surplus produce to these centers where the goods were weighed (or counted), classified, and stored. This information was collected and coordinated by the different technical sections (mentioned above) of the Regional Administrative Commission in Valencia. Through this arrangement, the District Federations always knew exactly how much surplus there was and where it could be exchanged.[3]

The organization of economic justice was not the only achievement of the collective. . . . Each collective organized one or two free schools for the children. Under the new order, the collectives of the Levant, like those in Aragon, Castile, Andalusia, and Estremadura almost wiped out illiteracy (70% of rural Spain was illiterate before the Civil War). In 1937 a school for accounting and bookkeeping was also opened with an attendance of 100. In Valencia, capital of the Levant, the Peasant Federation established its own hotel welcoming the collectivists and their families to good meals and comfortable sleeping accommodations. . . .

The peasant collectives were especially proud of their "University of Moncada," which the Regional Federation of Levant placed at the disposal of the Spanish National Federation of Peasants. The university gave courses in animal husbandry, poultry raising, animal breeding, agriculture, tree science, etc. . . . The campus was installed amidst the orange groves in the countryside. . . .

To conclude: the spirit of solidarity was as great among the Valencia collectives as among their brother workers in Aragon. The Levant collectives harbored a great many refugees, mostly women and children, from Castile. The collectives voluntarily donated great stocks of food and supplies to the fighting anti-fascist troops on the Madrid and Aragon fronts. Five tiny

---

[3] That is, made available to collectives in short supply, for export, etc. Souchy observed that: " . . . the commercial transactions became so complex that the Federation decided to organize a bank only to expedite the purchase and sale of products at home and abroad . . . " Souchy stresses that it was *not* a capitalist bank making profit through usury. (*Nacht über Spanien*, p. 156)—Ed.

villages in a few months donated 187 truckloads of food. A single telephone call, shortly before the fall of Malaga, was enough to dispatch instantly, and as always free of charge, seven truckloads of food to the hungry refugees in Almeria. Multiply all these contributions from all the collectives in Levant—generosity as radiant as the life-giving sun—and you will have a new insight into the inspiring character of their social life. . . .

The Aragon Federation of Collectives: The First Congress[4]
by Jose Peirats

Aragon embraces 47,391 square kilometers with a total population before the Civil War of approximately one and a half million. About three-fourths of the area remained in the Republican zone, embracing 500 collectives with 433,000 members [Souchy's estimate]. The aims and functions of the Aragon Federation of Collectives are defined in the extracts from the following declaration and resolutions adopted by the founding Congress in the little town of Caspé, Saragossa province, February 14th, 1937:

1)The purpose of the AFC is to organize in Aragon an association to defend and promote the interests of all the workers belonging to the collectives.
2)The functions of the Federation will be as follows: . . .
   Point 4)The AFC is organized to coordinate the economic resources of the region, in accordance with the principles of federalism. The Regional Federation will be structured as follows:
      a)The collective will be federated into districts.
      b)For cohesion and control, the District Committees will unite into the Regional Federation of Collectives. . . .

The Internal Structure of the Federation
1)The collectives will supply correct statistics on production and

[4]From José Peirats, *La CNT en la Revolución Española*, vol. I, pp. 340—342.

consumption to their respective District Committees, which will in turn add up and send the statistics for the district to the Regional Committee, thus creating the structural basis for real human solidarity.

2) The circulation of money (or various types of exchange) within and between collectives is abolished in favor of a uniform ration booklet (to be issued by the AFC) leaving it to the collectives themselves to determine their own rations according to available supplies.

3) In accordance with the resources of the collectives and to facilitate procurement of outside commodities the collectives or the districts will accumulate funds [official national currency] for the creation of a Regional treasury. . . . In organizing the District (county) Federations as well as the Regional Communal (provincial) Federation, the *traditional boundaries must be eliminated*, so that the tools and materials of production shall be freely available to all the collectives as needed. . . . In the collectives where there is at certain seasons of the year a surplus of agricultural labor, the District·Committees agree to ask the comrades to work where they are most needed. . . . [5]

Increasing the Output and Bettering the Quality of Agriculture
   a) Greatly expand the benefits of collectivism by the practice of mutual aid.
   b) Try to organize in the most suitable areas experimental farms and stations.
   c) Encourage the formation of special technical schools for the most gifted young people.
   d) Organize a corps of technicians who will study how to get the maximum yields in different branches of agriculture.
   e) To yield more and better animal production, it is also necessary to organize in each collective modern scientific stock-breeding methods and facilities . . . which must be guided by qualified experts. . . . Animal husbandry and agricultural production must be fully integrated. . . .
   f) Organize international exchange by establishing statistics on the surplus production of the region. . . . [6]

---

[5] We emphasized the phrase *traditional boundaries must be eliminated* because it stresses the determination of the assembled collectivists to do away with the arbitrary territorial barriers imposed upon the people by the state, and transcend—to use Leval's phrase—"the kind of petty local and even regional patriotism which springs from a narrow and false conception of true communalism."—*Ed.*

[6] Applying the same principle to exchange of commodities between collectives, the Federation arranged for the exchange of surplus products for goods in short supply.

On the problems of relations with small peasant landholders, and distribution of expropriated land to tenant farmers, sharecroppers, and landless laborers, the Congress endorsed the following measures:

1) Small proprietors desiring to remain outside the collectives, who think they can go it alone, will not be entitled to the benefits of the collective. However, their rights will be respected, provided they do not infringe on or affect the interests of the collective.

2) Small landholders outside of the collectivity can keep only land that they themselves can cultivate; hired help for wages is absolutely prohibited.

3) All lands formerly worked by tenant farmers or share croppers will be taken over by the collectivity.

4) All property, agrarian or urban, as well as goods taken by the workers from the fascists, are to remain in the custody of these organisations, on the condition that they will join the collective. . . .

On public education the AFC resolution pledged the Federation to:

a) Furnish the collectives with everything needed to advance education and culture.

b) Organize seminars to advance the education of the peasantry (night schools, evening motion pictures and theatres, excursions, etc.) and all sorts of propaganda and cultural projects. . . .

The last resolution of the Congress outlined how to block the counter-attack of the Central Government in Valencia. It wanted to destroy the collectives by instituting a dual power, displacing the independent collectives and syndicates created by the Revolution with the restoration of the Municipal Councils (the legal organs of the Central Government composed of counter-revolutionary, anti-collectivist political parties, bourgeois socialists, left-and right-wing republicans, reactionary small landholders, etc.).

The realization of these libertarian projects was abandoned with the destruction of the collectives by the combined military might of the fascist powers and (to their everlasting disgrace) the attacks of the Communist armies and their civilian allies in August, 1937, six months after the conclusion of the Congress.

It is axiomatic that revolutionary programs, however important, do not make revolutions. The impact of Revolution must be studied at its source: among the people, in the cities and the villages, the factories and the farms, where the creative efforts of the workers shaped the character of the Revolution.

Where this was not feasible, the surplus was simply to be donated to needy collectives with no strings attached.—*Ed.*

chapter 10
The Rural Collectives

Introduction

All participants and observers agree that the extent and nature of the agrarian collectives were more widespread and thorough than were the industrial collectives. Often separated from the seats of State power and with their long tradition of rural communism and militant agitation, the rural collectives were able to thrive for a period of time.

The extent to which theories are valid can be determined only by the extent to which they are practical. Theories that do not correspond to the acid test of real life are worse than useless as a guide to action. For this reason this chapter consists of eyewitness reports from a number of typical rural collectives, from direct contact with the landworkers who made the agrarian revolution a success. These experiences renew faith in the constructive, creative capacities of "ordinary" people, to make and sustain the social revolution and successfully tackle their everyday problems. Spontaneity, solidarity and mutual aid enriched and broadened their lives (if only for a few years and under the constant threat of attack). Nor must we forget that collectivization led to modernization of facilities and methods, and cultural opportunities for all. All this, and more, achieved by the workers themselves!

A Journey Through Aragon[1]
by Augustin Souchy

Calanda

The libertarian youth is the moving spirit of the Revolution in Calanda. The Revolution radically altered the lifestyle of this village, and to the libertarian youth belongs all the credit for the innovations introduced after July 19th.

As we approach the village square, we hear the refrain from the theme song of the Revolution: "To the Barricades! To the Barricades! All for the victory of the Confederation!" (CNT-FAI is sometimes referred to as "our Confederation.") The youth play recordings of the old anarchist hymn, "Hijos del Pueblo" ("Sons of the People"), recalling the heroic struggles of past centuries.

On the village square, facing the church, stands a new granite fountain. On its base, engraved in bold letters, is the inscription: "CNT-FAI-JJLL" (JJLL is the libertarian youth organization). The fountain is the pride of the village, erected on their own initiative by the construction workers as sketched out by the young anarchists.

Of the 4,500 inhabitants, 3,500 belong to the CNT. Production and distribution are organized on libertarian principles. Although there were no such organizations in Calanda before July 19th, 1936, the anarchists practiced tolerance and welcomed the republican and socialist groups.

The relations between the libertarian collectivists and the "individualists" (small peasant proprietors) are cordial. There are two cafés: the collective's café serves free coffee and in the other café the "individualists" have to pay for their coffee. The collective operates a barber shop, giving free haircuts and (if desired) free shaves twice weekly.

[1] From Augustin Souchy, *Nacht über Spanien*, pp. 137–139; 145–147; 147–149, 151.

Money is abolished and has been replaced by vouchers. Food, meat, and all other provisions are distributed in quantity when plentiful or equitably rationed when in short supply. The collective allows 5 liters of wine per person weekly. Medical care and medicines are free. Even postage stamps are free. There is no rent. Housing, building repairs, water, gas, electricity—all are supplied gratis, not only to the collectivists but also to the "individualists." The village generates its own power from a waterfall. There is no scarcity of clothing. By arrangement with a Barcelona textile plant, oil is exchanged for cloth, dresses, etc. Garments are distributed in rotation to 40 persons daily.

The Municipal Council consists of 6 members, 3 from the CNT and 3 from the Libertarian Youth. The youth are very active. They have built public baths, a library, conducted cultural events, etc. Cinema is collectivized. Except for some small shops that prefer to remain independent, everything is collectivized. The land is worked by teams of ten, each team cultivating a zone. Every team chooses its own delegates. The work teams are freely formed by "affinity."[2] The bank was closed down, and the assets of 70,000 pesetas confiscated by the municipality to purchase supplies.

The showplace of the collective is the newly organized Ferrer (libertarian progressive) School, housed in an old convent. The collective requested the services of 10 more teachers from Barcelona. School supplies, desks, stools, and other equipment are donated by the collective. The school is equipped with a hatchery and greenhouses. From a comparative handful of privileged children, the school now accommodates 1,233 pupils. Gifted children are sent at the expense of the collective to the high school in Caspé. The Calanda militiamen voluntarily send their savings not to relatives but to their communal family, the collective.

Muniesa

The 1,700 inhabitants of Muniesa felt no great urge to collectivize before July 19th. There were no Fascist threats in the area and there had been no fighting. There had been no big landlords (and consequently no expropriations). There were only poor peasants struggling hard to eke out a living from their small properties.

But after July 19th, a new spirit shook Muniesa out of its lethargy. The moving spirit of the new order was Joaquin Valiente. He had lived in Barcelona for 17 years and there came to know libertarian ideas. He returned to Muniesa a convinced anarchist and fiery exponent of the "new"

---

[2] That is, by personal preference. An "affinity grouping" could be called a working partnership of close friends.—*Ed.*

ideology. His proposal to collectivize fell on fruitful ground. Things had not been going well for the peasants and they had become receptive to change—they decided to collectivize. Joaquin Valiente . . . was elected mayor.

The libertarian communist commune was organized at a general meeting of the villagers. Valiente presided. On the table lay an open copy of Kropotkin's classic, *The Conquest of Bread.* One of the members read aloud extracts from the book. "Here is the new gospel! Here, in black and white, is written how to institute well-being for all!"

Bread, meat, oil, wine, and certain other products were distributed gratis from the community center where the peasants deposited their products. But many commodities had to be purchased elsewhere. The Communal Council did the shopping for everyone, buying in quantity. It was decided that these supplementary supplies (aside from goods it was decided should be free) should be paid for by the individual consumers. For this purpose, the Council printed 100,000 pesetas in local currency (not negotiable anywhere else). To buy whatever supplementary commodities they wanted from the commune, every adult man and woman was allotted one peseta, and children 50 centimes, per day.

"Are you not afraid," I asked, "that unlimited quantities of free wine will lead to excessive drinking?"

"By no means. No one gets drunk here. We have been living under this system for a year, and everyone is satisfied. . . . "

Of the 100,000 pesetas in local money, only 11,000 are circulated. The remaining 89,000 pesetas are held in reserve by the Communal Council. This local currency is only a token of exchange and carries no interest. Everyone is (as noted above) alloted an equal sum. No one dreams of hoarding because no one can accumulate capital.

The greatest problem of the village elders is the education of the children. There are no teachers nor sufficient educational supplies. The commune is willing to do anything to attract teachers. The teachers' union in Barcelona promised to send teachers. In the meantime, two villagers are, at least, teaching the older children to read and write.

Early in the evening, as I and my travelling companion reclined in our improvised lodging (we left next morning), I remarked:

Early in this century, some sociologists and economists thought that socialism was realizable; others that it was only a utopian dream. When we see with what confidence, dedication, and practical common sense the peasants of this village, through their cooperative labor, are, without compulsion, creating a new and better life in a free commune, these academic discussions seem singularly abstract and unrealistic. The peasants know nothing about theory. Nevertheless, their healthy common sense, confirmed by their own experience, tells that more can be achieved by working together than alone. And this same thing is taking place in hundreds of villages all over Republican Spain. . . .

Albalate de Cinca

The Aragon village of Albalate de Cinca is located not far from the Catalonian border. Here, as in Muniesa, the peasants know very little about politics or socialist theories. But, as in so many other places, the landless agricultural laborers and the small peasant proprietors routed the local fascists and organized their collective. Things were arranged too hastily and mistakes were made, but after a year under the new system conditions improved greatly. "Things are better now," said an old peasant. "Before we were always on the brink of starvation; now we have plenty to eat and other things gratis. . . . "

By 7 a.m., the village is at work. A woman suffering from rheumatism comes to the community center. She wants travel expenses to Lerida to consult a specialist. Although money was abolished within the village, the commune reserves cash for necessary outside services. The village clerk asks her, "Have you a doctor's certificate?" "No." "Then I cannot give you money for transportation. The general meeting ruled that travel funds will be provided only when authorized by the village physician." The woman leaves to get authorization from the village doctor. The clerk explains, "Before, hardly anyone went to the city (Lerida), but now that it costs them nothing, everybody suddenly finds reasons to go." Perhaps the clerk is too strict. Anyhow, the doctor will decide.

Doctor José Maria Pueyo, a middle-aged man from Saragossa, now lives in Albalate de Cinca. He has been treating the villagers for 12 years, and understands their physical condition and health needs. Dr. Pueyo is a liberal, but belongs to no party. He is well liked. Here in Albalate de Cinca, as in many other Spanish villages, health care was customarily provided by paying the doctor a stipulated yearly sum. . . . After collectivization, the situation was radically altered. Since money was abolished, we asked Dr. Pueyo:

"How are you paid?"

"The collective takes care of me."

"Surely you have other needs than eating, drinking, and being clothed. You need medical instruments, books, and many other things."

"The collective takes care of all this, just as in city hospitals where the management provides the doctor with all supplies and services. . . . "

Dr. Pueyo shows us some new medical books. He had spent a few days in Barcelona where he bought everything he needed at the collective's expense. Since there is no pharmacy in the village, the doctor fills his own prescriptions and supplies patients with other medical necessities.

"What do you think of collectivization, doctor?"

"Collectivization, in my opinion, is morally superior to capitalism. It assures the greatest possible amount of social justice. The new system is not yet perfected. . . . The principal shortcomings spring from the uneven rate of development. . . . While the cities retained the money system, most of the rural collectives abolished money. Many villages issued their own currency. This is very impractical. If money is to be abolished, it should be abolished everywhere, all over Spain. If money is retained there must be a fixed, uniform currency, negotiable everywhere. Issuing local money for different localities is not practical. I repeat: from the standpoint of social justice, money should be abolished, and libertarian communism is infinitely superior to capitalism. . . . "

A few days later, while on our way to visit the Federation of Workers' Collectives in Barbastro, we talked about a collectivized economy and I referred to our conversation with Dr. Pueyo:

"Dr. Pueyo's criticism of collectivism is well grounded only insofar as it concerns the need for a uniform currency throughout Spain. But the establishment of a uniform economic system, on the contrary, destroys freedom and leads inevitably to economic totalitarianism. . . . Economic variety, for example coexistence of collective and privately conducted enterprises[3], will not adversely affect the economy, but is, on the contrary, the true manifestation and the indispensable prerequisite for a free society. But regimentation, the imposition of a uniform economic system by and for the benefit of the state, leads inevitably to economic and political slavery. . . . "

---

[3] Enterprises not employing wage labor.—*Ed.*

The Collectivization in Graus [4]
by Gaston Leval and Alardo Prats

Graus is a district situated in the mountainous northern part of the province of Huesca, a region less suitable for socialized agriculture than are the villages of southern Aragon that I have seen. In this isolated northern region, progress is slow in coming. New ideas have hardly penetrated these lonely hills, mountains, and valleys of Aragon. . . . The district consists of fourty-three villages and yet very few are disposed to accept large-scale collectivization. Only one, Secastiglia, is fully collectivized. . . . Ten others are only half socialized.

The place that I had time to study best is the village of Graus, the capital of the district, which I visited in June, 1937. Although its population is only 2,600, Graus is more like a city than a village. It is situated at the intersection of many roads and is a relatively important commercial center, with many small establishments serving the countryside. For lack of good land, agriculture is of relatively little importance. As of July, 1936, 40% of the working population was engaged in commerce. The rest were in industry and agriculture. Twenty percent of the land is irrigated. The main crops are cereals, grapes for wine, olives and olive oil, almonds, and vegetables. About one-fourth of the young workers left to work in Catalonia or in France and almost as many young girls worked as domestics in the cities or abroad. The living standards of various working layers of the population varied greatly. For example, a mechanic was paid more than twice as much as an agricultural laborer.

Guided by our comrades, the anti-fascists boldly introduced radical social reforms. The family wage was instituted immediately, assuring equal pay and equal rights for all. A married couple received 2 pesetas per day,

---

[4]This selection is divided into three parts. The first is from Gaston Leval, *Né Franco né Stalin*, pp. 234-252. The second is from Alardo Prats, a socialist observer quoted by Peirats, *La CNT en la Revolución Española*, vol. 1, p. 314. The last is from Leval, *Espagne Libertaire*, pp. 94-108.

plus one peseta per day for each additional family member. A month later, coupons divided into units of various denominations became the prevailing medium of exchange. Much later, the relative commercial importance of Graus as a trading center made necessary the restoration of the peseta, the official currency of Spain, as the measurement of all outside transactions. But the collective continued to issue its own currency valid in strictly local transactions.

Partially controlled establishments were soon fully socialized. Cooperative communal markets replaced privately owned retail shops. A textile, haberdashery, and clothing center replaced 23 out of the 25 small shops. Twenty-five or 30 privately owned retail food shops were consolidated into one food market. Two of the 3 shoe shops were collectivized. Two hardware stores were consolidated into one. Four bakeries and bread depots were merged into 2, and instead of 3 bakery ovens, 1 was sufficient for all needs.

As in the collectivization of industry, similar procedures were applied to agriculture. In Graus, as in many other places in Aragon, the first step toward socialization was organization of the agricultural collective. The Revolutionary Committee first tackled the most urgent problems: harvesting, planting, overcoming the shortage of young workers (many were away fighting on the Aragon front), and still getting maximum yields from the land. Thanks to the strenuous effort and initiative of the comrades of the CNT and UGT, better ploughs and stronger horses were procured, and other improvements were made. The land was cleared and fields sown with corn. The agricultural collective was established on October 16th, 1936, 3 months after the fascist assault was repulsed. On the same day, transportation was collectivized and other new collectivizations were scheduled by the two unions, the CNT (libertarian) and UGT (socialist). Printshops were socialized on Nov. 24th, followed 2 days later by shoe stores and bakeries. Commerce, medicine, pharmacies, horseshoers' and blacksmiths' establishments, were all collectivized December 1st, and cabinet makers and carpenters on December 11th. Thus all social economic activities were gradually integrated into the new social order. . . .

There was no forced collectivization. Membership in the collectives was entirely voluntary, and groups could secede from the collective if they so desired. But even if isolation were possible, the obvious benefits of the collective were so great that the right to secede was seldom, if ever, invoked. The Revolutionary Committee which initiated collectivization became the coordinating committee after the collective was established. With the reestablishment of the Municipal Council, as required by the government, the Committee was dissolved in January, 1937.

The Municipal Council was composed of 4 councilmen from the CNT and 4 from the UGT. A republican worker who acted as mayor was elected by the general assembly of all the inhabitants. Relations between the CNT and the UGT were cordial with no friction. Thus favoritism was avoided and harmony assured. The mayor's post was mostly ceremonial. He had no real power and could only carry out the instructions of the two unions that composed the Council. The Municipal Council represented the Central Government; it mobilized soldiers for the war, furnished identification papers for all the inhabitants, etc. The Collective was entirely independent and the Municipal Council did not interfere with any of its functions. This was true in almost all collectives.[5]

Ninety percent of all production, including exchange and distribution, was collectively owned. (The remaining 10% was produced by petty peasant landholders.) The collective's coordinating functions were conducted by an 8 member administrative commission. This was divided into 8 departments, each headed by a highly qualified secretary, delegated for no set term of office by the rank and file membership of the two unions. Both the CNT and the UGT were equally represented on the Commission—4 for each union. All delegates were subject to instant recall by the General Assembly. The departments were: Culture and Public Health, Statistics and Labor, Industry, Transportation and Communications. . . .

In industrial organization, each factory and workshop selected a delegate who maintained permanent relations with the Labor secretariat, reporting back to and acting on the instructions of his constituents.[6]

Accounts and statistics for each trade and enterprise were compiled by the statistical and general accounting department, thus giving an accurate picture of the operations of each organization and the operations of the economy as a whole. The list that I saw included: drinking water, bottle making, carpentry, mattress making, wheelwrights, photography, silk mills, candy, pork butchershops, distilleries, electricity, oil, bakeries, hairdressers and beauty parlors, soap makers, house painting, tinware, sewing machines, shops and repairs, printing, building supplies, hardware, tile shops, dairies, bicycle repairs, etc.

Everything was coordinated both in production and in distribution. For

[5] Later, as Leval himself recounts, the Municipal Council turned out to be the entering wedge for the destruction of the collectives by the government. This was precisely why the government insisted that they be restored and the independent Revolutionary Committees be dissolved.—*Ed.*

[6] In general this form of organization was suitable for a village of a few thousand, where people knew each other and face-to-face democracy and surveillance could more effectively detect and check any incipient abuse of power. —*Ed.*

example, the tiny privately owned liquor and soft drink bottling enterprises had been collectivized and installed in a single up-to-date building. There they bottled wine, lemonade, soda water, beer, and liquors under the most sanitary conditions, at less cost and better quality than before collectivization.

One may have the impression that the kind of idyllic regime developed in Graus was too impractical and was bound to collapse. But this way of life was based not upon fantasy but on a solid organization, perfectly balanced, coordinated and in harmony with practical needs, resources, and potentialities. . . . Everything was systematically organized. Exact statistic were compiled on the hourly, daily, and yearly condition and possibilities of each branch of industry, thus insuring the highest degree of coordination.

The collective modernized industry, increased production, turned out better products, and improved public services. For example, the collective installed up-to-date machinery for the extraction of olive oil and conversion of the residue into soap. It purchased two big electric washing machines, one for the hospital and the other for the collectivized hotel. . . . Through more efficient cultivation and the use of better fertilizers, production of potatoes increased 50% (three-quarters of the crop was sold to Catalonia in exchange for other commodities . . .) and the production of sugar beets and feed for livestock doubled. Previously uncultivated smaller plots of ground were used to plant 400 fruit trees, . . . and there were a host of other interesting innovations. Through this use of better machinery and chemical fertilizers and, by no means least, through the introduction of voluntary collective labor, the yield per hectare was 50% greater on collective property than on individually worked land. These examples finally induced many more "individualists" to join the collective.

I saw many other revolutionary changes. In the converted corset factory girls sewed shirts and underwear for the militiamen while singing revolutionary hymns in honor of Durruti, killed on the Madrid front. . . . These girls were not obliged to work—they were covered by the family wage—but nevertheless donated their labor for the common cause. . . . With increased output the family wage had also been increased by 15%. The increase was all the more meaningful when we consider that housing was free, gas and electric rates had been cut 50%, and medical treatment and medicines had been free since these services had been socialized. Men over 60 were exempt from work with full pay but they refused to stay put and insisted on donating their labor where most needed. Full wages were paid to the unemployed, 52 weeks a year. As one organizer in Graus told me, "Work or no work, people must eat . . . "

Before the July, 1936, fascist attack, animal husbandry in Graus was neglected in favor of commerce. But with the lessening of traffic because of interrupted communications with the rest of Aragon, the collective turned to the intensive raising of livestock.[7]

In the vicinity of the town, first class piggeries have been constructed containing about 2,000 animals. In Aragon as well as in other parts of Spain the pig is one of the basic family staples. Pig killing is an institution of some standing.[8] In the winter each family is given a pig. Feeding of the animals is conducted on strict scientific lines. I asked the comrades in charge of pig and cattle raising what methods they used and they told me that after various experiments they decided to adopt the system used in Chicago.

In other districts outside the city other breeding establishments have set up chicken farms with research laboratories. The main center occupies the site of an old camp. The most varied kind of fowl are to be found in this establishment. About 10,000 animals will be bred by next fall.

All systems are completely new. The head of this establishment invented a new type of incubator with enormous yielding powers. Thousands of baby chicks jump around in specially heated rooms, as well as ducklings and geese. Observers from all parts of Aragon visit this unique laboratory to learn the new methods.

When a collectivist wants to marry, he is given a week's holiday with full pay. The collective's cooperative provides a house completely equipped and furnished. All the services of the collective are available to the collectivist. From birth to death he is protected. His rights are respected and his obligations are voluntarily assumed. All decisions affecting him and his fellow workers are democratically made in the full and open assembly of all the collectivists. . . . Children are given special attention. They are not allowed to work until they reach the minimum age of 14. . . . Pregnant women are accorded the most tender pre-natal care. . . .

Every family is allotted a piece of land for its own use, be it to raise some chickens, rabbits, or whatever. Seed and fertilizer are also provided to grow vegetables. There is no longer any need to employ hired labor nor is it any longer necessary for young girls to seek employment as servants in Catalonia or in France. The collective has made truly remarkable progress in raising the standard of living by 50% to 100% in a few months. And this is all the

---

[7] The construction of piggeries and poultry houses had not yet been completed when Leval was there. Another observer, the socialist Alardo Prats, who saw them when completed, gives this interesting account. Then he also depicts other innovations.—*Ed.*

[8] It was done collectively, like a fiesta.—Ed.

more remarkable in that this was achieved under the stress of war and in the absence of the youngest and most active workers, now in the armed forces. This miracle is due not only to collective enthusiasm but also to a better and more economical use of productive labor and resources. . . . Bear in mind that 40% of the work force, formerly engaged in socially useless activity, is now directed to useful projects for the benefit of all. . . .

And the spirit of mutual aid and solidarity is not confined to each little section of the collective, but embraces all the different branches of the economy so that the unavoidable deficit of one branch is balanced by the surplus of another branch. For example: deficits of hairdresser and beauty shops are made good by the more profitable trucking industry or the enterprises distilling alcohol for medicinal and industrial purposes.

Yet other examples of mutual aid: harboring 224 refugees from villages seized by the fascists (only 20 are able to work and 145 are at the fighting front). Twenty-five families whose breadwinners are sick or permanently disabled receive the regular family wage. Despite these extra expenses, the collective has been able to carry through considerable public improvements (paving roads, enlarging and deepening irrigating canals, providing water power, etc.). . .

One of the most popular measures of the collective was the expropriation of the holdings of a landlord who sealed off, even to his own laborers, all access to a magnificent stream of clear water running through his property. For the enjoyment of the public it was decided to construct a beautiful scenic roadway sloping gently toward the waterway (even the deposed landlord and his former employees helped!). When the project was completed with that love for water so characteristic of semi-arid Spain (and in so many other lands!), I read, etched in gold on the marble base of a graceful fountain spurting crystal clear water, this tribute to the Revolution: *Fountain of Liberty, July 19, 1936.*

As in the other collectives, Graus paid special attention to education. The School of Fine Arts was attended in the afternoon by elementary school pupils and in the evenings by young people who worked during the day. It was primarily the striking creation of a dedicated man, an apostle of culture. The evening session taught choral singing (always popular in Spain), design, painting, sculpture, etc.

When I visited the school, 80 little refugees from the Franco zone were housed in a beautiful estate expropriated by the collective situated some kilometers from the village. Two male teachers and one female teacher conducted classes, shaded by the great trees. In the main dormitory the children slept on plain but clean and comfortable beds donated by the villagers. Two women prepared delicious meals in the vast kitchens which

Woman on a collectivized farm.

Above—Farmers with a new mechanized tractor on a collectivized farm.
Below—The grain harvest with horse drawn reaper.

the wealthy former owners used only a few weeks a year. Food, furnishings, linen, wages of personnel, everything was supplied gratis. The children were visibly delighted with this place, with its splendid woods fronting the river, its park, its swimming pool, its farmyard, and its buildings. Doubtlessly they had never known so beautiful a life. If the circumstances had been favorable, our comrades of the UGT and the CNT would have converted this vast estate (till now so ostentatious, garish, and humanly sterile) into a permanent colony in which all the children of Graus would take turns living, learning, and enjoying the wholesome air and the sunshine. . . .

Libertarian Communism in Alcora [9]
by H. E. Kaminski

The village of Alcora has established "libertarian communism." One must not think that this system corresponds to scientific theories. Libertarian communism in Alcora is the work of the peasants who completely ignore all economic laws. The form which they have given to their community corresponds more in reality to the ideas of the early Christians than to those of our industrial epoch. The peasants want to have "everything in common" and they think that the best way to achieve equality for all is to abolish money. In fact money does not circulate amongst them any longer. Everybody receives what he needs. From whom? From the Committee, of course.

It is however impossible to provide for five thousand people through a single center of distribution. Shops still exist in Alcora where it is possible to get what is necessary as before. But those shops are only distribution centers. They are the property of the whole village and the ex-owners do not make profits instead. The barber shaves only in exchange for a coupon. The coupons are distributed by the Committee. The principle according to which the needs of all the inhabitants will be satisfied is not perfectly put in

[9] From H.E. Kaminski, *Ceux de Barcelone*, pp. 156–158. The translation is taken from *Anarchy* #5, July, 1961.

practice as the coupons are distributed according to the idea that everybody has the same needs. There is no individual discrimination: the family alone is recognized as a unit. Only unmarried people are considered as individuals.

Each family and person living alone has received a card. It is punched each day at the place of work, which nobody can therefore leave. The coupons are distributed according to the card. And here lies the great weakness of the system: for the lack hitherto of any other standard they have had to resort to money to measure the work done. Everybody, workers, shopkeepers, doctors, receive for each day's work coupons to the value of five pesetas. On one side of the coupon the word bread is written: each coupon is worth one kilogram. But the other side of the coupon represents explicitly a counter-value in money. Nevertheless these coupons cannot be considered as banknotes. They can only be exchanged against goods for consumption and in only a limited quantity. Even if the amount of coupons was greater it would be impossible to buy means of production and so become a capitalist, even on a small scale. Only consumer goods are on sale. The means of production are owned by the community. The community is represented by the Committee, here called the Regional Committee. It has in its hands all the money of Alcora, about 100,000 pesetas. The Committee exchanges the village products against products which it does not possess, and when it cannot obtain them by exchange it buys them.   But money is considered an unavoidable evil, only to be used as long as the rest of the world will not follow the example of Alcora.

The Committee is the *pater familias*. It possesses everything, it directs everything, it deals with everything. Each special desire should be submitted to it. It is, in the last resort, the only judge. One may object that the members of the Committee run the risk of becoming bureaucrats or even dictators. The peasants have thought about that too. They have decided that the Committee should be changed at frequent intervals so that every member of the village should be a member for a certain period.

There is something moving about the ingenuity of all this organization. It would be a mistake to see in it anything more than a peasant attempt to establish libertarian communism and unfair to criticize it too seriously. One must not forget that the agricultural workers and even the shopkeepers of the village have lived very poorly up till now. Their needs are hardly differentiated. Before the revolution a piece of meat was a luxury for them: only a few intellectuals living among them wish for things beyond immediate necessities. The anarchist communism of Alcora has taken its nature from the actual state of things. As a proof, one must observe that the family card puts the most oppressed human beings in Spain, the women, under the control of men.

"What happens," I ask, "if somebody wants to go to the city for example?"

"It is very simple," someone replies. "He goes to the Committee and exchanges his coupons for money."

"Then one can exchange as many coupons as one wants for money?"

"Of course not."

These good people are rather surprised that I understand so slowly.

"But when can one have money then?"

"As often as you need. You have only to tell the Committee."

"The Committee examines the reasons then?"

"Of course."

I am a little terrified. This organization seems to me to leave very little liberty in a "libertarian communist" regime. I try to find reasons for travelling that the Alcora Committee would accept. I do not find very much but I continue my questioning.

"If somebody has a fiancée outside the village will he get the money to go and see her?"

The peasant reassures me: he will get it.

"As often as he wants?"

"Thank God, he can still go from Alcora to see his fiancée every evening if he wants to."

"But if somebody wants to go to the city to go to the cinema. Is he given money?"

"Yes."

"As often as he wants to?"

The peasant begins to have doubts about my reason.

"On holidays, of course. There is no money for vice."

I talk to a young, intelligent looking peasant, and having made friends with him, I take him to one side and ask him:

"If I proposed to give you some bread coupons would you exchange them for money?"

My new friend thinks for a few moments and then says: "But you need bread too?"

"I don't like bread, I only like sweets. I would like to exchange all I earn for sweets."

The peasant understands the hypothesis very well, but he does not need to think very long. He starts laughing.

"It is quite simple! If you want sweets you should tell the Committee. We have enough sweets here. The Committee will give you a permit and you will go to the chemist and get them. In our village everybody receives what he needs."

After this answer I had to give up. These peasants no longer live in the capitalist system, neither from a moral nor a sentimental point of view. But did they ever live in it?

The Collective in Binefar[10]
by Gaston Leval

In the province of Huesca, the village of Binefar was beyond doubt the chief center of collectivization. . . . The district embraced 32 villages, 28 of them wholly or partially collectivized. In Binefar itself, 700 of the 800 families belonged to the Collective.

There had long been a sizable social movement in Binefar, despite the fact that the small local industries (mills, factories, clothing and shoemaking shops, foundries, etc.) employed only a tenth of the 5,000 inhabitants. In the local CNT syndicate most of the members (600 members in 1931) were peasants. . . . The syndicate, founded in 1917, had experienced the typical ups and downs—times of relative quiet, then persecution, suppression and imprisonment of militants. When the fascist threat appeared in July, 1936, our forces, though disorganized from the last persecution, rose to meet the danger and took the initiative in forming a revolutionary committee on July 18th (two popular front representatives served on the committee). Within two days, the barracks where the fascist Civil Guard retreated in the first fighting were taken by assault, and our victorious comrades departed to help liberate other villages.

The fields of the big landowners, who fled at the first sign of anti-fascist victory, had not yet been harvested. The revolutionary committee took possession of the reapers and mowers and summoned the peasants who had previously worked on these lands as laborers. The peasants decided that

[10]From Gaston Leval, *Né Franco né Stalin*, pp. 133—143, the translation is taken from *Resistance* as reprinted in *Views and Comments*, Oct., 1958. The rules of the popular assembly are added by the editor and are from *Espagne Libertaire*, pp. 118—119.

they would work the land in common in the interests of the whole village. To organize the work they formed groups and elected delegates. . . .

After the harvest, industry and eventually commerce were socialized. The following are the rules that the popular assembly of all the inhabitants approved:

1. Work shall be carried on in groups of ten. Each group shall elect its own delegate. . . . The delegates shall plan the work, preserve harmony among the producers, and if necessary apply the sanctions voted by the popular assembly. (At first the delegates met every night after work, and when work was normalized, once a week.)

2. The delegates shall furnish the Agricultural Commission a daily report of the work done.

3. A central committee, consisting of one delegate from each branch of production, shall be named by the general assembly of the Community. The committee shall report monthly on consumption and production, and supply news about other collectives and events in Spain and abroad. . . .

5. Directors of labor for the collective shall be elected by the general assembly of all the collectivists.

6. Each member shall be given a receipt for the goods he brings to the Collective.

7. Each member shall have the same rights and duties. Members shall not be compelled to join either union (the CNT or the UGT). All that is required is that members accept the decisions of the Collective.

8. The capital of the Collective belongs to the Collective and cannot be divided up. Food shall be rationed, part of it to be stored away against a bad year (harvest).

9. When needed, as for urgent agricultural work (the harvest), women may be required to work, and do the work assigned to them. Rigorous control shall be applied to insure that they contribute their productive efforts to the Community.

10. No one shall work before the age of 15, or do heavy work before the age of 16.

11. The general assembly shall determine the organization of the Collective, and arrange periodic elections of the administrative commission.

In Binefar, the Collective was all-embracing. Despite its past influence and importance, the syndicate had almost no role . . . nor was it, in the traditional sense of the word, strictly a municipality. . . . Just as the Soviet was the typical type of organization emerging from the Russian Revolution, the Collective was the typical organization of the Spanish Revolution. Binefar spontaneously and naturally followed norms generally and tacitly accepted without formal discussion.

It was no longer a matter of fighting the employers but of assuring production, and this meant planning and direction and calculation of local needs and exchange needs. . . . Everything was linked like the gears of a machine. There was a joint treasury for both agricultural and industrial enterprises. There was no jurisdictional rivalry between the various units of the economy, and there were equal wages for all. . . . An administrative commission, composed of a president, a treasurer, a secretary, and two councillors, coordinated activities and kept daily records. . . .

In case of need the peasants' section could call upon industrial workers, including technicians, to work in the fields. In the July, 1937 harvest (when labor was short because of war mobilization), when it was necessary to save the wheat crop, the clothing workers helped with the harvesting. . . . Young women, and housewives who did not have to look after young children or old people, were summoned to work by an announcement of the town crier on the preceding evening. . . . Attendance records of regular workers were kept by the delegates . . . and violations could not be repeated without calling down open public disapproval, or, failing that, the necessary disciplinary measures. . . .

Food and other goods were distributed in municipal stores. There were wine, bread, and oil cooperatives, one for dry goods, three dairy stores, three butcher shops, a hardware store, and a furniture store. Bread, olive oil, flour, potatoes, meat, vegetables, greens, and wine were free when plentiful and when scarce, rationed. Each person had a piece of land to raise whatever he wanted. Electricity and telephones were installed throughout the region. Commodities not distributed free of charge were paid for in local currency. In Binefar, as in many other communes, the wage scale varied according to the number of persons in each family (the "family wage"). . . .

As the capital of its district, Binefar coordinated trade among its 32 villages. Each village informed the office of the surplus food it had. From October to December, 1936, 5,000,000 pesetas worth of goods were exchanged with other collectives in Aragon and Catalonia, including 800,000 pesetas worth of sugar and 700,000 pesetas worth of olive oil. . . . Abandoned by the government, the militiamen (on the Aragon front) lacked food. Binefar gave everything it could, sending from 30 to 40 tons of food every week. On one occasion, in addition to the regular contributions, Binefar gave Madrid 340 extra tons of food. In a single day, 36,000 pesetas worth of olive oil was sent to the Ortiz, Durruti, and Ascaso columns (anarchist columns on the Aragon front). . . . The generosity and the solidarity of the Collective did not flag. 500 militiamen permanently quartered in Binefar were provisioned by the Collective. . . .'. [11]

In June, 1937, I attended a district congress where a grave problem had come up. The harvest was at hand. Sacks, wire, gas, and machinery were needed to be distributed among the villages, and they would cost hundreds of thousands of pesetas that the Collectives did not have. It seemed that the only way to get money was to sell the foodstuffs normally donated to the soldiers. This seemed to be the choice: either lose a good part of the crop, or else not send the free food. The assembly chose unaminously to try to find another solution. They sent a delegation to the government in Valencia. Their effort was foredoomed: the abandonment of the combatants on the Aragon front was a calculated plan of the cabinet majority (Largo Caballero was in power at the time). They hoped that, in desperation, the militiamen would sack the Collectives.

The machinations of the reactionaries fell through. In *Solidaridad Obrera* (organ of the CNT) of Barcelona, I published an appeal to the militiamen, advising them of the situation and asking them to send part of their pay to help the peasants. Hundreds of thousands of pesetas were sent to the collectives and the harvest was saved. . . .

I do not say that there were no exceptions to the generous spirit of the Collectives. I remember a dispute between a woman of 50 and a comrade assigned to control labor and housing. She lived with her husband, their son, daughter-in-law, and grandchildren. "My daughter-in-law and I can't get along. I want to live separately!" This comrade had the soul of a child, a voice of thunder, and the heart of a lion. He argued his best to persuade her to give up her demand. Finally she left. I asked the delegate why he had refused. He told me that, since the rate of pay diminished as the number in the family increased, some families in which material interests predominated agreed on a feigned separation in order to get more income. The case had already been looked into. Under the circumstances, the shortages of houses made it out of the question.

The incident was minor but there were others like it. The directors of the Collective had to face up to all these troubles, to touch-and-go food problems, and to the anti-collectivist minority (UGT, Communists, etc.) It is impossible not to admire these men who gave themselves to the cause

---

[11] Since Leval's account of health care, education, and other welfare measures instituted in Binefar did not differ substantially from those instituted in other libertarian collectives, it is here omitted.—*Ed.*

with abnegation, and knew how to get so much done in a short time and in the best way.

In Binefar as in the other Aragon collectives all the interlocking units of the economy (factories, workshops, systems of distribution, etc.) functioned harmoniously without a hitch. I often made trips from Barcelona to Tamarite and Binefar. This time accompanied by a friend, a doctor from Barcelona, I pointed out with pride the newly planted fields of wheat, the vineyards, and the olive groves, where flourishing kitchen gardens and orchards alternated with fields of gold flax. "These miles of cultivated plantations," I exclaimed, "where everything is carefully and lovingly tended, and nothing is neglected, belong to the Collective!!" Two days later we visited Esplus, where we beheld vast fields of potatoes and more vineyards. As we travelled, we marvelled at this revolution, this dream, at last come true. With near religious fervor, I exclaimed again and again, " . . . The Collective! the Collective! created this miracle!"

Miralcampo and Azuqueca [12]
from Cahiers de l'Humanisme Libertaire

The collectivization of the land properties of Count Romanonés in Miralcampo and Azuqueca by the Castilian Regional Peasant Federation merits special attention. The peasants altered the topography of the district by diverting the course of the river to irrigate new land, thus tremendously increasing cultivated areas. They constructed a mill, schools, collective dining halls, and new housing for the collectivists.

A few days after the close of the Civil War, Count Romanonés reclaimed his domains, expecting the worst, certain that the revolutionary vandals had totally ruined his property. He was amazed to behold the wonderful

---

[12] From *The History of Spanish Anarcho-Syndicalism*, published in 1968 in Franco Spain! It was reprinted in Gaston Leval's monthly *Cahiers de l'Humanisme Libertaire*, Aug.–Sept., 1969, under the title, "An Example from the Spanish Revolution," demonstrating once again, writes Leval, "the remarkable constructive abilities of the libertarian militants during the Spanish Revolution. . . . "

improvements made by the departed peasant collectivists. When asked their names, the Count was told that the work was performed by the peasants in line with plans drawn up by a member of the CNT Building Workers' Union, Gomez Abril, an excellent organizer chosen by the Regional Peasant Federation. As soon as Abril finished his work he left and the peasants continued to manage the collective.

Learning that Gomez Abril was jailed in Guadalajara and that he was in a very precarious situation, the Count succeeded in securing his release from jail and offered to appoint him manager of all his properties. Gomez declined, explaining that a page of history had been written and his work finished.[13]

Collectivization in Carcagente[14]
by Gaston Leval

Carcagente is situated in the southern part of the province of Valencia. The climate of the region is particularly suited for the cultivation of oranges. Carcagente is completely surrounded by orange groves. The orange trees, with their abundance of golden fruit, present a truly magnificent picture.

In Carcagente, as in so many other Valencian towns and villages, the organizational capacity and the spirit of sacrifice of a handful of militant and determined workers, who labored incessantly in spite of all the

[13] It is worth noting that in one year the area seeded with wheat increased from 1,938 to 4,522 hectares (one hectare is about 2½ acres), and with barley increased 323 hectares to 1,242 hectares. There were even greater increases in wine production. The value of melons jumped from 196,000 to 300,000 pesetas, and of alfalfa from 80,000 to 250,000 pesetas. . . . The collective installed splendid facilities for raising rabbits and new pigsties for 100 animals, as well as a foodmarket serving 800 persons.—*Note by Leval.*

[14] This selection has two parts. The first is by Gaston Leval, from *Tierra y Libertad*, January 16, 1937. This was translated in *Spain and the World*, March 5, 1937. The second part is from Leval's *Espagne Libertaire*, pp. 171–174.

persecutions to prepare for the revolution, are now bearing fruit. The anarcho-syndicalist organization was deeply rooted, and this fact, together with the prestige of its militants, induced the majority of the people, once the revolution was initiated, to join or support our movement.

On visiting the Local Federation of Syndicates our attention was drawn to a showcase, once used to protect the image of Christ, but now harboring a magnificent photograph of Francisco Ferrer—a most agreeable substitution! (Ferrer was a libertarian educational pioneer, murdered in 1909 by the State in collusion with the Church).

A high percentage of the work force (the total population is 20,000) are members of our syndicates (the CNT). Here are a few statistics:

```
Peasant union . . . . . . . . . . . . . . . . . . . . . . . . . . . . . . .2,700 members
Orange packers(mostly women) . . . . . . . . . . . . . . . . .3,400 members
Construction . . . . . . . . . . . . . . . . . . . . . . . . . . . . . . 340 members
Carpenters(packing cases) . . . . . . . . . . . . . . . . . . . . . 125 members
Wood-workers . . . . . . . . . . . . . . . . . . . . . . . . . . . . . 230 members
Railway workers . . . . . . . . . . . . . . . . . . . . . . . . . . . 150 members
Miscellaneous . . . . . . . . . . . . . . . . . . . . . . . . . . . . . 450 members
```

Most of the land consisted of large estates. The poverty stricken peasants were forced to work on the estates of the rich landlords or do odd jobs to supplement their incomes. The syndicalists immediately broke up the monopoly, and now see to it that new forms of privilege are not created.

The small proprietors are treated differently. Their rights are respected and they are not forced to join the collective. But the syndicalists gradually introduce socialization by consolidating small parcels of land into larger areas in order to render the land suitable for collective cultivation. At first only the property of peasants who willingly joined the collective was socialized. Later, hesitant peasants who became convinced of the advantages of the new system also joined the collectives. A favorite tactic is to offer better land to recalcitrant peasant proprietors, just to convince them that they will still be better off if they become members of the collective. . . .

But this does not mean that those small proprietors who still prefer to cultivate their own land are left to do as they please. The local Agricultural Labor Commission is on the alert for possible sabotage and sees to it that both private and socialized agriculture (where it is even more necessary) make proper use of the land.

And the collective is really making good use of the land. We have looked over very large cultivated areas, among them one so vast that it falls within the radius of 7 municipalities. All of the socialized land, without exception, is cultivated with infinite care. The orchards are thoroughly weeded. To assure that the trees will get all the nourishment needed, the peasants are incessantly cleaning the soil. "Before," they told me with pride, "all this belonged to the rich and was worked by miserably paid laborers. The land was neglected and the owners had to buy immense quantities of chemical fertilizers, although they could have gotten much better yields by cleaning the soil. . . . " With pride, they showed me trees that had been grafted to produce better fruit.

In many places I observed plants growing in the shade of the orange trees. "What is this?," I asked. I learned that the Levant peasants (famous for their ingenuity) have abundantly planted potatoes among the orange groves. The peasants demonstrate more intelligence than all the bureaucrats in the Ministry of Agriculture combined. They do more than just plant potatoes. Throughout the whole region of the Levant, wherever the soil is suitable, they grow crops. They take advantage of the four month interval between the harvest and the next planting to grow early wheat in the rice fields. Had the Minister of Agriculture followed the example of these peasants throughout the Republican zone, the bread shortage problem would have been overcome in a few months.

The work of the agricultural collective is organized in the following manner: the general membership meeting of all the peasants (even including the few peasant landholders) elects the Technical Committee of six comrades to take care of technical matters, and the five member Administrative Committee, to look after the expropriated big estates, payment of wages, sale of produce, bookkeeping, etc. There is also a committee concerned with export of oranges and other products.

Industrial socialization began in Carcagente *not before, but after* agrarian socialization. Industrial organization, from the very outset, inspired confidence. Building was taken care of by the Building Workers' Industrial Union, and metal work by the Metal Workers' Union. The Wood Workers' Industrial Union included cabinet makers, joiners, carpenters, etc. The same principle held true in all the other trades. The artisans and small workshops consolidated their enterprises into vast workshops where each received a commonly agreed upon payment, and where no one would ever again have to wait for a customer and worry about being paid. Other less important trades also united into one union (like hairdressing salons or lamp makers). Small, unsatisfactory, outdated facilities were replaced by sunny, comfortable, well-conducted collectives. Yesterday's competitors became today's cooperating fellow workers.

Dwellings belonging to the rich and to the local fascists were allocated to those most in need of better housing. The most numerous groups of men were the workers in the socialized orange industry engaged in packing and processing fruit for export. Many plants were used for this work. Each plant was managed by a committee chosen by the workers, consisting of a commercial expert and of a delegate for each departmental function (box-making, packing, sorting, storage, shipping, etc.). Fruit had to be shipped to England, Sweden, Holland, France, and other countries. "We want people abroad to tell," said the workers, "from the quality and packaging of the fruit, that we work better in socialized industry than we did before. . . . "

Slowly rising prices, due in part to the persistence of little retail shops competing to make a living out of their meager trade (against which I warned), lagged far behind and threatened to partly offset the gains made by socialized production. Clearly the time had come to socialize distribution and exchange to the same degree as production. . . . My friend Gramén (later shot by the fascists) proposed the organization of socialized distribution centers in different areas, which would make the people themselves the true masters of prices and distribution. This policy soon brought results. A month and a half later, half the commune of Carcagente was already fully socialized and Gramén had good reason to expect that socialization of the other half would also be shortly achieved.

On the evening of my first visit, in November, 1936, at the request of my comrades I delivered a lecture. I resolved to speak constructively. I then learned how little I really had to say. And when I spoke to these men and saw how fervently they awaited my words, I frankly and humbly confessed that it was I who had to learn from them, not they from me, and I said this sincerely.

An added touch to this tableau: my comrades, in the very finest tradition of Spanish hospitality, invited me to dine with them in the garden of the most luxurious and beautiful expropriated pavillion, located in the countryside near Carcagente. My friends were enchanted by the beauty of the site, the healthy climate, the restful surroundings. It immediately occurred to me that this would make an ideal place to erect a rest and convalescent home. But once again they were way ahead of me. They did not need my advice. After consulting the Carcagente doctors, it was decided to convert this beautiful estate into a first-class sanitarium.

Collectivization in Magdalena de Pulpis[15]
by Gaston Leval

It used to be *Santa* Magdalena de Pulpis, but the revolution dropped the "saint." A little village (population 1,400), it serves as a typical example of revolutionary changes in many other villages in the Levant (the region on the east coast of Spain embracing 5 provinces, including the metropolis Valencia). Almost all of the few revolutionaries living in the village belonged to the CNT. Our comrades took advantage of the occasion of the Civil War to spearhead the social revolution. The majority of the inhabitants were petty peasant landholders owning 6,254 hectares out of the total of 6,654 hectares. The rest was owned by four or five big landlords. Though small in area, this land has the best irrigation, was suitable for intense cultivation, and was at least ten times more productive.

Our comrades, who knew nothing about the intricacies of a money economy, simply resolved to introduce libertarian communism at once. In this little village this was not very difficult. All that was needed was tact (which our comrades possessed in abundance). After clearing out the fascists, they proceeded to organize the collectives. They asked those who wanted to join to sign up. All the residents (including some who had misgivings) became members of the collective. Except for personal belongings, everything was turned over to the collective: land, money, livestock, tools, and other property. And the people began the new way of life.

We repeat here what we have said on other occasions; the commune (synonym for collective) prevailed. The syndicate was only one of its constituent organs. The function of the syndicates was limited strictly to the technical administration of production. But the Communal Assembly of all the members controlled everything. When the fascist invasion began, the

---

[15] From Gaston Leval, in *Cahiers de l'Humanisme Libertaire*, March, 1968. Also in *Né Franco né Stalin*, pp. 182-186.

Revolutionary Committee immediately began to introduce far-reaching changes affecting the social life of the village (housing, health, food supplies, education, public services). It took care of exchange and set the income of each family. In short, the Committee became the administrator of local life.[16]

To assure the equitable distribution of commodities, it became necessary to fix the income to which each family was entitled. The quantity of goods was measured in terms of the peseta, the standard national currency. No money standard was set for oil or firewood, which were free in any quantities. The same held true for wine, but since our comrades wanted to promote sobriety, quantities were limited. . . .

Things were arranged very simply. The remaining commodities were distributed as follows: each family was given a card stating the size of the family and the name and age of each member. Every adult was entitled to a "ration" of 1 peseta, 50 centimes for men, 1 peseta, 10 centimes for women, and for children over six, a graduated amount according to age. . . . A notebook kept track of the value in pesetas of the ration consumed each quarter of the year. Unused rations were credited to the next quarter. For example: if a family entitled to consume the equivalent of 150 pesetas in one quarter actually expended 100 pesetas, the difference of 50 pesetas was carried over to the next quarter.

No one paid rent. Housing was free and completely socialized, as was medical care. There were two doctors. Both spontaneously welcomed the new way of life. But one doctor moved to Castellón, the provincial capital. The other doctor remained, receiving the same rations as the rest of the people. The pharmacist also joined the collective. Medicines, supplies, transfer to hospitals in Barcelona or Castellón, surgery, services of specialists—all was paid for by the collective.

The collective obtained money by selling products outside the village, which were paid for in pesetas. The retail merchants closed their shops and voluntarily joined the commune. They organized themselves into a cooperative, where everyone could purchase all available commodities. The cooperative was installed in a former chapel big enough to meet all needs. Some of the merchants worked in the new cooperative. The hairdressers also got together and opened one spacious, well-equipped salon. The dressmakers

---

[16]It would appear at first sight that the extensive administrative functions of the Committee could easily lead to the abuse of power. But the Committee, the creation of the whole commune, is under its constant control, and is directly responsible to the parent body, i.e., all the people.—*Ed.*

Revolutionary slogans decorate the collectivized railroads.
Above—Slogan reads, "The land is yours, workers!"
Below—Working together, people paint slogans on a train.

Education was of great importance to the libertarian movement. Schools throughout revolutionary Spain came under popular control and many new ones were started.

Above—Young children enter a libertarian school.

Left—The popular university in Barcelona associated with the Libertarian Youth organization.

and tailors, housed in a single large workshop, offered better clothes and services. The carpenters also installed their collective. . . .

As for the organization of agricultural labor, we must first of all take into account that out of 265 men able and available for work, 65 voluntarily left to fight the fascists. Nevertheless, the amount of wheat and potatoes planted increased threefold. . . . and this increase was achieved not by cultivating more land, but primarily because many peasants (oh, miracle of private property!) never had had enough money to buy enough seed and fertilizer, and could only work part of their land.

Farming was organized in the following fashion: The cultivatable land was divided into 13 sections, with 15 men and equipment for each section. Each section was represented by a delegate. As in almost all other collectives, the delegates met weekly. Equipment was dispatched from one section to another as needed. Work animals and farm tools were intelligently used so as to get the best results.

We asked for information on marriages. Although the comrades naturally favored free love, the people enjoyed lawful marriage because a marriage ceremony in these peaceful villages is a festive occasion, celebrated with great gusto by the whole community. On the other hand, legal marriage does violate libertarian principles.

Our comrades met this problem by going through all the legal procedures and then rendering the marriage legally meaningless by destroying the documentary proof of marriage, as if no marriage had taken place. (Since the revolution, four couples have married). The couple, accompanied by relatives and friends, was married in the presence of the secretary of the Committee as a witness. After registering their full names and ages, and reaffirming their desire to marry, the legal requirements were fulfilled. But while the couple was descending the stairway the secretary hurriedly shredded paper which included the page on which the marriage was registered into confetti and showered it over the couple as they reached the street. Thus everybody was satisfied and the festival began.

I explained that indispensable social studies and planning are impossible without vital statistical information and that records of marriages, births, deaths, and other such information must be kept and readily available. The comrades understood and promised to reconstitute the missing records.

While promenading leisurely down the streets to the village square, we watched young people playing the Basque game, "Pelote," while the elders watched and made occasional comments. Things moved unhurriedly. Life flowed serenely through this village, as it had in bygone days, but now with a new feeling of confidence and security never known before. And we would have dearly loved to linger in these antiquated houses (which the commune will doubtless soon replace) but tranquilly, without despair without the uneasiness about the bleak prospects for tomorrow that had for so many centuries plagued the good people of Magdalena de Pulpis.

The Collective in Mas de las Matas[17]
by Gaston Leval

On my last visit in May, 1937, almost all the villages in the district were entirely socialized. The anarchist movement in this village dates from the turn of the century and precedes the establishment of the CNT union movement. The first syndicates were organized in 1932. On December 8th of the same year, an insurrection which enveloped all of Aragon and part of Catalonia proclaimed libertarian communism. The insurrection was suppressed. The CNT was outlawed, and was reconstituted only after the victory of the popular front government in April, 1936.

In mid-September, 1936, two months after the local fascists were driven out, our comrades proposed the establishment of agrarian collectives. At a general membership meeting of the agricultural associations, the proposal was unanimously adopted. Small landholders who refused to join formed their own organization. Out of a total of 600 families, 550 joined the collective. The remaining 50 families, members of the UGT, were instructed by their leaders not to join the collective. The collective does not interfere with their rights to continue private ownership as long as they do not infringe on the rights of the collective.

The extent and character of socialization varies according to the decision of each village collective. All of the collectives in the entire district function without written rules or constitutions. All business is simply conducted at monthly membership meetings of each collective. The meeting usually elects a committee of five to carry out the instructions of the membership on how to handle current problems.

[17]From Gaston Leval, *Espagne Libertaire*, pp. 142–149.

Depending on the condition of the land and various other factors, the work of the collective is carried on by 32 teams of workers. Each group cultivates a portion of dry as well as irrigated land. And each group, in rotation, performs its share of more agreeable work as well as especially unpleasant work. In all the collectives of the district, work groups select their own delegates to the Administrative Committee. The delegates meet once a week to plan the next week's work. The collectives constitute a continuously coordinated work organization.

In livestock raising, the number of sheep has increased 25%; sows for breeding, from 30 to 60; milk cows, from 18 to 24 (the land is not suitable for the pasturage of cows). Until such time as the collective constructs its own piggeries, it has purchased a great number of young piglets which are to be raised by the families of the collectivists. For meat each family raises one or two porkers, which are salted and stored at the communal slaughter house.

But production is not limited solely to agriculture or stock breeding. Small industries (building, leather goods, shoes and slippers, garments and underwear, etc.) have been set up in the larger centers and in the more important collectivized villages. As in Graus and other areas, each enterprise constitutes a section of an overall organization of the whole community, "the general collective." Here is an example to illustrate the mechanism through which the production of each group, as well as the transactions of each family is recorded and coordinated. If the agrarian section needs certain tools, its delegate files the order with the Administrative Committee, which sends the order to the metallurgical syndicate, where it is filled and registered. If a family needs furniture, the same procedure is followed. The order is transmitted via the Administrative Committee to the delegate of the wood workers' syndicate (which includes the cabinet and furniture workers) where the order is filled and registered.

Money has been abolished. Neither the standard currency of Spain (the peseta) nor local money is used in transactions within or between any of the collectives of the county or district. The socialization of commerce was one of the first steps. On my first visit to Mas de las Matas, there were only two small grocers who refused to cooperate. But they had to close their stores for lack of supplies. In general, municipal markets have replaced the old mode of distribution.

It is most difficult to transmit in writing an adequate description of this vast movement which both enhances and exceeds the scope of agrarian socialization per se. Here in Mas de las Matas, as in any other collectivized village, there are not only the familiar outward signs of community enterprise, which we have seen in Graus (like the red and black signs designating factories, communal markets, and hotels) but something far more substantial: the installations which constitute the lifeblood of collective life. The district warehouses (for chemical products, cement, raw materials for all the industries) are here, where other village collectives deposit needed surplus commodities, and in exchange pick up necessary goods according to arrangements worked out by the assemblies of fraternal delegates. In the spacious premises of a wealthy fascist who fled are kept stocks of clothing to be distributed to the people of the district. Here also is the place where the individual peasant owners can pick up goods they need and where the amount of goods supplied to each family is recorded.

In the newly built distillery cooperative, organized by the district villages, tartaric acids and ninety-proof medicinal alcohol are extracted from the residue of raisins. In the tailoring shop, men and women cut and sew clothes to order for the collectivists in a good variety of cloth and colors. A family of four (mother, father, and two children) is entitled to 280 pesetas worth of clothing, which is two or three times more than an average peasant family spent for clothes under the old order.

Women shop for provisions in well-appointed sanitary markets done in white tile and marble. Tasty bread of the highest quality is now baked in the collective bakeries at less cost. Dress shops not only make fashionable clothes for women and girls, but as in many other villages young girls are taught how to sew clothes for their future children.

A sign reads "Public Library." It is surprisingly well stocked with a good selection of books on academic subjects—sociology, literature . . . and a good variety of school textbooks. . . . The library is free to all including the "individualists" (nonmembers of the collectives). There are also educational activities for young and old.

In the spirit and practice of solidarity for all through respect for the individuality of each, every family is allotted a small parcel of land to use as it wishes, supplementing their diet by growing certain fruits and vegetables, raising rabbits, etc. Rationing is not therefore synonymous with uniformity.

If clothes, for example, are also rationed, it is not because the collectives in this part of Aragon lack the necessary purchasing power. There are many products, principally wheat, which could be exchanged for clothing manufactured in Catalonia. However, enormous quantities of wheat, meat, vegetables, and olive oil, which could be exchanged for other goods, but are sorely needed to sustain the armed forces in the anti-fascist war, are donated free of charge to the soldiers. Likewise, great quantities of goods are donated to Madrid, besieged by the Franco armies.

Medical care and medicines are free. Free eyeglasses are provided for both collectivists and "individualists." Public instruction is obligatory for children up to the age of fourteen. A new rural school some distance from the village has just been built and opened for all older children who have never before attended school. And in Mas de las Matas, two young teachers graduated from colleges in Saragossa, Valencia and Teruel have been placed in charge of two new classrooms providing for the education of 50 children in each room.[18]

According to the norms established throughout Aragon, Castile, and the Levant, no collective is allowed to go into business for itself for its own profit. This avoids the tendency towards speculation, which is made easy by the war situation and is fairly common (a type of competition which so often characterizes certain collective factories, especially the textile mills in Barcelona). These measures of a moral character are on a par with the sense of organizational responsibility prevailing in the socialized villages. Each collectivized village provides a list of its surplus products and the products in short supply to the Cantonal (district) Committee. The Committee headquarters in Mas de las Matas keeps track of the surplus commodities and needs of each collective village. It knows exactly what reserves of wine, meat, olive oil, wheat (flour), potatoes, sugar, and other supplies each village has on hand. If, for example, a collective furnishing oil does not need wine, it can order other articles, or reserve them until they become available, or hold surplus commodities for exchange with other collectives in the district. The Cantonal Committee is actually a kind of clearing house for exchange or barter. In addition, through the general market and the communal warehouse, the facilities for exchange within and outside the village are always at hand.

This system of exchange is practiced without the slightest reservation because the spirit of profiteering no longer motivates the collectivists. A village which, because of unusually difficult circumstances, has nothing to exchange will not therefore be condemned to poverty, or be compelled to mortgage itself and its economy for years and years. For example: this year the principal crops of Mas de las Matas, Seno, and La Ginebrosa were destroyed by hailstorms. In a capitalist regime, such natural disasters would have meant endless privations, heavy debts, foreclosures, and even

---

[18] Fifty children per classroom may appear excessive, but considering the backwardness of educational organization in Spain, this represents progress. The important thing is to combat illiteracy. The author taught as many as 52 students in one class (ranging in age from 5 to 15) in the progressive "rationalist" school organized by the Spanish radicals and liberals.—*Ed.*

emigration of some workers for several years. But in the regime of libertarian solidarity, these difficulties were overcome by the efforts of the whole district. Provisions, seeds, etc., everything needed to repair the damage, were furnished in the spirit of brotherhood and solidarity—without conditions, without contracting debts. The Revolution has created a new civilization!

chapter 11

An Evaluation of the
Anarchist Collectives

Introduction

In the concluding chapter of his pioneering work, Né Franco né Stalin *Gaston Leval, on the basis of his exhaustive first hand studies, enumerates both the achievments and the setbacks of the libertarian revolution on the land and in the cities. In so doing he summarizes various themes outlined in preceding chapters.*

The Characteristics of the Libertarian Collectives[1]
by Gaston Leval

1. In juridical principles the collectives were something entirely new. They were not syndicates, nor were they municipalities in any traditional sense; They did not even very closely resemble the municipalities of the Middle Ages. Of the two, however, they were closer to the communal than the syndicalist spirit. Often they might just as well have been called communities, as for example the one in Binefar was. The collective was an entity; within it, occupational and professional groups, public services, trade and municipal functions were subordinate and dependent. In forms of organization, in internal functioning, and in their specialized activities, however, they were autonomous.

2. The agrarian collectives, despite their name, were to all intents and purposes libertarian communist organizations. They applied the rule "from each according to his abilities, to each according to his needs." Where money was abolished, a certain quantity of goods was assured to each person; where money was retained, each family received a wage determined by the number of members. Though the technique varied, the moral principle and the practical results were the same.

3. In the agrarian collectives solidarity was practiced to the greatest degree. Not only was every person assured of the necessities, but the district federations increasingly adopted the principle of mutual aid on an inter-collective scale. For this purpose they created common reserves to help out villages less favored by nature. In Castile special institutions for this purpose were created. In industry this practice seems to have begun in Hospitalet, on the Catalan railways, and was applied later in Alcoy. Had the political compromise not impeded open socialization, the practices of mutual aid would have been much more generalized.

[1] From Gaston Leval, Né Franco né Stalin, pp. 306–320. The translation is from Anarchy #5, July, 1961.

4. A conquest of enormous importance was the right of women to livelihood, regardless of occupation or function. In about half of the agrarian collectives, the women received the same wages as men; in the rest the women received less, apparently on the principle that they rarely lived alone.

5. The child's right to livelihood was also ungrudgingly recognized: not as a state charity, but as a right no one dreamed of denying. The schools were open to children to the age of 14 or 15—the only guarantee that parents would not send their children to work sooner, and that education would really be universal.

6. In all the agrarian collectives of Aragon, Catalonia, Levant, Castile, Andalusia, and Estremadura, the workers formed groups to divide the labor or the land; usually they were assigned to definite areas. Delegates elected by the work groups met with the collective's delegate for agriculture to plan out the work. This typical organization arose quite spontaneously, by local initiative.

7. In addition to these methods—and similar meetings of specialized groups—the collective as a whole met in a weekly, bi-weekly or monthly assembly. This too was a spontaneous innovation. The assembly reviewed the activities of the councillors it named, and discussed special cases and unforseen problems. All inhabitants—men and women, producers and nonproducers—took part in the discussion and decisions. In many cases the "individualists" (non-collective members) had equal rights in the assembly.

8. In land cultivation the most significant advances were: the rapidly increased use of machinery and irrigation; greater diversification; and forestation. In stock raising: the selection and multiplication of breeds; the adaption of breeds to local conditions; and large-scale construction of collective stock barns.

9. Production and trade were brought into increasing harmony and distribution became more and more unified; first district unification, then regional unification, and finally the creation of a national federation. The district (*comarca*) was the basis of trade. In exceptional cases an isolated commune managed its own, on authority of the district federation which kept its eye on the commune and could intervene if its trading practices were harmful to the general economy. In Aragon, the Federation of Collectives, founded in January, 1937, began to coordinate trade among the communes of the region, and to create a system of mutual aid. The tendency to unity became more distinct with the adoption of a single "producer's card" and a single "consumer's card"—which implied suppression of all money, local and national—by a decision of the February,

1937 Congress. Coordination of trade with other regions, and abroad, improved steadily. When disparities in exchange, or exceptionally high prices, created surpluses, they were used by the Regional Federation to help the poorer collectives. Solidarity thus extended beyond the district.

10. Industrial concentration—the elimination of small workshops and uneconomical factories—was a characteristic feature of collectivization both in the rural communes and in the cities. Labor was rationalized on the basis of social need—in Alcoy's industries and in those of Hospitalet, in Barcelona's municipal transport and in the Aragon collectives.

11. The first step toward socialization was frequently the dividing up of large estates (as in the Segorbe and Granollers districts and a number of Aragon villages). In certain other cases the first step was to force the municipalities to grant immediate reforms (municipalization of land-rent and of medicine in Elda, Benicarlo, Castillone, Alcaniz, Caspe, etc.).

12. Education advanced at an unprecedented pace. Most of the partly or wholly socialized collectives and municipalities built at least one school. By 1938, for example, every collective in the Levant Federation had its own school.

13. The number of collectives increased steadily. The movement originated and progressed swiftly in Aragon, conquered part of Catalonia, then moved on to Levant and later Castile. According to reliable testimony the accomplishments in Castile may indeed have surpassed Levant and Aragon. Estramadura and the part of Andalusia not conquered immediately by the fascists—especially the province of Jaen—also had their collectives. The character of the collectives varied of course with local conditions.[2]

15. Sometimes the collective was supplemented by other forms of socialization. After I left Carcagente, trade was socialized. In Alcoy consumers cooperatives arose to round out the syndicalist organization of production. There were other instances of the same kind.

16. The collectives were not created single handedly by the libertarian movement. Although their juridical principles were strictly anarchist, a great many collectives were created spontaneously by people remote from our movement ("libertarians" without being aware of it). Most of the Castile and Estramadura collectives were organized by Catholic and Socialist peasants; in some cases of course they may have been inspired by the propaganda of isolated anarchist militants. Although their organization opposed the movement officially, many members of the UGT entered or

---

[2] Number 14 deals with the number and extent of collectivization. Since we have included more complete information elsewhere in the book (see page 71), this point is omitted.—*Ed.*

organized collectives, as did republicans who sincerely wanted to achieve liberty and justice.

17. Small landowners were respected. Their inclusion in the consumer's card system and in the collective trading, the resolutions taken in respect to them, all attest to this. There were just two restrictions: they could not have more land than they could cultivate, and they could not carry on private trade. Membership in the collective was voluntary: the "individualists" joined only if they were persuaded of the advantages of working in common.

18. The chief obstacles to the collectives were:

a) The existence of conservative strata, and parties and organizations representing them. Republicans of all factions, socialists of left and right (Largo Caballero and Prieto), Stalinist Communists, and often the POUMists. (Before their expulsion from the Catalan government— the *Generalidad*—the POUMists were not a truly revolutionary party. They became so when driven into opposition. Even in June, 1937, a manifesto distributed by the Aragon section of the POUM attacked the collectives). The UGT was the principal instrument of the various politicians.

b) The opposition of certain small landowners (peasants from Catalonia and the Pyréenées).

c) The fear, even among some members of collectives, that the government would destroy the organizations once the war was over. Many who were not really reactionary, and many small landowners who would otherwise have joined the collectives, held back on this account.

d) The open attack on the collectives: by which is not meant the obviously destructive acts of the Franco troops wherever they advanced. In Castile the attack on the collectivists was conducted, arms in hand, by Communist troops. In the Valencia region, there were battles in which even armored cars took part. In the Huesca province the Karl Marx brigade persecuted the collectives. The Macia-Companys brigade did the same in Teruel province. (But both always fled from combat with the fascists. The Karl Marx brigade always remained inactive, while our troops fought for Huesca and other important points; the Marxists troops reserved themselves for the rearguard. The second gave up Vivel del Rio and other coal regions of Utrillos without a fight. These soldiers, who ran in panic before a small attack that other forces easily contained, were intrepid warriors against the unarmed peasants of the collectives).

19. In the work of creation, transformation and socialization, the peasant demonstrated a social conscience much superior to that of the city worker.

Conclusion

S.D.

In our introductory remarks we indicated, in broad outline, important things that modern radicals and particularly those involved in the worldwide movement for workers' self-management of industry (a more accurate term than "workers' control") could learn from the rich experience of the Spanish Revolution. Attempting to provide the reader with at least enough essential background information to make his own assessment, we refrained from going into a detailed discussion of the lessons of the Spanish Revolution. This much, however, is clear: the embattled workers and peasants of Spain had successfully translated the libertarian principles of self-management into concrete achievements. This was not done in some isolated experimental commune made up of select individuals but on a vast scale, involving the lives of millions of ordinary men, women, and children. This was the "popular consciousness" of the Spanish Revolution. In the last chapter of his *Né Franco né Stalin* Leval sums up the nature of this grass roots popular control.

The revolution developed in extremely complicated circumstances. Attacks from within and without had to be fought off. It took fantastic efforts to put the anarchist principles into practice. But in many places it was done. The organizers found out how to get around everything. I repeat: it was possible because we had the intelligence of the people on our side. This is what finds the way, and meets the thousand needs of life and the revolution. It organized the militia and defeated fascism in the first phase of the war. It went to work instantly, to make armored cars and rifles and guns. The initiative came from the people, above all from those influenced by the anarchists. For example the Aragon collectives: among their organizers I found only two lawyers, in Alcorina. They were not, strictly speaking, intellectuals. But if what they did, together with their peasant and worker comrades, was well done, it was no better than what could be seen in Esplus, Binefar, Calanda, and other collectives. What was a surprise was to find that a great many of these peasants were illiterate. But they had faith, practical common sense, the spirit of sacrifice, and the will to create a new world.

I don't want to make a demagogic apology for ignorance. Those men had a mentality, a heart, a spirit, of a kind that education cannot give and official education often smothers. Spiritual culture is not always bookish, and still less academic. It can arise from the very conditions of living, and when it does, it is more dynamic. By adapting themselves to what was being done, by coordinating the work, by suggesting general directions, by warning a certain region of industry against particular errors, by complementing one activity with another and harmonizing the whole, by stimulating here and correcting there—in these ways great minds can undoubtedly be of immense service. In Spain they were lacking. It was not by the work of our intellectuals who are more literary than sociological, more agitators than practical guides—that the future has been illuminated. And the peasants—libertarian or not—of Aragon, Levant, Castile, Estramadura, Andalusia, and the workers of Catalonia, understood this and acted alone.

The intellectuals, by their ineptitude in practical work, were inferior to the peasants who made no political speeches but knew how to organize the new life. Not even the authors of the syndicalist health organization in Catalonia were intellectuals. A Basque doctor with a will of iron, and a few comrades working in the hospitals, did everything. In other regions, talented professional men aided the movement. But there, too, the initiative came from below. Alcoy's industries, so well organized, were all managed by the workers, as were those of Elda and Castillon. In Carcagente, in Elda, in Granollers, in Binefar, in Jativa, in land transport, in marine transport, in the collectives of Castile, or in the semi-socialization of Ripolls and Puigerda—the militants at the bottom did everything.

As for the government, they were as inept in organizing the economy as in organizing the war.

In assessing the profound impact of the Spanish Revolution, anarchist and non-anarchist critics of the conduct and policies of our comrades must never lose sight of the fact that these constructive achievements were made under the worst possible circumstances. They would do well to ponder deeply these words of Bakunin, which, though made about the Paris Communards, are still relevant to the kind of problems the Spanish workers had to face:

> I know that many socialists, very logical in their theory, blame our Paris friends for not having acted sufficiently as socialists in their revolutionary practice. The yelping pack of the bourgeois press, on the other hand, accuses them of having followed their program too faithfully.... I want to call the attention of the strictest theoreticians of proletarian emancipation to the fact that they are unjust to our Paris brothers, for between the most correct theories and their practical application lies an enormous difference that cannot be bridged in a few days.... They had to keep up a daily struggle against the Jacobin majority. In the midst of the conflict they had to feed and provide work for several thousand workers, organize and arm them, and keep a sharp lookout for the doings of the reactionaries. All that in an immense city like Paris, besieged, facing the threat of starvation, and a prey to the shady intrigues of the reaction. (Dolgoff, pp. 266–267)

We don't want to pass judgment on what the Spanish anarchists should or should not have done—playing the fruitless game of "what if...." We are concerned with the indispensable prerequisites for the realization of a libertarian society based upon worker's self-management of industry—rural and urban. We are concerned with the fundamental principles which must not only underpin such a society but which must also determine the character and direction which struggles leading to the realization of the free society must take. It is here that we find

> the precise significance of Spanish anarchism. It voices more clearly and intelligently than any other Iberian movement the resistance offered by the whole Spanish people to the tyranny and soullessness of the modern machine serving age.... It accepts the benefits to be obtained from machine production, but it insists that nothing whatever should curtail the right of all men to lead dignified human lives. (Brenan, pp. 196–197)

What are these basic principles of workers' self-management? Let us go through them briefly.

By definition, "self-management" is self-rule. It excludes rule over others—domination of man by man. It excludes not only the permanent, legally sanctioned authority of the state through its coercive institutions but demands the very extirpation of the principle of the state from within the

Poster of the CNT-FAI. "Liberty!"

unofficial associations (miniature states) of the people: from within the unions, from the places of work, and from within the myriad groupings and relations which make up society.

By definition, "self-management" is the idea that workers (*all* workers, including technicians, engineers, scientists, planners, coordinators—*all*) engaged in providing goods and services can themselves efficiently administer and coordinate the economic life of society. This belief must of necessity be based upon three inseparable principles: 1) faith in the constructive and creative capacity not of an elite classs of "superior" individuals but of the masses—the much maligned "average man"; 2) autonomy (self-rule); and 3) decentralization and coordination through the free agreement of federalism.

By definition, "self-management" means that workers are equal partners in a vast network of interlocking cooperative associations embracing the whole range of production and distribution of goods and the rendering of services. It must of necessity be based upon the fundamental principle of free communism, that is, the equal access to and sharing of, goods and services, according to needs.

The contemporary significance of the Spanish Revolution lies not so much in the specific measures improvised by the urban socialized industries and the agrarian collectives (most of them outdated by the cybernetic-technological revolution) but in the application of the fundamental constructive principles of anarchism or free socialism to the immediate practical problems of the Spanish social revolution. These principles are beginning to be understood more and more today.[3] It is hoped that this collection will contribute to that understanding.

---

[3] A fuller discussion of workers' self-management and of how modern technology (cybernetics, the transportation and the information revolutions, etc.) renders these principles even more relevant is beyond the scope of this work. But there can be no doubt that such an investigation is bound to yield fruitful results and expedite the solution of the problems of social reconstruction which have impeded the development of past revolutions.

Glossary

Assault Guards (Guardia de Asalto). The police organization formed in 1932 consisting of pro-Republican elements, but which was used in the suppression of workers and peasants.

Carabineros. The traditional force of customs officers that was built into a large national police force after 1936.

Civil Guards (*Guardia Civil*). The traditional highly-disciplined and reactionary police force much hated by the Spanish people.

CNT (*Confederación Nacional del Trabajo*: National Labor Confederation). The CNT, founded in 1910, was the large anarcho-syndicalist labor union closely associated with the FAI. CNT members were referred to as *ceneteistas*.

FAI (*Federación Anarquista Ibérica*: Iberian Anarchist Federation). The FAI, formed in 1927, was the militant anarchist organization of committed libertarians that worked closely with the much larger CNT. FAI members were referred to as *faistas*.

Generalidad The autonomous government of Catalonia province.

POUM (*Partido Obrero de Unificación Marxista*: Workers' Marxist Unification Party). A united party formed in 1936 of two small left-communist dissident groups.

PSUC (*Partit Socialista Unificat de Catalunya*: Catalan United Socialist Party). Formed in 1936, it included many *petite bourgeoisie* elements and was dominated by the Communists.

UGT (*Unión General de Trabajadores*: General Workers' Union). The UGT, founded in 1888, was the reform-oriented socialist labor union, the leadership of which came under the influence of the Communist Party during the Civil War.

Bibliography

I. The following is a list of the authors and works from which the selections in this book were drawn. Included is a short biographical sketch of each author.

H.E. Kaminski:
> *Ceux de Barcelone*. (Paris, 1937)

A radical French historian, Kaminski was friendly to libertarian ideas and movements and wrote an excellent biography of Bakunin. He visited Spain during the Civil War, where he traveled and interviewed prominent anarchists.

Gaston Leval:
> *Ne Franco ne Stalin*, (Milan, 1952)
> *Espagne Libertaire: 1936-1939*. (Paris, 1971)

Gaston Leval is a French anarchist whose father fought in The Paris Commune of 1871. He is an outstanding theoretician and militant, and has written a great many works on the economic and sociological problems of anarchism, with special reference to Spain. A conscientious objector in World War I, he took refuge in Spain, where he was active in the revolutionary labor movement and was imprisoned many times. He represented the CNT of Spain at the Congress of the Red International of Trade Unions in Moscow, 1921. He was among the first to expose the true nature of the Bolshevik dictatorship. Under the dictatorship of Primo de Rivera, he took refuge in Argentina. With the outbreak of the Civil War he illegally emigrated to Spain to participate in the revolution. Knowing that the war was lost, he made a first-hand study of the collectives and socialized industries, leaving for posterity the fullest and most reliable reports ever written of the constructive work of the revolution. He now lives in Paris, where he works as a printer and edits the *Cahiers de l'Humanisme Libertaire*, one of the best anarchist journals.

José Peirats:

> *La CNT en la Revolución Española.* (documentary history in 3 volumes, Toulouse, 1951, 1952, 1953)
> *Los Anarquistas en la Crisis Política Española.* (Buenos Aires, 1964)

An outstanding militant and historian of the Spanish anarchist movement, he wrote a three-volume documentary history of the CNT in the Spanish Revolution and other works. During the Civil War he edited an anarchist publication opposed to the participation of the CNT-FAI in the government of the Republic.

Diego Abad de Santillán:

> *Por Que Perdimos La Guerra: Una Contribución de la Tragedia Espanola.* (Buenos Aires, 1940)

Born in Spain, Diego Abad de Santillán was raised in Argentina. He has been a prolific writer and historian of the Spanish and Latin-American anarchist and anarcho-syndicalist labor movements. He has translated the works of Bakunin; Kropotkin; the great German writer, militant, and historian, Rudolf Rocker; the works of the historian of anarchism, Max Nettlau; etc. Before the outbreak of the Civil War he edited many anarchist newspapers and magazines (*Timon, Tierra y Libertad,* etc.). He was one of the founders of the FAI in 1927. After the outbreak of the Civil War he became Minister of the Economy in the Catalonian Government. He is now living in Argentina.

Augustin Souchy:

> *Nacht über Spanien.* (Damstadt, 1957)

Augustin Souchy is a German anarcho-syndicalist. He was also a delegate of the German syndicalist union to the Congress of the Red International of Trade Unions in Moscow, 1921. He was one of the founders and Secretary of the anarcho-syndicalist International Workingmen's Association organized in Berlin in 1922, to which the CNT was affiliated. From 1912 to the end of the Civil War, Souchy was in constant touch with the Spanish revolutionary movement. During the whole duration of the Civil War he remained in Spain, in charge of international propaganda. He wrote hundreds of articles in the Spanish anarchist press. Souchy observed and lived in many of the collectives and is an outstanding authority on all phases of the Spanish anarchist movement—particularly the collectivizations. He left Spain only a few hours before Barcelona was occupied by the Franco troops. With the coming of World War II, he lived as a refugee in France, and later traveled extensively throughout Latin America, Israel, etc., to study at first hand collectivization and cooperative movements in semi-developed countries. He lives in Munich, Germany.

Isaac Puente:
    El Comunismo Anarquico. (Havana, 1934)
Isaac Puente was an anarchist popular theoretician. He wrote many articles and pamphlets on the practical application of anarchist theory. In particular, he was one of a "school" of anarchists who combined anarcho-communism and anarcho-syndicalism. His *El Comunismo Anarquico* was widely known. The edition we have used was published by Ediciones Federacion de Grupo Anarquistas de Cuba, Habana.

    Collectivisations: L'Oeuvre Constructive de la Revolution Espagnole (1936-1939). (second edition, Toulouse, 1965) Augustin Souchy and P. Folgare, editors.
First published in 1937 in Barcelona by the FAI press, Ediciones Tierra y Libertad, this is a collection of documents by those involved in the collectivization movement including decrees, resolutions and reports from both industrial and rural collectives.

II. Works cited in the text.

Bolloten, Burnett, *The Grand Camouflage: The Communist Conspiracy in the Spanish Civil War.* (London, 1961)
Brenan, Gerald, *The Spanish Labyrinth.* (London, 1962)
Broué Pierre, and Emile Témime, *Revolution and the Civil War in Spain.* (London, 1972).
Bulletin of the Institute of Workers' Control. (Nottingham, Eng.)
Dolgoff, Sam, ed., *Bakunin on Anarchy.* (New York, 1972)
Guérin, Daniel, *Anarchism.* (New York, 1970)
Kaminski , H.E., *Ceux de Barcelone.* (Paris, 1937)
Leval, Gaston, *Espagne Libertaire: 1936-1939.* (Paris, 1971)

—Né Franco né Stalin (Milan, 1952).

Lorenzo, Cézar, *Les Anarchistes Espagnols et le Pouvoir: 1868-1969.* (Paris, 1969)

Malefakis, Edward E., *Agrarian Reform and Peasant Revolution in Spain.* (New Haven, 1970)

Mintz, Frank, *La Collectivisation en Espagne de 1936 à 1939.* (Thesis presented 1965-66, later published in Paris)

Paz, Abel, *Durruti: Le Peuple en Armes.* (Paris, 1972)

Peirats, José, *Los Anarquistas en la Crisis Political Española.* (Buenos Aires, 1964)

—La CNT en la Revolucion Española. (Toulouse, 1951-53)

Puente, Isaac, *El Comunismo Anarquico.* (Havana, 1934)

Richards, Vernon, ed., *Malatesta: His Life and Ideas.* (London, 1965)

Santillán, Diego Abad de, *After the Revolution.* (New York, 1937)

—Por Que Perdimos La Guerra: Una Contribución de la Tragedia Española. (Buenos Aires, 1940)

Serge, Victor, *Memoirs of a Revolutionary: 1901-1941.* (London, 1963)

Souchy, Augustin, *De Julio a Julio.* (Valencia, 1937)

—Nacht über Spanien. (Damstadt, 1957)

Souchy, Augustin and P. Folgare, eds., *Collectivizations: L'Oeuvre Constructive de la Révolution Espagnole (1936-1939).* (Toulouse, 1965)

III. The literature of the Spanish Revolution in English is at best meager. The following annotated list may be helpful to the reader who wants to pursue the subject.

A. Books

Brademas, Steven J., *Revolution and Social Revolution: A Contribution to the History of the Anarcho-Syndicalist Movement in Spain, 1930-37.* (PhD. thesis, Oxford, 1953) A scholarly approach.

Brenan, Gerald, *The Spanish Labyrinth: An Account of the Social and Political Background of the Civil War.* (London, 1962) Not much about the revolution itself, but excellent as background.

Bolloten, Burnett, *The Grand Camouflage: The Communist Conspiracy in the Spanish Civil War* (original subtitle). (London, 1961) A pioneering work.

Borkenau, Franz, *The Spanish Cockpit.* (London, 1962) Read with care. As a former Marxist he is inclined to be hypercritical of the anarchists. A useful book nonetheless.

Broué, Pierre, and Emile Témime, *Revolution and the War in Spain*. (London, 1972) Probably the best all-around book in English.

Carr, Raymond, ed., *The Republic and the Civil War in Spain*. (London, 1971) Interesting but read with caution.

Cattell, David T., *Communism and the Spanish Civil War*. (Berkeley, 1957)
—*Soviet Diplomacy and the Spanish Civil War*. (Berkeley, 1957) Among the finest on their subject.

Chomsky, Noam, "Objectivity and Liberal Scholarship," in *American Power and the New Mandarins*. (New York, 1969) A superb critique of Jackson's book with good new material of its own.

Jackson, Gabriel, *The Spanish Republic and the Civil War in Spain*.(Princeton, 1965) Valuable for the Republic of 1931 but not an objective history.

Jellinek, Frank, *The Civil War in Spain*. (London, 1938) The first part is useful but beware of his pro-communist bias.

Malefakis, Edward E., *Agrarian Reform and Peasant Revolution in Spain*. (New Haven, 1970) Read for factual background information. Very anti-anarchist.

Orwell, George, *Homage to Catalonia*. (London, 1938) Tries to deal objectively with the revolution. Gives a vivid portrayal of events.

Santillan, Diego Abad de, *After the Revolution*. (New York, 1937) A realistic and constructive formulation of what the revolutionary economy could look like.

Thomas, Hugh, *The Spanish Civil War*. (London, 1961) Readily available, but we *don't* recommend this book.

B. Pamphlets

Dashar, M., *The Origins of the Revolutionary Movement in Spain*. (New York, nd)

Leval, Gaston, *Social Reconstruction in Spain*. (London, 1938)

Rocker, Rudolf, *The Tragedy of Spain*. (New York, 1937)

Souchy, Augustin, *The Tragic Week in May*. (Barcelona, 1937)

C. Periodicals

Spain and the World. (Freedom Press, London, 1936-39)

The Spanish Revolution. (United Libertarian Organizations, New York, 1936-39)

Spanish Labor Bulletin. (Chicago, 1936-39?)

Index

Note: collectivization is abbreviated "coll." in this index.

SAM DOLGOFF, a house painter by profession, now retired, was born in 1902. At an early age he was "riding the rails," an itinerant laborer working in lumbercamps, steel mills, construction, etc. He has been involved in radical movements since the age of fifteen when he joined the Socialist Party youth organization.

His radical bent then began to turn towards anarchism and he became involved with the anarchist group and journal *Road to Freedom* which printed his first article about Mahatma Gandhi. In the early 1920's he met the well known Russian revolutionary anarchist Gregory Petrovich Maximoff who became his close friend and mentor. Maximoff helped clarify his ideas about anarchism as a genuine constructive social movement. To better study the literature of anarchism, Sam taught himself to read several languages.

Under the *nom de plume* Sam Weiner, he has written widely in radical and anarchist periodicals. Two of his pamphlets have been recognized as important critiques of the labor scene in America: *Ethics and American Unionism* (1958) and *The Labor Party Illusion* (1961). He has also been a correspondent for a number of radical papers in Europe. Through the years Sam helped found and edit a number of important anarchist magazines including *Vanguard* (1932-1939), *Spanish Revolution* (1936-1938), and *Views and Comments* (1955-1965). In addition to *The Anarchist Collectives*, Sam recently edited and translated *Bakunin On Anarchy* (Knopf, 1972).

An active "anarcho-pluralist" (as he calls himself), Sam is still deeply absorbed in the radical labor movement and especially with the IWW. He is a frequent speaker to labor groups, at informal get-togethers, and at such colleges as Antioch, Columbia, Williams, Oregon University, and San Jose. He is currently working on a supplement to his *Bakunin on Anarchy* and also on a book on the American labor movement and workers' self-management of industry.

MURRAY BOOKCHIN currently lives in Vermont and teaches Social Ecology at Goddard College. A prolific writer and speaker, he is the author of *Our Synthetic Environment* (1962) and *Crisis in Our Cities* (1965), both written under the pseudonym "Lewis Herber," *Post-Scarcity Anarchism* (1971), and the forthcoming *The Limits of the City*. He was formerly involved with *Anarchos* magazine and is currently associated with the Center for New Studies.

He is currently working on books including *The Ecology of Freedom* and *The Spanish Anarchists*, a two volume history. The first volume is completed and concerns the development of the Spanish Anarchist movement from 1870-1936.

The staff of Free Life Editions, Chuck Hamilton, Mark Powelson, and Sharon Presley, would like to thank the following people who assisted in the preparation of this book: D. Rosen, Bertch—Art, OBU Typesetters, Diane Radycki, Renna Draynel, Paul Avrich.